DICTATORSHIP
ACROSS BORDERS

DICTATORSHIP ACROSS BORDERS

BRAZIL, CHILE, AND THE SOUTH AMERICAN COLD WAR

MILA BURNS

THE UNIVERSITY OF NORTH CAROLINA PRESS

Chapel Hill

Designed by Jamison Cockerham
Set in Scala and Trade Gothic
by codeMantra

Cover art by Jr korpa / Unsplash.

"Canto a Gabriela" by Héctor Sandoval Torres used by permission.

Manufactured in the United States of America

LIBRARY OF CONGRESS CATALOGING-IN-PUBLICATION DATA
Names: Burns, Mila author
Title: Dictatorship across borders : Brazil, Chile, and the South American
Cold War / Mila Burns.
Description: Chapel Hill : The University of North Carolina Press, [2025] |
Includes bibliographical references and index.
Identifiers: LCCN 2025013297 | ISBN 9781469689623 cloth alk. paper |
ISBN 9781469689630 pbk alk paper | ISBN 9781469688039 ebook |
ISBN 9781469689647 pdf
Subjects: LCSH: Dictatorship—Chile—History—20th century | Dictatorship—
Brazil—History—20th century | Chile—History—Coup d'état, 1973 | Chile—Politics
and government—1973–1988 | Brazil—Foreign relations—Chile—20th century |
Chile—Foreign relations—Brazil—20th century | Chile—History—1973–1988
Classification: LCC F3100 .B866 2025 | DDC 983.06/5—dc23/eng/20250521
LC record available at https://lccn.loc.gov/2025013297

For product safety concerns under the European Union's General Product
Safety Regulation (EU GPSR), please contact gpsr@mare-nostrum.co.uk or
write to the University of North Carolina Press and Mare Nostrum Group B.V.,
Mauritskade 21D, 1091 GC Amsterdam, The Netherlands.

Para Chico e Matias, meu coração inteiro.

Dulce Patria, recibe los votos

Con que Chile en tus aras juró

Que o la tumba serás de los libres,

O el asilo contra la opresión.

NATIONAL ANTHEM OF CHILE

CONTENTS

ILLUSTRATIONS

ACKNOWLEDGMENTS

This book has been a major part of my life for a long time. Since I first started my research, I have published another book and its translation, moved three times, changed jobs, and had a child. Many people supported me throughout these projects, and I am deeply appreciative.

I want to express my profound gratitude to the Brazilians who had the courage to stand against the civilian-military dictatorship from its earliest days and later sought exile in Chile. These individuals are vital witnesses and narrators of this history. Unfortunately, many of them are no longer here to see the result of the project to which they contributed so much. I owe a special thanks to Marcos Arruda, Wilson Barbosa, Solange Bastos, Otto Brockes, Rene de Carvalho, Eliete Ferrer, Reinaldo Guarany, Anivaldo Padilha, Aluízio Palmar, Ubiramar Peixoto de Oliveira, Nielsen Pires, Jovelino Ramos, Vera Vital Brasil, Jean Marc von der Weid, and many others. Cabo Anselmo, Aristóteles Drummond, and Orlando Saenz Rojas also granted interviews, for which I am appreciative.

To the entire team at the University of North Carolina Press, especially Elaine Maisner, who believed in this book from day one, Debbie Gershenowitz, who took over with generosity and expertise, Alexis Dumain, who supported me through the final and crucial stages, grammar master Erin Granville, and Alex Martin, whose eagle eyes made me a better writer—thank you. I also want to acknowledge the anonymous reviewers, whose insights pushed me to work harder when necessary and fall in love with this work all over again. I am also indebted to Sandra Paine for being my patient copyeditor for more than a decade.

Given the notorious practice of destroying evidence during the dictator-ship, I long believed it would be difficult to find documents attesting to the Brazilian influence in Chile. However, it was not by chance that I found box after box of still uncatalogued materials. It was the result of the hard work of those involved in the Brazilian Truth Commission and state-level truth com-missions, and the keen eye of the staff at the Brazilian National Archives, es-pecially Paulo Augusto Ramalho. I am also grateful to the Coordenação-Geral de Documentação Diplomática at the Arquivo Central do Itamaraty. During my visits to Brasília, I was fortunate to find friendship, support, and lodging with Monica and Luiz Marcelo Pinheiro Chaves.

At the Cancillería de Chile, Carmen Gloria Duhart facilitated my re-search. I also appreciate the team that made the documents of the Archivo del Terror and the National Security Archive accessible online. The National Archives, along with the John F. Kennedy Library and the Nixon Library and Museum, guided me at different stages of this research. I am particularly grateful to the Gerald Ford Library and the LBJ Presidential Library, which awarded me fellowships that enabled me to conduct in-person research. In Austin, I had in Lynore and Jonathan Brown the best company. Just as crucial as these major impressive archives is Documentos Revelados, an online archive created by the tenacious Aluízio Palmar, who was among the Brazilians exiled in Chile.

The images in this book come from the Brazilian National Archives, the Richard Nixon Library, the Colección Museo Histórico Nacional de Chile, and the Centro de Pesquisa e Documentação (CPDOC) at the Fundação Getúlio Vargas. The director at the CPDOC, Celso Castro, has been not only an inspiration but a friend for over a decade, someone I always make sure I see, anywhere in the world, not only because of his unwavering support but because he has an adorable family.

Many sparks for this research emerged from informal conversations with my professors Pablo Piccatto and James Naylor Green during my master's studies at Columbia University. In addition to them, I had the support of Kate Hampton, Marc Hertzman, Roberto Santamaría, and Tom Trebat.

At the City University of New York, where I pursued my doctorate, I was fortunate to have the marvelous Amy Chazkel as an adviser. Mary Roldán epitomizes generosity, having offered me countless hours of her intellectual marathons, a gift she continues to give her current students. I also extend my thanks to Joel Allen, Herman Bennett, Joshua C. Brumberg, Steve Everett, Dagmar Herzog, David Nasaw, Helena Rosenblatt, Karen Sander, Jonathan Sassi, Marilyn Weber, and the always insightful writer Thomas Kessner.

I was lucky to encounter brilliant minds in the classroom, such as Gordon Barnes, Jonathan Hill, Abigail Lapin, Glen Olson, Chelsea Schields, and Krystle Sweda.

Laird Bergad has been a rigorous professor, a generous mentor, and a great friend. He and Fatima have welcomed me with open hearts and gave me a family far from home. He also opened the doors of the Center for Latin American, Caribbean, and Latino Studies (CLACLS), which provided me with travel support, study space, and the best friends I made during my academic career, including my friends for life Amanda Marin, Karen Okigbo, Victoria Stone, and Sebastián Villamizar; partners in the CLACLS road Justine Calcagno, Lawrence Capello, Laura Limonic, and Andreina Torres; and my brilliant team Juan Acevedo, Cathy Cabrera-Figueroa, Gloria Caminha, Marco Castillo, Diomelca Rivas, Lidia Hernández-Tapia, and Fátima Vélez. Without CLACLS's support, this book would not exist.

Over the years, I taught at various universities within the CUNY system, and my students have influenced not only this work but my life. To those who shared their knowledge with me in the classrooms of Borough of Manhattan Community College, Hunter College, and Lehman College—please forgive the cliché, but I have learned more from you than you from me. I consider myself especially fortunate to have returned to the Graduate Center, now as a professor in the history department. Maricarmen Canales Moreno contributed directly with revisions. Lemann College, the Graduate Center, and CUNY supported me with grants and fellowships on multiple occasions and have been crucial for this work.

At Lehman, I am fortunate to be part of an incredibly prolific department, alongside intellectuals like David Badillo, Laird Bergad, Forrest Colburn, Alyshia Gálvez, John Gonzalez, Teresita Levy, Sarah Ohmer, Milagros Ricourt, Magdalena Sagardia, and Xavier Totti. Bertrade Banoum, Karin Beck, James Mahon, Eileen Markey, Julie Maybee, and my *hermanita* LaRose Parris have been sources of support and inspiration.

I feel extremely fortunate and honored to work at public universities in the United States, and I want to take this opportunity to express my immense gratitude to the Federal University of Rio de Janeiro (UFRJ), where I completed my bachelor's in journalism and master's in social anthropology with the mentorship of some of the greatest minds in these fields. This would never have been possible for me if they were not institutions free of charge. Access to top-tier education should be a right, not a privilege. In memory of my principal mentor, Gilberto Velho, I want to express my debt to ECO-UFRJ and Museu Nacional-UFRJ.

My amazing friends made sure I continued appreciating life beyond these pages. The writing goddesses Susanne Ferguson, Marianne González Le Saux, Katy Lasdow, and Rachel Newman held my hand in moments of despair and joy. Maria Braeckel, Barbara Condliffe, Alex Drake, Genevieve Hanson, Jessica Kessler, Sophie Marks, Chi Nguyen, Huong Pham, and Kiti Kajana Phillips, I feel lucky to have you around the corner. I also want to thank Paula Abreu, Silvio Almeida, Martin Alvarez, Zoy Anastassakis, Pedro Aquino Paiva, Juliana Barbassa, Marina Bedran, Adriana Carranca, Neia Carvalho, Hector Celis, Mayra Cotta, Margarita Fajardo, Fan Fan, Flavia Jacomo, Karina Kushnir, Ernani Lemos, Juliana and Rodrigo Maroni, Andreia Marreiro, Sandra Moreyra (in memoriam), Oliver Murphey, Marcelo Noah, Antonio Oliveira, Carla Ribeiro, Maria Fernanda Rodrigues, Aníbal Rodríguez-Montas, João Luiz Sampaio, Fernanda Santos, Fernanda Sofio, Daniel Wiedemann, and Juliana Yonezawa for their friendship and support.

This book follows in the footsteps of scholars who raised questions, unearthed documents, and paved the way for a deeper discussion about the relations among South American countries during the Cold War, including Vânia Bambirra, Patrick Barr-Melej, Alessandra Castilho, Michelle Chase, Benjamin Cowan, René Armand Dreifuss, Monica González, James Naylor Green, Horacio Gutiérrez, Tanya Harmer, Renata Keller, Peter Kornbluh, Felipe Loureiro, Luiz Alberto Moniz Bandeira, Pio Penna Filho, Carlo Patti, Rodrigo Patto, Luiz Bernardo Pericás, Margaret Power, Daniel Aarão Reis, Denise Rollemberg, Marlise Simons, Rogério de Souza Farias, Matias Spektor, Samantha Vaz, Alejandro Velasco, and Paulo Fagundes Vizentini.

My mother Denise, my father João Marcos, and my sister Julia were part of this conversation for many decades, giving me insights and, more important, love. So were their friends and my "aunts and uncles" Paulo, Rita, Niltinho, Walderléa, Paulo Roberto, Adauto, Tarcísio, Sônia, and many others.

I never take for granted the luck to share life with my favorite two people in the world. Francisco Quinteiro Pires's intelligence, sense of humor, and love make me happier every day. Thank you for the little things (like charging my phone without my noticing) and the big ones (like raising a person). There has never been a moment when I didn't feel completely supported. My son, Matias, reminds me every day of what really matters. Witnessing you grow expands my brain, body, and soul in unimaginable ways. You are my pride and joy.

ABBREVIATIONS

ADELA Atlantic Community Development Group
       for Latin America (Agrupación Atlántica
       de Desarrollo para América Latina)

  AI-5 Institutional Act no. 5
       (Ato Institucional Número Cinco)

  AILA Latin American Industrial Association
       (Asociación de Industriales Latinoamericanos)

   ALN National Liberating Action (Ação Libertadora Nacional)

 CAMDE Brazilian Campaign of Women for Democracy
       (Campanha da Mulher pela Democracia)

CENIMAR Navy Intelligence Center
       (Centro de Informações da Marinha)

   CIA US Central Intelligence Agency

  CIEX Brazilian Foreign Office's Intelligence Center
       (Centro de Informações do Exterior)

   COA Council of the Americas

   CSN Brazilian National Security Council
       (Conselho de Segurança Nacional)

DSN	National Security Doctrine (Doutrina de Segurança Nacional)
DOPS	Department of Political and Social Order (Departamento de Ordem Política e Social)
ECLAC	Economic Commission for Latin America and the Caribbean
EMFA	General Staff of the Armed Forces (Estado Maior das Forças Armadas)
ESG	Brazilian War College (Escola Superior de Guerra)
IBAD	Brazilian Institute for Democratic Action (Instituto Brasileiro de Ação Democrática)
IPES	Institute for Social Studies and Research (Instituto de Pesquisas e Estudos Sociais)
MAPU	Popular Unitary Action Movement (Movimiento de Acción Popular Unitaria)
MIR	Revolutionary Left Movement (Movimiento de Izquierda Revolucionaria)
MR-8	October 8 Revolutionary Movement (Movimento Revolucionário 8 de Outubro)
OAS	Organization of American States
PAEG	Government Economic Action Program (Programa de Ação Econômica do Governo)
SNI	Brazilian National Intelligence Service (Serviço Nacional de Informações)
SOFOFA	Federation of Chilean Industry (Sociedad de Fomento Fabril)
UP	Chilean Popular Unity (Unidad Popular)
VAR-Palmares	Palmares Armed Revolutionary Vanguard (Vanguarda Armada Revolucionária Palmares)
VPR	Popular Revolutionary Vanguard (Vanguarda Popular Revolucionária)

DICTATORSHIP
ACROSS BORDERS

INTRODUCTION

When Salvador Allende was elected president of Chile in 1970, Brazil had been a right-wing dictatorship for over six years. At the height of the Cold War, a socialist leader in the neighborhood was not good news. The Brazilian government was dissatisfied with the choice of Chilean voters and lawmakers for multiple reasons. Allende embodied the menace of communism, represented the destabilizing of a long tradition of cooperation between the countries, and offered a potential harbor for political adversaries of the Brazilian dictatorship. This book argues that for years Brazil actively sought to undermine Allende's government. Whether working with US intelligence services or acting independently, spying on supporters of the Chilean leader or sending torturers to the National Stadium, the Brazilian dictatorship worked to put an end to the Marxist administration.

Many Brazilians who went into exile in Chile have been denouncing these actions for decades. Today, additional evidence makes clear that the speculation about Brazilian support of the Chilean coup was not the result of their faulty memories but instead was yet another true story of US-backed interference in a sovereign nation.[1] Brazil was a key regional ally against the spread of communism in Latin America. Furthermore, the country had its own anticommunist agenda. Businesspeople and politicians were interested primarily in protecting their economic and political interests amid fears of a growing leftist movement and the high inflation, slow growth, and rising unemployment experienced during the João Goulart government. They feared that center-left policies would exacerbate these problems by undermining free-market principles and private property rights. Leading up to and after

1

Brazil's 1964 coup d'état, these fears, combined with a growing anticommunist sentiment and the military aim of "restoring order," became the narrative to support dictatorship as the only way to prevent Brazil from slipping into chaos. A similar rationale would later justify interference in Chile.

Over the past decade, an abundance of new sources has become available due to the work of truth commissions, activists, and historians of Latin America and the Cold War. This book leans heavily on such sources, including documents in more than a dozen archives in Brazil, Chile, Paraguay, and the United States, as well as a plethora of scholarly works that pioneered the investigation into Brazil's role in the installation of dictatorships in the region. It departs from a US–Soviet Union approach to focus instead on the complex, multinational history of the South American Cold War. It calls for a closer examination of interactions between local powerhouses, especially Brazil, the first to embrace anticommunism as state policy.

Submerged in the West-East Cold War narrative, researchers have examined Chile-US relations before, during, and after Allende's presidency and blamed the US Central Intelligence Agency (CIA) for weakening the Popular Unity government.[2] In light of disturbing images of the bombing of the Chilean presidential palace, this first wave of scholarship mostly focused on US influence as the only external factor leading to the coup. It was especially motivated by the revelations of the 1975 Church Committee—when it became public that President Nixon had demanded that the CIA make the Chilean economy "scream" to "prevent Allende from coming to power or to unseat him."[3] Before committing suicide in La Moneda Palace, Allende addressed his countrymen for the last time, blaming his fall on "foreign capital, imperialism, united to conservatism."[4] He nominally pointed to members of the military but did not mention the United States or the Chilean leftist groups that had been pressuring him to deliver his promise of a Chilean path to socialism.[5]

Although trained historians may be inclined to consider official documents more reliable than people's voices—even though written words are still products of human minds—this book relies on eyewitness accounts by exiles, torturers, businesspeople, and other actors involved in the political scenario of the South American Cold War. While some of the exiles interviewed for this book seemed eager to talk about their experiences; others were reticent. None were indifferent. Many of their memories were impacted by time and sorrow. Some could not be corroborated by official documents. Nevertheless, the difficulties of finding sources about this period due to the destruction of evidence and the fact that many documents remain classified should not prevent the testimony of people who experienced the South American Cold War from being included in its narrative.

It is impossible to confirm how many Brazilian exiles lived in Chile at the time of the 1973 coup or if they were a majority group among exiles in other places. Historian Denise Rollemberg wrote in 1999 that "the goal of quantifying the number of exiles was completely frustrated by the total lack of data with real meaning. Any attempt to do so would be mere supposition without any foundation."[6] This remains true. The survival of a political exile depends on secrecy; it can be dangerous for someone with powerful enemies to reveal their name, address, and nationality. The French newspaper *Le Monde* estimated that there were around 1,200 Brazilians in Chile, while other publications offered higher figures. According to the Committee Carlos de Ré for Truth and Justice of Rio Grande do Sul, at least 123 Brazilians were detained in Chile's National Stadium. The Pinochet regime killed six of them.[7] They had ended up in Santiago for different reasons: Brasília established agreements with Chile to receive some of them; others chose the country because they had friends, family, or professional contacts, especially at universities. There were also supporters of Allende who decided to assist in the development of Chile's path to socialism. Although many were members of guerrilla and resistance groups, most were not in Chile to develop military strategies that would allow them to go back to Brazil and fight the dictatorship, as was the case of exiles in Cuba. Rather, they were students, intellectuals, artists, and educators, looking for a safe place.

Vânia Bambirra developed some of her most pathbreaking works in political science while at the University of Chile.[8] Educator Paulo Freire understood the instrumentality of reading words as a precursor to reading the world when working with educators in rural Chile. These ideas would later be developed in his book *Pedagogy of the Oppressed*, one of the most cited works in the social sciences.[9] In 1966, while teaching in Santiago, Fernando Henrique Cardoso and Enzo Faletto cowrote their seminal book about dependency theory, *Dependência e desenvolvimento na América Latina*.[10] Cardoso would later be elected president of Brazil for two terms, serving from 1995 to 2003.

There were three major waves of Brazilian political exiles to Chile. The first took place right after the 1964 coup and was comprised of professors, politicians, and other professionals who had lost their jobs for being considered enemies of the regime.[11] From leftist political activists and labor organizers to intellectuals, guerrilla fighters, and human rights defenders, the dictatorship operated under the belief that opposition to its policies was enough for an individual to be deemed a threat to national security, stability, and its anticommunist agenda, justifying extreme measures to repress opposition and maintain power.

The second wave of exiles came in 1968 and 1969, after the promulgation of Institutional Act no. 5 (AI-5), when political persecution of the government's enemies reached its zenith.[12] The decree, approved on December 13, 1968, gave President Artur da Costa e Silva the authority to order the National Congress and the state legislative assemblies into forced recess. Under the pretext of "national security," AI-5 authorized the government to appoint *interventores* (federal officers) to run states and municipalities. Censorship prevented the press from circulating freely and the government demanded, with an iron hand, the revision or simply prohibited music, films, plays, and television programs.[13] The new legislation also deemed political meetings illegal and suspended habeas corpus for political crimes.[14] The torture, murder, and imprisonment of anyone perceived as an adversary intensified. Official data attest that this was the most violent period of the Brazilian dictatorship, with more than 400 deaths.[15] Students and young activists became the most common victims of state repression, and, for many, the only way to survive was to leave the country.

The third and last major wave of Brazilian exiles began with Allende's election in 1970, when supporters of his socialist government fled to Chile with the hope of witnessing the development of a nation where their ideals would be at the center of policymaking.[16] Otto Brockes, a physician in Brazil, moved to Santiago with the intention of being part of Allende's *via chilena al socialismo*, which included the nationalization of copper mining and other large-scale industries, the expansion of a land redistribution program initiated by his predecessor Eduardo Frei, and increased investment in welfare programs.[17] "Allende was a very evolved person who had clear beliefs, and had a governmental program dedicated to greatly improving life conditions of the Chilean people," Brockes observed more than four decades after the Chilean coup.[18] Allende was careful not to create a diplomatic crisis with his most powerful neighbor, but his support for Brazilian exiles was enough to intensify the tension between the two countries. The Brazilian government increased its monitoring of exiles, who lived in a permanent state of distrust and anxiety.

For the exiles, this constant surveillance was the first indication that the Brazilian authoritarian regime was cooperating with Chilean military and right-wing groups who planned to overthrow the democratically elected socialist president. However, the collaboration had started much earlier. As soon as the candidacy of Salvador Allende began to gain momentum leading up to Chile's 1970 presidential election, the governments of Brazil and the United States colluded with the antisocialist opposition, including the Federation of Chilean Industry (SOFOFA). They used political repression and intelligence services to intimidate Allende supporters and weaken the connections among leftists in the Southern Cone. The yearslong infiltration of agents of the Brazilian Foreign Office's Intelligence Center (CIEX) among Brazilian exiles was essential for the success of the 1973 seizure of power.

On the day of the coup, the Brazilian ambassador to Chile, Antônio Cândido da Câmara Canto, sent several telegrams to Brasília celebrating the violent events and recommending that Brazil become the first to officially congratulate the new regime.[19] Counselor Tomas Amenabar Vergada, chief of staff of Chile's Ministry of Foreign Affairs, went to the Brazilian embassy to inform the friendly nation of the new governmental organization.[20] A month after the coup, an extensive report from CIEX celebrated the return to "normality" in Chile. It stated that schools were open, the police continued searching for weapons, nine people were "summarily shot" on September 30, another three were executed in Santiago on the same day, and another six were shot in Iquique.[21] The Brazilian government defined this as "normal."

The support of the largest country in South America was also instrumental for the solidification of the Augusto Pinochet regime. When the Soviet Union canceled the export of wheat to Chile, a month after the coup, the United States opened a line of credit to allow the country to buy the grain. Brazil went further. A few days later, the nation donated a shipful of corn flour. It also sent forty tons of sugar as soon as Cuba cut exports to Chile, and even redirected to Santiago bags of sugar that had already been sold to other buyers.[22] The Brazilian government opened a $50 million line of unrestricted financial credit to Chile, which encouraged Argentina to offer another $25 million.[23] The Brazilian military fueled the National Stadium—the main center of murder and violence in the first months of the Chilean dictatorship—with torturers and medical supplies.[24] When the Pinochet military needed to expand its arsenal, Brasília sent weapons from its own arms reserves, with the coat of arms carefully erased—an acknowledgment of the need to hide the extensive aid.[25] Although these efforts to keep secret the Brazilian participation in the overthrow of Allende were successful, and such interference remained obfuscated by the US role, it is finally possible to establish that responsibility and demand accountability.

The hypothesis that the Brazilian government conspired for years, even before Allende's election, to prevent him from taking power and later played a substantial role in his overthrow, has been raised not only by exiles but also by diplomats in the region.[26] Former US ambassador to Chile Nathaniel Davis wrote about the "Brazil Connection" in 1985. He stated that his Brazilian counterpart, Câmara Canto, had approached him to suggest an "inter-embassy coordination" to provoke the demise of the Allende government.[27] Davis also mentions the support of Brazilian businessmen for anti-Allende groups in Chile, including the fascist Patria y Libertad (Homeland and Freedom). He affirmed that he had no "real doubt" that the allegations of a Brazil connection were true and provided firsthand accounts to corroborate the accusation. The recent discovery of systematic, primary-source documentation, combined with oral histories of Brazilian exiles, confirms that Davis's assessment was accurate and that the scope of such interference was much larger than previously known.

Ultimately, what we know is this: the Brazilian government provided money, weapons, medicine, expertise, intelligence reports, and torturers to the enemies of the Allende government prior to the coup and after the Chilean military took power. In Chile, Brazil internationalized its model of state terror and political repression beginning in the 1960s. It helped launch the infamous Operation Condor, implemented in 1975 by the Southern Cone dictatorships of Chile, Uruguay, Argentina, Paraguay, Bolivia, and Brazil with the support of the United States. This campaign caused 60,000 deaths and 400,000 imprisonments throughout Latin America.[28] The interchange of ideas, strategies, military supplies, and diplomatic policies between Brazil and Chile facilitated the fall of Allende, the strengthening of the authoritarian Pinochet regime, and the intergovernmental terror cooperation that ultimately resulted in Operation Condor.[29]

This book does not deny the role of the United States in the Condor years, much less in the derailment of the Salvador Allende presidency. It does not diminish in any way the violence of US covert action in Chile, which culminated in popular disapproval of the government.[30] Instead, this work intends to reframe the United States as merely one of many countries that influenced Chile, among which Brazil appears as central.[31] It goes beyond the role of the United States and the Soviet Union in the shaping of democracies and dictatorships in the region, concentrating, instead, on a new understanding of the Cold War that privileges an interregional approach.[32]

In contrast with recent scholarship that investigates the relations between Brazil and Chile during the Allende presidency, this book begins just before the implementation of the Brazilian dictatorial regime, in 1964.[33] The periodization not only allows for a broader understanding of diplomatic, political, and economic relations between the two countries but also permits an analysis of how policies evolved before, during, and after the Allende years. The socialist leader was already a prominent political figure in Chile during the Eduardo Frei Montalva administration (1964–70).

As early as 1966, the Brazilian minister of foreign affairs, General Juracy Magalhães, and his Chilean counterpart, Gabriel Valdés, discussed potential outcomes should Allende win the presidency.[34] The multitude of forces that culminated in the 1973 coup in Chile started being constructed as soon as the Brazilian dictatorship was established—almost a decade earlier. The two nations had been commercial, cultural, and diplomatic partners for centuries. However, between 1964 and 1973, when Brazil was a dictatorship and Chile remained a democracy, there were inevitable conflicts. The Brazilian government policy toward Chile after 1964 was shaped by the National Security Doctrine (Doutrina de Segurança Nacional; DSN), which urged a focus on "national defense."[35] A clear reaction to the Cold War, the doctrine, which became law in Brazil in 1968, indicated that it was necessary to identify "domestic enemies" of the regime, even if they were abroad. These policies would later be embraced by Augusto Pinochet, who declared the doctrine to be the official ideology of Chile on the third anniversary of the coup, in 1976.[36]

A firm believer in the DSN, the Brazilian ambassador in Chile guided his country's military regarding the situation in the region, influenced government decisions, and offered support to the Chilean military. The Brazilian embassy in Santiago served as a meeting place for coup plotters, a source of information about the internal affairs of Allende and his staff, and a hub to exert pressure on supporters of the Popular Unity (UP) administration through the monitoring of Brazilian exiles. Câmara Canto was the most famous face of the civilian branch of the military dictatorship, which also included other diplomats, businesspeople, intellectuals, and right-wing institutions.[37] In the past decade, the debate over the nature of the authoritarian regime—which for decades was called a "military dictatorship"—resulted in a broader investigation of its civilian actors.[38]

The dictatorships in Chile and Brazil cannot be understood as isolated effects of the Cold War, domestic issues, and international economic crises. They were part of historical processes of both societies with the engagement of multiple actors from the civilian and military sectors. This book adopts the term "civilian-military dictatorship" not only because historians have demonstrated the role of civilians in these periods of military rule, but especially because one of its main goals is to unveil the contribution of Brazilian diplomats to the overthrow of Allende.

For decades, the Brazilian government has denied the existence of the Brazilian Foreign Office's Intelligence Center, which was at the heart of these actions.[39] Recently declassified documents, nevertheless, not only confirm but also detail the scope of its activities. CIEX was an arm of the Brazilian National Intelligence Service (SNI).[40] During the entire Allende presidency, its agents spied on exiles, with the goal of repressing left-wing groups and collecting inside information about the socialist leader.[41] The secret intelligence service was initially founded to report on the situation of Brazilians in Uruguay, where deposed president João Goulart and his family lived in exile.[42] However, after Institutional Act no. 5 in 1968 and the election of Salvador Allende in 1970, Chile became a central focus of CIEX.

Military attachés and agents who had infiltrated among exiles wrote reports on the activities of political enemies of the regime and on the Allende administration. Spies befriended leftist militants who had close ties with the Chilean government, allowing Brazilian authorities to build an extensive source of information about socialist leaders. CIEX agents reported on domestic problems, such as demonstrations, strikes, and economic indicators. In many instances, they discussed, foresaw, and even started preparing a military coup. The Brazilian dictatorship had always known that guerrilla groups, exiles, and intellectuals were circulating widely in the region and perceived such connections as a menace. The best way of combating the internationalization of the Left was to promote dictatorship across borders.[43]

One of the main reasons for the lack of research into these activities was the absence of documentation. The secretive nature of dictatorships and the need to hide state-sponsored crimes, including systematic torture and murder, account for the destruction of much evidence.[44] The Brazilian regime, however, tended to methodically document its activities.[45] Additionally, much of Brazil's interference in Chile was part of transnational cooperation, so several records survived on one end of the line or another. Some of the first clues came from the efforts of the National Security Archive to declassify the conversations between Richard Nixon and his Brazilian counterpart, Emílio

Garrastazu Médici. The details of the latter's visit to Washington, DC, in December 1971, when the two leaders openly discussed strategies to topple Allende, were clear indicators of the Brazilian-US collusion that culminated in the coup in Chile.[46]

In 2011, the approval of Legislative Act 12.527, known as the Access to Information Law, gave Brazilians the fundamental right to obtain data about the government.[47] A year later, in 2012, the establishment of the Brazilian Truth Commission determined that documents related to the 1964 coup and the subsequent dictatorship should become available at the Brazilian National Archives in Brasília.[48] The initiative, however, had its constraints. First, access to documentation came much later than in other countries of the Southern Cone.[49] For example, the Chilean National Commission for Truth and Reconciliation (Comisión Nacional de Verdad y Reconciliación), also known as the Rettig Commission, was created in 1990, immediately after the end of the Augusto Pinochet regime, with the objective of documenting "human rights abuses resulting in death or disappearance during the years of military rule, from September 11, 1973, to March 11, 1990."[50] Second, the Brazilian Truth Commission did not uncover many of the documents belonging to the military intelligence services, such as the Navy Intelligence Center (CENIMAR), the Air Force's Aviation Information Service, and the Army Intelligence Service.[51] Nevertheless, in addition to several bureaucratic documents reporting day-to-day activities, the files included correspondence between military authorities from several countries that attest to the fact that the Brazilian regime's influence was much broader than once imagined, encompassing the export of military equipment and the monitoring of Chilean leftist movements as well as the Allende government itself.[52]

As previously noted, this book acknowledges the role of the United States in the coups of 1964 in Brazil and 1973 in Chile.[53] In that sense, it also considers prior studies suggesting that the United States "attempted to modify or perpetuate the internal balance of political forces in Brazil" through strategies such as scare-mongering among business elites about the expansion of emerging Peasant League movements and policies of the Goulart government in general, exaggerating the importance of maintaining a close relationship with the military.[54] This strategy resonated with the anticommunist struggle in Brazil much earlier than the 1970s.

However, the perception that Brazil was a mere pawn of the United States, attempting to exercise a kind of "subimperialism," could not be further from reality. President Médici was eager to pursue exclusively Brazilian policies without direction from the United States.[55]

When Richard Nixon and Emílio Garrastazu Médici met, in December 1971, Brazil was in a strong economic position. From 1968 to 1973, its gross domestic product grew at an impressive yearly rate of 11 percent. The foreign investment rate reached 19 percent.[56] At the same time, the country faced growing international criticism. Médici saw the trip as an opportunity to silence the opposition and reinforce the country's economic strength.[57] For Médici, Nixon's preoccupation with Allende coupled with international criticism of the slow US withdrawal from Vietnam empowered Brazil to take the lead in the fight against communism in South America.[58] At dinner in the State Dining Room at the White House on the day of Médici's arrival, Nixon famously said, "We know that as Brazil goes, so will go the rest of that Latin American Continent," presaging the series of military coups that would take place in the following years, with the support of the United States and Brazil. Nixon stated, "We shall work together for a greater future for your people, for our people, and for all the people of the American family, for which we have a special place in our hearts."[59]

The following day, Nixon proposed the creation of a secret line of communication, to which only the two presidents and one designated authority on each side would have access. Nixon named his national security adviser, Henry Kissinger, and Médici enlisted his minister of foreign affairs, Mário Gibson Barbosa. That way, the Brazilian president stated, "not even typists had knowledge of them."[60]

Nixon then asked about the political situation in Chile and Médici reassured him that "Allende would be overthrown for very much the same reasons that Goulart had been overthrown in Brazil." The US president asked Médici if he thought that the "Chilean Armed Forces were capable of overthrowing Allende," referring unflinchingly to a coup d'état. The Brazilian dictator responded straightforwardly "that he felt that they were, adding that Brazil was exchanging many officers with the Chileans, and made clear that Brazil was working towards this end." Nixon then reinforced the importance of the partnership between Brazil and the United States to achieve their objectives in Chile. "If money were required or other discreet aid, we might be able to make it available. This should be held in the greatest confidence. But we must try and prevent new Allendes and Castros and try where possible to reverse these trends," summarized Nixon.[61]

By 1975, most of South America was under the control of dictatorships: Argentina, Bolivia, Chile, Paraguay, Uruguay, and Brazil had experienced the consolidation of authoritarian governments. In November, these countries' leaders met in Santiago to discuss the rise of left-wing movements. Chile provided most of the funding for this meeting, and Manuel Contreras, the head of its National Intelligence Directorate (Dirección de Inteligencia Nacional), the Chilean secret police, played a key role.[62] The Brazilian Department of Political and Social Order (DOPS) also actively supported these efforts.[63] This meeting marked the beginning of Operation Condor, which with the support of the United States delivered one of its longest-running objectives for the region: "coordination of the struggle against 'Communism' and 'subversion,'" as stated by the head of the US Southern Command, General Robert W. Porter, as early as 1968.[64] The plan focused on the eradication of leftist ideas from the continent and, to achieve this end, the assassination of political enemies.[65]

Recently, multiple groups have begun investigating whether João Goulart was one of the victims of Operation Condor. He died on December 6, 1976, at his farm in Corrientes, Argentina, of an alleged heart attack. In 2000, the Brazilian House of Representatives created a special commission to investigate Goulart's death. It did not reach a conclusion, but the official report stated, "It is not possible to affirm peremptorily that Goulart was murdered. But it would be deeply irresponsible of us, after all the interviews and facts here consolidated, to conclude that João Goulart's death occurred under normal circumstances."[66] A former member of Uruguay's intelligence service declared that Goulart was poisoned, on the order of DOPS chief Sérgio Fleury.[67] The Goulart family has long called for a deeper investigation into his death, highlighting the political tensions and surveillance they faced in exile. Goulart's widow, Maria Thereza, released documents to prove that the family was being monitored while living in Uruguay.[68] These allegations reflect the broader climate of suspicion and fear surrounding political dissidents before and under Operation Condor, a transnational network of repression in South America.

OVERVIEW OF THE BOOK

This book is divided into six chapters that address one overarching question: What was the influence of the Brazilian dictatorship on the violent end of the Allende administration, culminating in the 1973 Chilean coup d'état? Chapter 1 contends that preparation for the overthrow of the socialist government in Chile did not start with the election of Salvador Allende, in 1970. The actions of the Brazilian government in the decade before the coup d'état of 1973 were key precursors. Opponents of socialism in Brazil, Chile, and the United States strategized and discussed the need for a coup as early as 1966, when the Brazilian minister of foreign affairs, General Juracy Magalhães, met with his Chilean counterpart, Gabriel Valdés, to discuss the possible victory of "the communists" in the 1970 elections.[69] The blueprint for what would happen in Chile was developed even earlier, during the first years of US covert action in Brazil. Dissatisfaction with Goulart increased after the 1962 Meeting of the Organization of American States (OAS), when his administration voted against the boycott of Cuba.[70] In the meantime, Chile was chosen to be the showcase for the Alliance for Progress.

Chapter 2 follows the waves of exiles from Brazil to Chile, starting in 1964, peaking in 1968, and continuing with the Quarenta and the Setenta, political prisoners exchanged for the release of foreign ambassadors to Brazil. The celebrity-like status they achieved when arriving in Santiago did not translate into a comfortable life, as a series of oral histories and documents demonstrate. By focusing on a group that tried to influence Chilean politics while being monitored by Brazilian intelligence services, this chapter offers evidence of the state-sponsored policies to destabilize the government and leftist groups in Chile.

Chapter 3 examines the transnational partnership between Brazil and the United States to influence Chilean politics; Brazil wanted to have as much power as the United States. For that, it created a model of action to fight communism in the region that had diplomats at the center, including the country's ambassador in Santiago, Antonio Cândido da Câmara Canto.[71] The Brazilian dictatorship relied on an apparatus of espionage that CIEX implemented in Chile, enabling a surge of inside information about the socialist government.

Chapter 4 considers the various groups that acted against Allende: Brazilian intellectuals, policymakers, and businesspeople. Although the economic policies of the Chilean and Brazilian dictatorships differed widely, they had in common a business sector supportive of authoritarian regimes and economists aligned with the US liberal school that rejected Keynesianism in favor of the state's playing a less interventionist role in the economy. In the early years of the Brazilian dictatorship, this was the predominant outlook, as can be seen in Roberto Campos and Otávio Gouveia de Bulhões's 1964 Government Economic Action Program (PAEG), which focused on cutting spending to combat inflation.[72] In tune with the policies of the Pinochet era, the Brazilian intellectuals who formed what René Dreifuss called the "organic elite" of the country never supported nationalist and populist approaches.[73] The Brazilian Institute for Social Studies and Research (IPES) advised Chilean businessmen on how to organize for the military coup by using the same strategy that the CIA had applied in the "spoiling operations" in Brazil as part of its efforts to destabilize perceived communist influences in the country.[74] These operations were designed to undermine political opponents, disrupt social movements, and create an environment of fear and distrust. By sabotaging progressive political initiatives, labor movements, and left-leaning governments, they sought to ensure that Brazil remained aligned with capitalist, anticommunist interests, particularly those favored by the United States during the Cold War. The women's organization El Poder Feminino (Female Power), which coordinated the March of the Empty Pots (*cacerolazo*), and the *gremios empresariales* (business guilds), which contributed to the weakening of Allende, pursued actions inspired by the Brazilian Campaign of Women for Democracy (CAMDE), an IPES creation.[75]

During the Brazilian civilian-military dictatorship, relations with the United States were cyclical. At times, alignment reigned. At others, it was replaced by the foreign policy of "responsible pragmatism," which focused on the economic needs of Brazil.[76] Chapter 5 investigates the relations among Chile, Brazil, and the United States and how their disputes influenced the first steps in the planning of the 1973 coup. The Brazilian diplomatic approach turned the most powerful nation in the world into an equal partner in the fight against communism in the region, as Operation Condor would later demonstrate.

Chapter 6 begins just before the September 1973 coup and analyzes how the "Brazil Connection" contributed to this violent outcome.[77] Through the testimonies of exiles, this chapter demonstrates that the Brazilian government acted to support the new authoritarian regime in its first days, sending torturers, money, and intelligence to Santiago. At the same time, it refused to protect its own citizens who were among the victims of human rights abuses in Chile.

Fifty years after the Chilean coup, Brazil and Chile still struggle with the legacy of the dictatorships that ruled the two countries in the second half of the twentieth century.[78] In October 2020, Chileans rushed to the polls in the midst of a pandemic to scrap the constitution designed during Pinochet's regime, but not quite two years later, 62 percent of voters decided to keep the text in place.[79] The previous years were marked by Chile's Estallido Social (Social Explosion), when hundreds of people occupied the streets of Santiago to protest neoliberal policies established during the authoritarian regime.[80] Decades after the fall of the dictator, the country's leaders still include heirs of the authoritarian rule. The chief of national defense who declared a state of emergency during the Estallido was Javier Iturriaga del Campo, whose uncle was accused of human rights violations.[81] Andrés Chadwick, interior minister between 2012 and 2014 during the first government of Sebastián Piñera, was a member of the *pinochetista* National Unity Youth Front (Frente Juvenil de Unidad Nacional) and of the military junta's legislative commission.[82] Piñera is Chadwick's cousin and the younger brother of José Piñera Echenique, one of the Chicago Boys who served as minister of labor and social security, and of mining, under Pinochet.[83]

Despite the passage of time, the ideologies that once shaped these nations continue to resonate, as seen in their contemporary political landscapes. In 2018, Brazilians elected right-wing retired military officer Jair Bolsonaro as president, despite his lack of administrative qualifications. In twenty-seven years as a member of Congress, he approved only two projects.[84] During this same period, he paid homage to the dictatorship multiple times. In 2016, when announcing his vote to impeach democratically elected president Dilma Rousseff, Bolsonaro praised Carlos Alberto Brilhante Ustra, who had tortured Rousseff when she was a member of the guerrilla group Palmares Armed Revolutionary Vanguard (VAR-Palmares). It was a shock. Brazil's National Bar Association asked for his removal.[85] He received no punishment and rose to the most powerful position in the country two years later.

These recent developments attest to the enduring legacy of the South American dictatorships. In a period of tremendous political tension and polarization in the United States, Chile, and Brazil, this book places the three countries as powerhouses on their own, going beyond Cold War bipolarity to assess the impact of regional political forces. It argues that Brazil played a fundamental role in changing the course of the entire region. Furthermore, it documents the scope of human rights abuses by the Brazilian dictatorship, attesting that it went way beyond its own borders. This examination remains crucial today, as the echoes of past authoritarianism continue to shape contemporary politics, human rights, and regional dynamics. Understanding these historical forces is essential to sustaining a democratic future.

1

BEFORE ALLENDE

God is not a socialist. He created men deeply unequally.

ROBERTO CAMPOS

Four years before the election of Salvador Allende as president of Chile, Brazilian leaders were already debating ways to prevent him from taking office. On October 24, 1966, President Humberto de Alencar Castelo Branco convened his cabinet for the thirty-ninth meeting of the National Security Council (CSN).[1] The ministers of finance, agriculture, war, the navy, the air force, education, labor and social security, energy and commerce, among others, debated the rise of the socialist politician.[2] The center of attention was the minister of foreign affairs, General Juracy Magalhães, famous for coining the expression "What is good for the United States is good for Brazil."[3] He had served as the Brazilian ambassador to the United States until a year earlier, and that morning, he opened the meeting by sharing the impressions of his latest visits to Europe, North America, and "especially to Latin America."[4]

First, Magalhães briefly described his trips to Portugal, Italy, and the Vatican. He then detailed his meetings in Washington, where he complained about the need to improve communications, since Brazil had been "surprised" by the Bogotá Conference—a meeting of South American nations, with the main proposal of creating an economic bloc among Chile, Colombia, Venezuela, Peru, and Ecuador.[5] The Brazilian government had not been invited and sent a formal note to the press complaining about its exclusion. Magalhães was outraged. After years collaborating with the US State Department, he had been sidelined. Secretary of State Dean Rusk explained that he was also caught off-guard and was as shocked as the Brazilian diplomat. Rusk promised to exchange information about all the "problems" related to the continent and "unambiguously applauded the Brazilian government."[6]

Finally, the foreign minister transitioned to the most awaited part of his account: the trip to Chile.[7] The invitation came right after the Brazilian public outcry about the Bogotá Conference. According to Magalhães, Chile attempted to "back off of its Bogotana adventure" and sought to rebuild its ties with Brazil, as the diplomatic tradition between the two countries demanded. The Brazilian leader positioned himself against the formation of economic blocs in Latin America but defended the creation of an inter-American peace force, a suggestion rejected by his Chilean counterpart.[8] Despite all his enthusiasm, the trip brought few practical achievements, except for one agreement on transportation and some joint reports. The political gains, however, were surprisingly significant.

According to Magalhães, the Chilean minister of foreign affairs, Gabriel Valdés—who would later become one of the most ferocious critics of the Pinochet dictatorship—demonstrated concern with the rise of socialism in the country. First, as chief diplomat of Eduardo Frei's government, Valdés refused to make a statement against the Tricontinental Conference in Havana but took clear anticommunist stances and promised to act diplomatically to prevent the next Tricontinental from happening.[9] For Magalhães, this reaction represented a decisive commitment, since the Frei government engaged closely with the Communist Party, "which is very strong, representing around 30 percent of the Chilean electorate."[10] The Brazilian ministry felt emboldened to declare that its government was ready to coordinate the action of leaders in the hemisphere to protect Chile in the case of "a victory of the Communist Party in the next elections, still very far away, if the Frei Government cannot meet the aspirations of the Chilean population."[11]

To Magalhães's shock, Valdés did not contest the pledge of military action. On the contrary, he stated that if the Communist Party became the majority, the "life forces of the nation would act in Chile, as they had in Brazil and in Argentina," where, only four months earlier, Juan Carlos Onganía had overthrown Arturo Illia.[12] Magalhães reinforced the importance of the commitment and assured the other ministers and the Brazilian president that "this is a declaration of the highest importance and completely surprising for us, since our impression was that Chile was moving in the direction of accepting an eventual result of the popular vote in favor of communism." Juracy Magalhães and Gabriel Valdés continued the conversation, talking

Ministers of foreign affairs of Chile, Gabriel Valdés, and Brazil, Juracy
Magalhães, in a meeting to celebrate Chilean president Eduardo Frei Montalva.
*Source: Centro de Pesquisa e Documentação de História
Contemporânea do Brasil / Fundação Getulio Vargas.*

about the economic integration of Latin America and the role of Brazil in
such a process.[13]

It is impossible to tell if Valdés was only trying to make amends after
the anger resulting from the Bogotá Conference. However, the conversation
between the two leaders and the weight it had during that National Security
Council meeting in 1966 demonstrates that the Brazilian government was
already worried about the rise of socialism and trusted that coordinated
military action would be the only way of averting it.[14] This chapter traces the
preoccupation among leaders of Brazil, Chile, and the United States with
the rise of Salvador Allende years before the 1970s elections and the 1966

meeting between Magalhães and Valdés. The anti-Allende agenda escalated with the inauguration of João Goulart, in 1961, reached a zenith as early as 1962, when Brazil voted against the boycott of Cuba at the meeting of the Organization of American States (OAS), and became part of state policy as soon as the military took charge of Brazil, in 1964.[15]

THE MANY FACES OF BRAZILIAN DIPLOMACY

In the decades between the start of the Great Depression of 1929 and the establishment of the Brazilian dictatorship in 1964, the country's foreign policy had dramatically different phases.[16] During the Getúlio Vargas era (1930–45), it shifted from a "pragmatic equidistance" to other countries to a progressive alignment with the United States.[17] After World War II and Vargas's fall, the fear of World War III led President Eurico Gaspar Dutra (1946–51) to pursue a different approach, in which alignment was not a means but an end. Historian Gerson Moura called the period "alignment without reward."[18] Its critics acknowledged that reciprocity was not possible for the United States and contended that instead of adopting a subordinating posture Brazil should embrace an anti-Yankee tone, which surged with Brazilian nationalism in the 1950s.[19]

That was the situation when Getúlio Vargas returned to power in 1951.[20] His protectionist promises during the campaign, however, did not result in a detachment from the United States. This was the time of the "nationalistic bargain," in which the government aimed to preach to both sides of the aisle, keeping aligned with Washington but ratcheting up the call for industrial development under state leadership and foreign capital investment.[21] After Vargas's suicide, political instability followed with three successive improvised administrations until the election of Juscelino Kubitschek in 1956.[22]

"JK," a charismatic politician from Minas Gerais, timidly but resolutely tried to break with a succession of administrations that failed to find a balance between US alignment and a "Brazil-first" narrative. Kubitschek emerged as the promise of a democratic future for the region, in contrast to the Eisenhower administration (1953–61), which seemed oblivious to the political shifts in Latin America and relegated the area to a secondary position, openly supporting dictatorships in Paraguay, Peru, and Venezuela while dedicating more attention to Europe and Asia.[23] Then–vice president Richard Nixon attended Kubitschek's inauguration in January 1956 and, two years later, in May 1958, went on a tour of Latin America that excluded Brazil. In Peru and Venezuela, he felt the anger of the population in a series of demonstrations against the United States.[24] In this climate, Kubitschek launched his "Operation Pan America," an economic development program to shrink development gaps between Latin America and the United States. A year later, in 1959, the Cuban Revolution emboldened political movements against US imperialism, stoking the sentiment that a foreign policy that privileged North American interests brought little to Brazil.[25]

This crusade gained media attention and became a preoccupation of the United States. A few days before the US presidential election of 1960, *New York Times* journalist Tad Szulc wrote about pro-Castro Marxists supporting Peasant Leagues in the Brazilian Northeast.[26] If the title, "Marxists Are Organizing Peasants in Brazil," was troubling, the subtitle was frightening: "Leftist League Aims at a Political Army 40 Million Strong." For then-candidate John F. Kennedy, the story was one more piece of evidence of subversive activity in the hemisphere.[27] The alarms were sounding, and he did not wait for his inauguration to start designing a program to curtail the threat of communist expansion in the region. With the help of Adolf A. Berle, ambassador to Brazil during the Vargas era, and Lincoln Gordon, who had served in the same position during the Goulart years, the Alliance for Progress began to take shape.[28]

Only a few days after JFK's inauguration, in January 1961, Brazilians also welcomed a new leader. Jânio Quadros was elected with the largest majority of any presidential candidate up until that point. However, he quickly displeased people across the political spectrum.[29] Despite his anticorruption platform, the rise of the national debt and inflation combined with a lack of political connections rendered Quadros unpopular with an overwhelming majority of the population. Even his own party, the conservative National Labor Party (PTN), turned against him. The rejection was not limited to the domestic sphere. Quadros's foreign policy of "neutrality" provoked unease in Washington. He visited Cuba, restored diplomatic relations with the Soviet Union, supported the independence of African countries, and fully embraced a nationalist and *terceiro-mundista* rhetoric.[30] The tipping point was his awarding Ernesto "Che" Guevara the most prestigious honor offered to foreign dignitaries, the National Order of the Southern Cross.[31] On August 25, 1961, less than seven months after his inauguration, Quadros resigned, enigmatically blaming "external forces."[32]

If Quadros was far from a reliable partner in the US anticommunist crusade, his successor was even worse.[33] João Goulart's progressive ideas were like kerosene to the incendiary growth of leftist movements in the biggest nation of the region.[34] The CIA launched a multimillion-dollar campaign to support the election of anticommunist candidates at the federal, state, and municipal levels. The money was channeled from the agency's Rio de Janeiro station and its many bases in consulates all over Brazil.[35] North American officials, who had for decades been providing anticommunist materials for gatherings to discuss the Cold War, intensified connections with right-wing groups in Brazil.[36] In 1962, the CIA spent at least $5 million in support of candidates who could defeat João Goulart's allies in the October 7 general elections.[37] US ambassador Lincoln Gordon used businessmen and institutions such as the Brazilian Institute for Democratic Action (IBAD) as intermediaries to donate money to the campaigns of governors, senators, and representatives.[38]

Goulart's nationalist rhetoric also disturbed Brazilian business groups and the military.[39] They embraced the mission of transforming Brazil into a modern nation and argued that democracy hindered this project and should be a privilege only of developed countries. Julio de Mesquita Filho, owner of *O Estado de S. Paulo*, one of the most widely read newspapers in Brazil, considered that the public sector invariably failed in business enterprises. Modern democracy, he defended, was only possible in a nation where the entire population had a "cultural level" that allowed them to understand that, due to the complexity of the political system, the people should delegate all the power to those "more capable to act."[40] He was one of the men behind the creation of think tanks to fight communism and promote free trade, with the support of the United States.[41] Among these organizations were the Institute for Social Studies and Research (IPES), the Federation of Industries of the State of São Paulo (FIESP), and the Brazilian War College (ESG).[42] They all worked to weaken Goulart and, years later, would be fundamental in supporting the coup in Chile, as we will see in chapter 4.[43]

The strategy implemented against Goulart in Brazil was a blueprint for what the most powerful nation in the hemisphere would put in motion a decade later, when Salvador Allende took office in Chile. First, the United States allied with local business groups to impede Goulart's inauguration. When that did not work, the United States acted to destabilize the government with "spoiling operations," in which agents infiltrated organizations of students, workers, and politicians to promote the impression that the already problematic economic crisis was even worse. This created a "long period of unrest, deep social disorganization, and intensification of class clashes which would destroy the social and political networks of support of the government and facilitate its fall through a military coup."[44]

In March 1961, when spoiling operations were still a well-protected state secret, John F. Kennedy spoke in a White House filled with more than 200 diplomats from Latin America to reinforce the objectives of the newly introduced Alliance for Progress.[45] The president maintained that Simón Bolívar's dream of freedom and glory had never, in the long history of the hemisphere, "been nearer to fulfillment and never has it been in greater danger."[46] A few months later, Kennedy announced that the Agency for International Development would lend more than $20 billion to Latin American countries to address the need for *techo, trabajo y tierra, salud y escuela* (homes, work and land, health, and schools).[47]

Chile was the perfect vitrine for the Alliance for Progress: it had had a solid democracy since 1932, was largely urban and industrialized, and virtually the whole population was literate—a stark contrast with most of the continent.[48] A presence in the country was also strategic to prevent the emergence of "another Castro" in the region, since the Chilean people had a "tendency to flirt with communism."[49] In 1958, Jorge Alessandri was elected president with 31 percent of the votes, only 33,416 more than Salvador Allende, then the candidate of the Popular Action Front, an alliance of the Chilean Communist and Socialist Parties. For the United States, the result was proof that the Chilean Left was gaining strength. It was clear that Allende needed to be tackled. In the years between 1962 and 1969, Chile received over $1 billion in direct US loans and grants, the largest per capita amount on the continent.[50] Besides the desire to prevent the spread of communism, there was a strong impulse to protect US industry. Chile was then responsible for 80 percent of the global manufacture of copper, and 75 percent of the production came from three North American companies: Braden Copper, Anaconda, and Kennecott.[51] Allende's campaign promises included the nationalization of the copper industry.

While Chile posed a potential danger, Cuba demanded immediate action. The year 1961 ended with attempts to address the failure at the Bay of Pigs, a prelude of the Cuban Missile Crisis. In a televised speech, Fidel Castro had proclaimed himself a Marxist-Leninist and declared the island a socialist state.[52] Under this tense climate, leaders of the member nations of the OAS met in Punta del Este, Uruguay, for ten days in January 1962. The main objective was to debate their differing perspectives on Cuba. Peru and Colombia, both supporters of sanctions against the island, set the agenda. The

Eighth Meeting of Consultation of Ministers of Foreign Affairs resulted in a resolution that clearly condemned a "communist offensive in America."[53] Except for Cuba, all of the countries agreed that "the principles of communism are incompatible with the principles of the inter-American system." The diplomats decided to "suspend immediately trade with Cuba in arms and implements of war of every kind."[54] However, instead of a condemnation of Fidel Castro's government, the gathering became a symbol of the political differences among the nations involved.

The expulsion of Cuba from the inter-American system was not unanimous. Following the tradition of alignment in foreign affairs, both Brazil and Chile abstained, and the motion was adopted by a vote of fourteen to one (Cuba), with six abstentions (the other four were Argentina, Bolivia, Ecuador, and Mexico). Remembering that "in the past three years, thirteen American states have found it necessary to break diplomatic relations with the present Government of Cuba," the resolution also ruled that the country-members of the OAS should study "the feasibility and desirability of extending the suspension of trade to other items, with special attention to items of strategic importance."[55] Chile and Brazil once again abstained en bloc, accompanied by Mexico and Ecuador.

The Brazilian independent foreign policy spoke volumes. João Goulart's diplomatic approach prescribed the freedom to trade with both sides during the Cold War, strengthening Brazil as a self-reliant player in the world economic system. Established during the Jânio Quadros presidency, in 1961, the policy defended the assumption that "although states acted on the basis of the principle of self-help, they sought not only relative but also absolute gains, thus enabling other states to benefit."[56] In summary, diversified relations would promote far more economic gains than an exclusive alignment with the United States.

Goulart also welcomed the policies of the Economic Commission for Latin America and the Caribbean (ECLAC), created in 1948 with the objective of uniting Latin American countries to demand different treatment from the larger economic powers.[57] ECLAC thinkers, the Cepalinos (from the commission's Spanish and Portuguese acronym, CEPAL), defended the idea that modern economic relations echoed colonial times, with wealthier countries focusing on producing and selling complex goods and poorer nations limited to exporting raw materials. The call to handle such inequality in international trade was foundational to dependency theory. Not coincidentally, the minister of planning under João Goulart, economist Celso Furtado, was one of its founders.[58] He would later become one of the Brazilians who sought exile in Chile.[59] Goulart's foreign policy was marked by a replacement of the "East-West disputes" with a North-South model, in which the preoccupation with development and underdevelopment became central to the commercial agenda.[60]

The Brazilian votes and arguments in Punta del Este were the result of such principles. Chancellor San Tiago Dantas positioned the country as repulsed by "interventionist formulas or punishments." Raúl Bazán Dávila, who had just stepped down as Chilean ambassador to Brazil, declared that the narrative was part of the principles of noninterventionism and self-determination while, at the same time, kept the "scrupulous caution of Brazilian sovereignty."[61] But he also claimed that Goulart's posture in regard to Cuba was mere "nationalist vanity" and left the country isolated, far not only from the United States but also from Argentina, which had broken off relations with Cuba in February 1962.[62] Chile nonetheless followed Brazil's example. The bigger country took the leadership of the moderate bloc, also influencing Argentina, Mexico, Ecuador, and Bolivia.[63] The United States had to accept halfway measures and seemed poised to cautiously partner with the Goulart government, allowing for social development projects while requiring economic measures to tackle inflation.

In April 1962, John Kennedy wrote to João Goulart delineating the terms of the Alliance for Progress plans for the development of the Brazilian Northeast.[64] During the missile crisis of October 1962, Goulart played a "double game," cautiously calming his US counterpart while buttering up the Soviet envoy to Brazil with words of support.[65] The Brazilian president avoided conflict with Kennedy but was firm in explaining his opposition to military intervention in Cuba because "we always recognize in every country, whatever their regime or governmental system, the right to sovereignly decide for themselves. . . . Although we do not recognize as legitimate the offensive weaponry that the United States claims exists in Cuba, we have never recognized war as an instrument capable of solving conflicts between nations."[66]

On November 8, Soviet premier Nikita Khrushchev declared that he was grateful to Brazil for its efforts in helping to solve the conflict.[67] Hermes Lima, who had been designated minister of foreign affairs only a month before the missile crisis, continued seeking to accommodate US and Soviet interests, a posture that generated even more discomfort between Goulart and Kennedy. This feeling was shared by Brazilian elites and military leaders who would, less than two years later, lead the 1964 coup that overthrew Goulart.

Although Chilean diplomacy remained aligned with Washington, the country privileged the friendship with Brazil. Foreign Minister Carlos

Martínez Sotomayor resisted breaking diplomatic ties with Cuba despite the trend in the region.[68] When asked if—in the name of the entire democratic history of Chile—one could attest that democracy existed throughout the Americas, he enigmatically replied that "the answer is in the collective consciousness of America."[69]

ALESSANDRI AND GOULART

After the close results of the elections of 1958 and seeing Salvador Allende's popularity increase year after year, Chilean president Jorge Alessandri tried different approaches to fight the rise of left-wing politicians in the country.[70] Known for his discretion and preference for avoiding public speeches, he soon understood that relying on his charisma, or lack thereof, would be a miscalculation. So, instead of grappling with the opposition, he decided that promoting a less conservative image of his administration was the best path. Curiously, his inspiration was then–Brazilian president João Goulart, whose foreign policy projected independence from the United States without adherence to communism. Following the suggestion of Chancellor Carlos Martínez Sotomayor, he invited Goulart to visit Santiago.[71] The recently nominated Chilean ambassador to Brazil, Marcelo Ruiz Solar, was in charge of the formal invitation. He received straightforward instructions about the reasons for the visit and how to proceed, since Chile "wants to keep and extend the practices of consulting between the two governments" to achieve common ground in their decisions.[72]

On April 22, 1963, the Brazilian president arrived in Santiago. He was celebrated by much of the Chilean media. The conservative publication *El Mercurio* saluted his arrival, stressing that the friendship between the two countries was old and had flourished in the "soul of their peoples."[73] The Brazilian president's nickname, Jango, was largely adopted by the Chilean press, which described him not only as the most important leader in the Southern Cone but also as a friend.[74] Alessandri's objective of showing tolerance and cautious alignment, however, did not work as planned. Jango's charisma was constantly linked to the Chilean Left. The newspaper *El Siglo* used the opportunity to connect him to Alessandri's rival, claiming that "the presidential candidate of the people, senator Salvador Allende, summoned the population to cheer President João Goulart," while he was in the country.[75]

Furthermore, at the height of the Cold War, the debates that predominated in the Chilean press were about Jango's support for communist ideals or, at least, his indifference to them. The João Goulart foreign affairs agenda that so fascinated Alessandri included the bold yet contentious neutrality of Brazil's independent foreign policy. In the regional realm, Brazilian and Chilean elites perceived Goulart's nationalist policies as a threatening path that would lead the region further away from developed nations.[76] The antipathy of the upper class toward a president who came from a wealthy family of landowners emerged from his alleged involvement with the Communist Party, as well as from his social and economic policies that focused on greater state intervention. The plan of "basic reforms [*reformas de base*]" included land expropriation, electoral and tax reforms, and the nationalization of strategic companies.[77] In 1962, the creation of Eletrobras, a state-owned energy company, enraged elites and foreign corporations.[78] The right-wing sectors of Brazilian society interpreted such moves either as state interventionism or as flirtation with communism. Neither was good.[79]

At the end of Goulart's visit to Chile, the two men issued the Joint Declaration of the Presidents of Chile and Brazil, in which they supported the end of nuclear tests, respect for all democratic regimes, and increased economic integration as essential to South America's development. The declaration attested to the asymmetric relationship between Chile and Brazil at that time, as all its topics were much more aligned with Goulart's independent foreign policy than with Jorge Alessandri's defense of a more intense partnership with the United States.[80] For Goulart, Chile was a useful ally, a country in South America with whom it shared strong diplomatic ties. For Chile, Brazil was an instrumental partner, with whom disagreements should be avoided at all costs. The Chilean president's acceptance of such an imbalance revealed the need to maintain a cordial dialogue with Brazil. Alessandri's "technocratic" philosophy was expressed even more explicitly in his relationship with Cuba. He ignored the status of anti-Castro Cuban asylum seekers who asked for support in the Chilean embassy, and he did not break diplomatic relations with the island.[81]

However smaller and weaker Chile was, in practice, it collected the biggest prize. The country received over $1.5 billion from US-controlled international agencies, reaching 13.4 percent of net per capita aid in Latin America.[82] Raúl Bazán Dávila, Chilean ambassador to Brazil until 1962, summarized Brazil's situation as being lost and "dazzled" about its role in the international system, and incapable of approaching the United States for financial aid. Chile, in contrast, had discovered an effective way to keep peace with its neighbor while getting tremendous support from the superpower. The recipe was not words, media coverage, or "political argument, based on the territorial importance," but the Alliance for Progress, as Chile had learned much earlier.[83]

GOULART OUT, FREIRE IN

João Goulart's unbending posture toward the United States ended up putting his government in a fragile position. In 1963, the country openly demonstrated frustration with the president's lack of support for the economic austerity policies suggested by his minister of finance, Carlos Alberto de Carvalho Pinto, who was forced to abandon the government after less than six months in the position. After that, the two countries stopped negotiating new aid programs. A confluence of powers with US support and supervision worked to destabilize the president. Business groups such as the Institute for Social Studies and Research (IPES) and the Brazilian Institute for Democratic Action (IBAD) intensified campaigns to enhance the crisis. Federal agencies went rogue; the Ministry of Foreign Affairs renewed the 1952 military agreement with the United States without the president's knowledge and distributed the money from the Alliance for Progress to state governors who opposed Goulart.[84] Carlos Lacerda of Guanabara and Aluísio Alves of Rio Grande do Norte benefited the most.

Although there is still debate on whether or not the US intervention was decisive in toppling Goulart, there is no question that the support was major and culminated with Operation Brother Sam, in which the United States sent four US Navy oil tankers to the Brazilian coast, in addition to ammunition, gasoline, and other materials, in case the Brazilian Army needed support for the coup.[85] After the fall of Goulart in April and the end of Alessandri's presidential term in November 1964, the Brazilian and US governments continued articulating with Chilean right-wing groups ways to counter the presidential campaign of Salvador Allende, who embodied the rise of communism and left-wing politics in Chile.[86] The CIA disbursed $3 million to impact the outcome of the country's 1964 presidential elections.[87]

The victory of Christian Democrat Eduardo Frei Montalva calmed tensions but was not enough to weaken Allende's popularity. During Frei's administration, the United States intensified a campaign to influence the political landscape in South America.[88] From propaganda to direct financial support of political parties, CIA resources interfered in Chilean politics and fomented the military coup.[89]

By November 1964, while Frei worked to establish his new government, the Brazilian dictatorship had been seven months in power and enjoyed the support of many in the United States. *Reader's Digest* published a twenty-six-page special feature titled "The Country That Saved Itself."[90] It told "the inspiring story of how an aroused Brazilian people stopped the communists from taking over their nation" and included step-by-step instructions on how to mail the article to other readers.

All this buzz encouraged the Brazilian government to position itself as a strong global player by building a relationship of equality with the United States that avoided both competition and passivity.[91] Publicly, Brazil and Chile were cordial during the Frei years, with Brazilian diplomats mostly reporting on trade and mundane activities. Ambassador Antônio Cândido da Câmara Canto wrote lengthy—and not particularly riveting—telegrams about Chilean domestic policies. The two countries also maintained a busy schedule of cultural events, such as film and arts festivals.[92] The trouble-free relationship lasted for Frei's entire tenure, eventually materializing in international support, as was the case in April 1970, when Chile championed the Brazilian candidacy for the UN Security Council.[93] A month later, Câmara Canto presented his government with his analysis of Frei's leadership. He evaluated his presidency by merely reporting on his speeches, avoiding any kind of judgment or opinion, in a tone very different from the harsh one that he would adopt routinely during the Allende presidency.[94]

In secret, however, espionage was already taking place. Officials and military attachés closely monitored exiles in the country and in other nations of the Southern Cone. The presence of hundreds of political enemies of the Brazilian dictatorship in Chile disturbed the military. To keep track of this group, the government created the Brazilian Foreign Office's Intelligence Center (CIEX) in 1966, while Eduardo Frei was Chile's president.[95] And it went beyond investigating Brazilians, stretching its tentacles into Chilean internal affairs. This can be seen, for instance, in a report from July 1967 that warned the Brazilian National Intelligence Service (SNI) of the creation of two "National Committees" of the Organization of Latin American Solidarity (Organización de Solidaridad Latinoamericana; OLAS) in Chile and Argentina.[96] OLAS had been founded in Cuba earlier that year with anti-imperialism as its guiding principle. Following ideals of the Cuban Revolution, it perceived the United States and Brazil as enemies.

Salvador Allende was the founder of the Chilean OLAS committee. The CIEX report charged Allende's party, the Popular Action Front, with coordinating actions to spread communism in Latin America.[97] Allende was then president of the Chilean Senate and went ahead with establishing the committee, despite reprimands from Frei and international leaders, including the head of the Christian Democratic Party in Venezuela, Edécio La Riva.

The United States worried about Allende but seemed unbothered by denunciations of human rights abuses in Brazil. On July 8, 1968, one of the most violent years of the Brazilian dictatorship, Charles Burke Elbrick was appointed US ambassador to the nation.[98] Weeks later, during a luncheon of the US Chamber of Commerce, he said that priorities in Latin America were unlikely to change. "Some people seem to feel that everything that has gone before in US–Latin American cooperation is perforce to be discarded or disregarded, and that drastic new departures are in the offing. I personally believe that this is too apocalyptic a view of the future."[99]

Ambassador Elbrick's assurances notwithstanding, the US reluctance to address its ally's violence became unsustainable with the increasing international criticism of Brazil after the proclamation of Institutional Act no. 5 (AI-5) in 1968. Many North Americans only became aware of what was going on in Brazil on December 15, 1968, when the *Washington Post* denounced the scope of AI-5.[100] The article began by noting that "Brazil's military-dominated government invoked sweeping new powers" and was arresting newspaper editors and politicians. It continued by mentioning the detention of former president Juscelino Kubitschek and the former governor of the state of Guanabara, Carlos Lacerda. Under the subtitle "Censorship Imposed," it informed its US audience about a few of the consequences of AI-5: "All papers appeared this evening, but with most news and all comments on the domestic crisis exorcized. Outgoing cables were censored. The move was the most massive interference with the press since the military coup of 1964."[101]

It would be the first of a series of articles that signaled a shift in the way the international press reported on the Brazilian government.[102] The tone of the *New York Times* was more reserved, replicating the US government's position on the political crisis: "The State Department said today that the situation in Brazil 'appears to have calmed.' Robert J. McCloskey, department spokesman, said that the number of arrests seemed to have diminished and that many of those seized over the weekend had been released or would be soon."[103] But the article also acknowledged that "United States economic aid to Brazil, which has been running at $250-million to $350-million yearly, will definitely be reviewed." The amount was equivalent to almost a third of the total aid distributed through the Alliance for Progress and was seen as key to Brazilian economic recovery.[104]

Henry Kissinger and Richard Nixon did not plan to restrain relations with Brazil, however. When the chief of the US National Security Council took office, in 1969, the Soviet Union was rising, student demonstrations and civil rights protests were spreading all over the United States, and the mood was generally pessimistic. Under these circumstances, the self-proclaimed leaders of the free world decided that there were multiple reasons to intensify the partnership with a dictatorship accused of torture, murders, and censorship. First, Brazil's authoritarian government appeared to have created more political stability than its Latin American economic rivals. Second, although intense, the US relationship with Brazil was not as closely watched as the one with Mexico, and this allowed for discretion in policies that had to remain secret and could influence the rest of the region. Third, Brazil's economic growth was impressive and trade with the country remained promising. Last but not least, geography played a role, since Brazil was located at the heart of South America, a crucial area where nationalist governments were ruling Argentina, Uruguay, Bolivia, and Chile.[105]

Brazilian foreign relations were also centered on the region. The government's top priority—and its most ambitious diplomatic project—was convincing other leaders in the neighborhood to join the fight against communism. Although the final objective was clear, however, the methods to achieve it were under debate. Most diplomats believed that regional control was the mission of the regime, but several saw the need for a more low-key approach. The founder of CIEX, Manoel Pio Corrêa, directly addressed the Brazilian State Department about the importance of focusing on Chile and Uruguay, where the Communist Party remained legal. He compared Eduardo Frei to the Russian Revolution's leader, Alexander Kerensky.[106] A few months before Allende's election, Brazilian president Emílio Garrastazu Médici would draw the same parallel.[107]

The aim of influencing South America was part of the spirit of the National Security Doctrine, established in Brazil with US mentorship.[108] After World War II, Brazilian military members flocked to the United States and brought back a strong sense of urgency for a policy of national defense dedicated to a systematic elimination of political opponents inside and outside the national territory.[109] A clear reaction to the South American Cold War, the National Security Doctrine, which became law in 1968, determined that it was necessary to identify "domestic enemies" of the regime, wherever they were.[110] A few years later, the military created the Brazilian War College (ESG), inspired by Washington, DC's National War College.[111]

The investigation of political, economic, and geographical aspects of neighboring countries was a usual practice for the military, especially the now defunct General Staff of the Armed Forces (Estado-Maior das Forças Armadas; EMFA).[112] The "mapping of the national territory and, in particular, the Border Areas" was made and remade constantly. The main targets of such strategic analysis were Chile, Bolivia, Ecuador, Paraguay, Argentina, and Peru.[113] Despite not sharing a border, the Brazilian government's preoccupation with Chile in this period was far more substantial than what has been acknowledged so far. It came from all the national intelligence services, including the diplomatic ones. The Brazilian ambassador in Santiago, Antônio Cândido da Câmara Canto, was a central actor in the interference in Chile.

Câmara Canto followed Allende's candidacy closely. The ambassador sent detailed reports about every Popular Unity demonstration, speech, or event to the Brazilian Ministry of Foreign Affairs.[114] He also measured the appetite of the Chilean population and leadership for socialism, following the series of demonstrations that took place in Santiago during the presidential campaign. While promoting Allende, supporters of Popular Unity, including workers and students, demanded that President Eduardo Frei deliver on his promises of land reform, wage increases, and copper nationalization.[115] The Brazilian dictatorship was constantly attacked and each new unfavorable story triggered Canto to write exasperated telegrams. In June 1970, a group of Brazilian students who had arrived at the University of Chile for an exchange program suffered threats from "leftist students" and were required to leave the campus. Canto considered the episode an indication of the "amplification and depth achieved in this country of the campaign of international defamation organized by the media against the Brazilian government."[116] When describing the repercussion of headlines about the Brazilian dictatorship, he stated that the regime had been the victim of a "terrible diatribe" in a segment about the kidnapping of the German ambassador in Rio de Janeiro broadcast by TV 7, "a company in which the state, through several state organizations, is the main shareholder." He complained that the political commentator Luiz Hernández Parker had urged Chileans to express solidarity with demonstrations "against the torture of political prisoners in Brazil with the objective of creating a broad global movement."[117]

In May 1970, months before the election in which the majority of the citizens would choose Salvador Allende as president, members of the Brazilian government were already predicting the 1973 coup d'état. On a breezy day in Santiago, Colonel Luiz José Torres Marques went to the Brazilian embassy with the mundane aim of introducing himself to his peers and was surprised when the military attaché invited him to join staff members and secretaries in a meeting behind closed doors. In the beginning, it felt like a dull discussion of Chilean domestic issues.[118] It only took a few minutes, however, for him to realize that it was a decisive moment, which inspired him to write a three-page letter to the vice chief of staff of the Armed Forces detailing the gathering.[119]

Câmara Canto led the conversation depicting a dramatic scenario and demanding action. He listed several reasons why the Brazilian government should worry: the Communist Party was legal; most of the population and the military were against dictatorships; the military police, known as *carabineros*, were more powerful than the army and "totally unpredictable"; the Revolutionary Left Movement (MIR) was gaining strength; and the Chilean population favored elections, whatever the outcome, an idea that was also "ingrained in the military sector."[120]

Torres Marques went on to describe the Brazilian ambassador's predictions for the upcoming presidential elections in case Congress needed to make the final decision. Câmara Canto claimed that the fifty-one votes of the Christian Democratic Party were "heterogeneous"; twenty-seven right-wing votes would go to conservative Jorge Alessandri; and fifty-four votes from the Popular Unity would go to Allende. This meant that the Christian Democratic candidate, Radomiro Tomic, would finish third. After affirming that both Allende and Tomic were communists, Câmara Canto declared his preference for Alessandri, "an austere man and worthy from all points of view, the favorite among the upper class." He was the best bet for "those who don't want to see communism in the country."[121]

More than a clear understanding of the trends in the Chilean Congress, Câmara Canto had a strategy of reaction to each possible outcome. The first possibility was Alessandri winning the majority of the votes, in which case no action from the Brazilian leadership would be required. Chile would remain a democratic government. The second was Alessandri winning a plurality, which would require congressional confirmation. In such a scenario, the diplomat suggested two possible outcomes: "Alpha: the Congress counter-signs Alessandri . . . Beta: the Congress countersigns Allende." In the "beta" case, the probable consequence would be a "military move against Allende." There was also a third possible outcome: Allende winning a plurality. In this case, the Brazilian ambassador expected military reactions if Allende was nominated president, and a "subversive reaction" in case Alessandri was nominated.[122]

In September, a month before Congress resolved the 1970 elections, the US ambassador to Chile, Edward Korry, asked to meet Canto and requested that he keep the gathering a secret even from the Brazilian Ministry of Foreign Affairs.[123] Korry suspected that Allende supporters might be planted in the US State Department. He then explained that, following White House instructions, he was directly appealing to all the relevant sectors to prevent "the tragedy" that an Allende presidency would be to the country. He also revealed that he had personally selected individuals with no clear political affiliation to distribute materials warning about the dangers of a Marxist administration among leaders of the military forces. Contradicting his efforts, nevertheless, Korry admitted that he was all but certain that Christian Democrats would vote to confirm Allende's victory on October 24.

Câmara Canto found the meeting with Korry so decisive that he wrote a letter to the Brazilian president contending that, as the embassy in Santiago already knew, Eduardo Frei was still not sure if he would support the socialist. For Korry, Chile's minister of justice, Gustavo Lagos, and its minister of foreign affairs, Gabriel Valdés, were the only two in the Chilean government directly championing Allende. Korry contended that the United States did not want a military intervention but would support it as long as new elections were called right away. He also shared a series of concerns: Allende had the support of 20 percent of the Air Force; the United Kingdom was trying to keep cordial relations with the socialists; and France had already unofficially recognized Allende's victory—and asked for protection for its four major companies: Peugeot, Citroën, the French and Italian Bank for South America, and the copper mine La Diputada. In contrast, Japan, Switzerland, and East Germany had already cut lines of credit to Chile, and the United States was ready to follow suit.[124]

Câmara Canto's letter ends with an analysis of a division inside the US government after the September 4 elections: the White House and the CIA wanted to prevent Allende from taking power; the State Department recognized the victory as a democratic one, which should be respected; and the Defense Department was unresponsive. Korry's loyalty remained to Nixon and that justified his unorthodox approach to Câmara Canto. The Brazilian diplomat, however, was assertive: it was too little too late and the only way to prevent Allende from being confirmed as president would be a military intervention. For that, however, leaders of the armed forces would need to conclude that a Marxist threat was more dangerous than the weakening of the Chilean democracy. "Unfortunately, however, the mere proclamation of the harm caused by Allende will not be enough to provoke such a reaction. Our hopes remain on a new event, such as the creation of a Military Cabinet or demonstrations from the anticommunist group Patria y Libertad, which will take place on September 24."[125]

His hopes would finally be dashed on October 24, 1970, when Congress confirmed the choice of the Chilean voters and elevated the socialist leader to the most powerful position in the country. The Brazilian newspaper *Folha de S. Paulo* printed on its cover, days later, Allende's promise that Chile would not become a Marxist nation.[126] Câmara Canto was doubtful. No more pleased were leftist movements in Brazil, who dreamed of the birth of a socialist republic on their continent.

2
LEAVING AND BEING LEFT
BRAZILIAN EXILES IN CHILE

Não permita Deus que eu morra
Sem que eu volte para lá;
Sem que desfrute os primores
Que não encontro por cá;
Sem que ainda aviste as palmeiras
Onde canta o sabiá.

[May God never allow me to die
Before I return home;
Without enjoying the wonders
That I cannot find here;
Without seeing the palm trees
Where the thrush bird sings.]

GONÇALVES DIAS, "CANÇÃO DO EXÍLIO," 1843

When Otto Brockes heard the news of Salvador Allende's election in Chile, he decided that it was time to go. He did not feel any sense of commitment to Brazil. His attachment was to the ideals of social equality that "only a person as evolved as Allende could deliver."[1] Working as a doctor at one of the largest hospitals in Rio de Janeiro, Brockes routinely dealt with death and often witnessed patients arriving when it was already too late. It was unbearable. "It felt as if we were 'using' the human being in its final stages as an experiment, to learn from death without guidance. It shook me deeply because I did not decide to become a doctor for profit. I had always dreamed of being a volunteer in Africa." It was 1970, the height of the civilian-military dictatorship in Brazil. In December 1968, dictator Artur da Costa e Silva had issued Institutional Act no. 5, suspending all constitutional guarantees and institutionalizing torture. The climate of fear encouraged Brockes to intensify his readings of Marxist authors. He concluded that socialism was the only path to a fair society and guerrilla fighting was the only path to socialism.[2] National borders were just an invention, unable to contain the limitless potential of these theories. "There came a day when I began to re-alize that formal democracy is an absurd idea. It only exists when the elites profit. When they lose, it loses its validity. So, I started embracing the ideas of communism and became a communist."[3]

For Aluízio Palmar, it was quite the opposite. Saving Brazilian democracy was all that mattered. The end of the dictatorship at home came before any ideology or political system.[4] Leaving the country, therefore, was simply a way of surviving to continue researching, establishing new methods of combating the regime, and fighting it when the time came.[5] He joined the Brazilian Communist Party (Partido Comunista do Brasil; PCB) at the age of sixteen. Later, he became one of the founders of the guerrilla October 8 Revolutionary Movement (MR-8). His role was one of outreach: he recruited former members of the PCB, contacted leftist organizations in Paraguay and Argentina, and connected with rural workers attracted by the prospect of fighting the regime.[6]

He managed to remain active in the movement until an accident liter-ally put him in the hands of the military. Palmar was in a car crash and the responding officers recognized him as a political enemy of the regime. He was then taken to the Ilha das Flores prison. The name means "island of flowers" in Portuguese, but that was the only pleasant thing about it. The place was an old hotel turned into one of the cruelest prisons of a cruel re-gime. In 1966, it became the National Training Center, a school for military training of Navy officers.[7] In 1969, Commander Clemente Monteiro Filho, in charge of the institution, converted it into a "small concentration camp."[8] Palmar was tortured multiple times, day and night. He attempted suicide, feeling that it was the only way out. Other companions of the MR-8 arrived there regularly. It was the end of the movement and the beginning of a new phase in Palmar's activism.[9]

Che Guevara and Régis Debray's writings about *foquismo* were the central inspiration for the MR-8, especially the belief that rural areas should be the focus of guerrilla strategy.[10] Although it dedicated its training and military tactics to developing the potential of rural guerrillas, the group was mostly formed of urban youth activists, and once its money ran short, they started to conduct armed bank robberies, attacks on armored cars, and other forms of what they call *tomas, grupos de expropriação* ("takings, groups of expropriation") or simply "political burglary."[11] Between 1968 and 1971 there were over 150 such robberies in Brazil, which generated almost $4 million for the guerrillas. There were also over forty bomb attacks and the hijacking of eight commercial airplanes. The abduction of ambassadors, something that had never happened in Brazil, became a major fear. In 1970, the *New York Times* declared that US officials were "increasingly worried that kidnapping of diplomats by Latin American extremists can become as epidemic a problem as airplane hijackings."[12] The latter was a source of money; the former, a way of freeing political prisoners who, in many cases, went into exile right after being released. Palmar would benefit from one of these exchanges in 1971, after the Popular Revolutionary Vanguard (VPR) kidnapped Swiss ambassador Giovanni Enrico Bucher.[13]

Aluízio Palmar and Otto Brockes had two very different intentions when they boarded the plane to Chile. Palmar joined the VPR and wanted his period in exile to be dedicated to developing strategies to return to Brazil. Brockes only thought about the international character of the revolution. Soon after arriving in Santiago, he started working in public hospitals as a volunteer. He then met a Chilean employed at the Ministry of Health who convinced him to formally apply for a job there. Brockes joined the Health Program for Schools. "I examined more than 15,000 kids while working there. Almost every day, after I was done with work, I would go to poor neighborhoods and work for free, to help the government."[14] He assisted the emergency teams when there were floods and worked day and night when the 1971 earthquake claimed 85 lives and injured more than 450 people.[15] Allende had been in office for only seven months then.

When I met Brockes, he was a skinny man in his eighties, with an astute mind and slow movements. He smiled like a monk and made me feel safe. Living in a small house in a small village in the state of Goiás, he avoided directly replying to questions about his role in guerrilla movements, always asking for more information before providing any details. Brockes had been a member of the Brazilian Revolutionary Communist Party (Partido Comunista Brasileiro Revolucionário; PCBR), a group formed by dissidents of the Brazilian Communist Party.[16] The PCBR diverged from the PCB on many issues, but the breaking point came from the continuing refusal of PCB leaders to condemn Soviet Stalinism, even after Nikita Khruschev's secret speech "On the Cult of Personality and Its Consequences," delivered in 1956.[17]

These differences notwithstanding, Palmar and Brockes had a lot in common. They were central witnesses to the Brazilian government's efforts to remove Allende from power. They were also victims of these very same actions, since a crucial part of the Brazilian government's espionage was to expand its monitoring of exiles. After the proclamation of Institutional Act no. 5 (AI-5) in 1968 and the election of Salvador Allende in 1970, Chile became a central focus of Brazilian intelligence services and the exiles were their principal target.

One of the biggest accomplishments of these clandestine operations was turning guerrilla members into informants for the military. They were the so-called *cachorros* (dogs), people who received money and other compensation to provide information on guerrilla leaders.[18] PCBR member Maria Tereza Ribeiro da Silva was one of them. On August 1, 1969, she wrote a letter to a friend complaining about the lack of support from the party and describing her fear of being arrested.[19] Three days later, agents of the Navy Intelligence Center (CENIMAR) detained her and immediately sealed a deal for collaboration. Her code name would be "Renata" and on her first day of work, she received 100 cruzeiros novos, the Brazilian currency at the time.[20] Ribeiro da Silva's whereabouts are a mystery today, but one known fact of her spy career is that in 1973 she infiltrated Brazilian exile circles in Chile. In a letter written to "Alfredo," her leader at CENIMAR, while still in Brazil, she claimed to be living in a house with no running water and having a hard time paying for food. The only silver lining was her upcoming trip to Chile, for which she had "great expectations," both in terms of gathering information and saving money.[21]

Many other spies acting in Chile worked for CENIMAR and other intelligence services of the military. However, one the most important sources of information came from the civilian branch of espionage, the Brazilian Foreign Office's Intelligence Center (CIEX). Although diplomats used CIEX as an incipient network to share information, military attachés and agents had two main goals when infiltrating the Brazilian exile community: to track these political enemies of the regime and to watch the Allende administration closely. Contact with exiles who had ties with the Chilean government gave the Brazilian authorities a privileged source of information about the socialist command. This chapter investigates the waves of people who moved from Brazil to Chile, starting in 1964, continuing in 1968, and culminating with the Setenta, the seventy political prisoners exchanged for the release of the Swiss ambassador Giovanni Enrico Bucher in 1971.

DISPLACEMENT, BELONGING, AND IDENTITY

As stated before, it is impossible to affirm the number of Brazilian exiles that went to Chile. Information was scarce and the nature of exile was secretive.[22] Amnesty International, however, states that approximately 1,200 Brazilians left the country for Chile between the start of the dictatorship, in 1964, and the fall of Allende, in 1973.[23] The virtual museum Memorial da Democracia classified exile during the dictatorship as "the greatest diaspora in Brazil's history" and stated that the majority of exiles went to France, although Argentina, Mexico, Algeria, Sweden, Canada, Italy, Cuba, United States, and the Soviet Union were also frequent destinations.[24] In Santiago, they never considered themselves free. From the language barrier to the lack of work and the monitoring by the Brazilian government, their daily habits were filled with boundaries. Building a new life away from the authoritarian regime installed in Brazil required finding new identities and spaces.

The first challenge in discussing this experience is the definition of "exile" itself.[25] Several issues have to be taken into consideration when conceptualizing the movement of people to a different country; namely, the reasons for the change, the objectives, the degree to which it is forced or voluntary, the ability to choose the destination, and the duration of stay.[26] The definition matters not simply for semantics but because it affects the very identity of this group.[27] The way this movement is explained has social, political, and emotional implications that may affect how one interprets its role in shaping Latin American politics. The word used to represent a person's immigration status is usually connected to a legal and diplomatic negotiation, something that did not always happen for Brazilian exiles in Chile.

An exile is a person who secures protection internationally due to disagreement with the political establishment in her or his nation of origin. Moving to Chile was not the result of economic inequality or the search for a better life. It was a forced displacement. In this sense, it becomes necessary to move away from the temptation of associating exile with immigration.[28] Unlike the refugee or beneficiary of asylum, most of the Brazilian political exiles in Chile had no legal support. If in Brazil the dictatorial government recognized them as political opponents, this role was also part of their identity in Chile.[29] Friends, enemies, immigration officers, and anyone they had to deal with classified them as a group of people who questioned and resisted their home country's authorities. Still, even during the socialist government of Salvador Allende, many of them did not enjoy permanent resident status or have a work visa. In this forced migration, most exiles continued to voice their opposition to the right-wing regime, thus creating networks of resistance in other countries.

In their reports, the Brazilian authorities refer to this group as *asilados* (asylees). The word "exile" is avoided, as it would have implied the recognition that the Brazilian government had expelled them. Furthermore, by choosing the term "asilados," the authorities suggest—intentionally but inaccurately—that the group enjoyed legal protection and support from the Chilean government. That was not the case for hundreds of Brazilians, either because they found no pathway to receiving a work visa or because they chose not to apply for refugee status, fearing that this would impair their mobility to other countries, including to places from which they could fight the dictatorship. According to a report from Amnesty International, the Allende government had no official data on foreigners who arrived in the country from 1970 onward and "some political refugees had no more than a stamp which permitted them to enter Chile."[30]

The stamp, however, was not easy to get. When Jean Marc von der Weid arrived in Santiago in 1971, he faced a long interview with Chilean authorities, who created detailed files about foreigners. He remembers spending over twenty-four hours in a room. "The place had a large garden. We were not locked in there. But without an official document one could not leave. It was a weird interrogation, it felt like the Brazilian police. After all, Allende had just started, so the police structure remained the same. They would ask us, 'So, what did you do? You must have done something. Why were you arrested, then? I must write *something* down.' I would say that I had done nothing and that this was exactly what a dictatorship looked like. It came to a point where we decided not to answer."[31]

For von der Weid, having dual citizenship was a privilege. As soon as he was free to leave the interrogation, he went to the Swiss embassy and received a passport. René-Louis de Carvalho also felt lucky. He was born in France, where his parents, Renée France Laugery and Apolônio de Carvalho, had been part of the French Resistance to the Nazi occupation.[32] Nancy Mangabeira Unger, however, saw her dual citizenship as a curse. Having US nationality, she asked von der Weid to go the US embassy with her, afraid of being arrested there. Von der Weid recalls that there was no violence. The diplomats recognized that she had a right to a passport but refused to give it to her unless she went to the United States. "I told her that we could find a leftist American who would help her," but Unger perceived the United States as a dangerous enemy and decided that it would be safer not to pursue this route.

The Brazilian government also refused to acknowledge the movement as an exile to prevent it from looking like a forced migration. Instead, authorities cast it as voluntary. After their removal from the country, however, it was all but impossible for these Brazilian citizens to return. During the period from 1964 to 1979, when the Amnesty Law was approved pardoning civilians and military personnel—including guerrilla members, state agents, and torturers alike—for all crimes committed during the dictatorship, several Brazilian intellectuals, teachers, artists, workers, and people the regime considered to be menaces could not easily reenter the country. Although the government's characterization of the movement as voluntary sounds almost ironic, considering that the alternative was, in many cases, torture, imprisonment, and death, many exiles referred to it as an expression of autonomy and agency. In *Memórias das mulheres do exílio* (Memoirs of exiled women), the authors state that "leaving the country—except in cases of banishment—is always, in a sense, an expression of will, although this choice could have been limited to absurd levels, the extreme example being the option between death and life, in parallel to that between staying and leaving." They also highlight the importance of the category "voluntary exile," which is preceded by "imprisonment, persecution, punishment, psychological pressure, reduction of mechanisms of professional, political, and even family expression."[33]

Deciding where to go when leaving Brazil depended on connections. Solange Bastos was only seventeen when she joined the Palmares Armed Revolutionary Vanguard (VAR-Palmares). "One of my roles was to conduct a political-military survey of thirty favelas in Rio de Janeiro. It was fascinating. We would arrive, say that we were looking for a room to rent, and gather information about the favela."[34] The political engagement came from home. Her father was military and union leader Paulo de Mello Bastos. In Rio de Janeiro, she met her first husband, Manoel Messias da Silva, who was then connected to the Communist Party of Pernambuco. Although she had never touched a weapon and was not affiliated with the party, the dictatorship arrested both of them. Bastos was tortured in front of her husband. Three months later, they were released with no job and a lot of fear. The best option was to leave. They went to Santiago, where other members of VAR-Palmares had found refuge.

The representation of the period of exile as one of prolific exchange of ideas and intellectual and artistic production, which still permeates the imaginary of many Brazilians, is a myth connected to the fact that some of the expelled citizens were professors, students, artists, and intellectuals who had achieved celebrity-like status, and used their public voice to echo their grievances against the dictatorship.[35] As thinkers in Brazil, and later in Chile, some of them shaped the intellectual and political structures of the countries in which they lived.[36] Among the Brazilian exiles in Chile were former Brazilian president Fernando Henrique Cardoso, former São Paulo governor and presidential candidate José Serra, economist and pioneer of structuralist development theory Celso Furtado, sociologist Vânia Bambirra, educator Paulo Freire, historian Caio Prado Júnior, and Fernando Gabeira, who has served as a representative in the federal legislature for the state of Rio de Janeiro for decades.[37]

José Serra remembers the period as an intellectual boom. Santiago was home to the Economic Commission for Latin America and the Caribbean (ECLAC) and its permanent body, the Latin American and Caribbean Institute for Economic and Social Planning (Instituto Latinoamericano y del Caribe de Planificación Económica y Social; ILPES). "It was a privilege to be in Chile at that time. There was dedication, serious research, discussion and renewal of ideas. It seemed possible to learn from the past, develop knowledge of the problems, and project a better future for Latin America."[38]

Transnational relations—as part of the institutions with which they dealt—defined the lives of exiles in their new home. German sociologist André Gunder Frank, who left Brazil with his Chilean wife, Marta Fuentes, and their Brazilian son, Paulo, conveyed his experience in a series of autobiographical essays. Gunder Frank summarized the sequence of forced migrations: "After our son Paulo was born there, Marta and I left Brazil again for Chile; later, for Mexico where Miguel was born, then to Montreal, and in 1968, back again to Chile."[39] Some of his closest friends and collaborators were Brazilian exiles Ruy Mauro Marini, Vânia Bambirra, and Theotônio dos Santos, professors at the University of Brasília, who were also forced to leave Brazil after the 1964 coup.[40]

Before 1964, several left-wing Brazilian intellectuals wrote about the possibility of capitalism coexisting with a more democratic society. After the coup, however, some began to argue for a different solution. Caio Prado Jr. proclaimed "the impossibility of a 'bourgeois revolution' and the incapability of the national bourgeoisie to go further with social reforms."[41] This debate was deepened in Chile, where a generation of Marxist thinkers emerged. Salvador Allende's "Chilean path to socialism" included the negotiation of social programs with members of the Chilean elite. This soft approach bothered many of these intellectuals who engaged with the Chilean Left. At the time, Ruy Mauro Marini served as the head of the foreign committee of the Revolutionary Left Movement (MIR) and echoed Prado Jr.'s position. For him, Latin America's revolutionary process could only develop in countries where "counterrevolution has succeeded in seizing power," among which Chile was the strongest example.[42] The secretary-general of MIR, Miguel Enríquez, complained that Allende was not delivering on his promises and suggested that the population seize farms and industries, taking forcefully what "belonged to them" instead of waiting for government restitution.[43] Like Marini, many Brazilian exiles were in tune with MIR's position. They fully engaged in the tension that was so decisive for the Chilean path to socialism.[44]

The connections between Brazilian guerrilla groups and the Chilean Left went beyond conversations. The Popular Unitary Action Movement (MAPU) had its roots in Brazilian Popular Action (Ação Popular).[45] Both were founded by leftist militants from the Catholic Church. The Brazilian organization inspired the Chilean group, which was created as a splinter group of the Christian Democratic Party, in 1969.[46] Brazilian exiles were crucial in the seminal phase of MAPU, especially José Serra—who would later be elected governor of São Paulo—and Herbert de Souza, known as Betinho, one of the most renowned sociologists and activists in Brazilian history.[47]

Jean Marc von der Weid remembers being asked to give guerrilla training to MAPU members. It was another moment when the discussion about the usefulness of foquismo became prominent. "The leftist groups in Chile occupied the factories around Santiago. So, you had blacksmiths in the base of MAPU, other workers, in the base of MIR, and so on. Still, they wanted me to train them, and I would say: 'Hey, I was a lieutenant in the Marines in Brazil. What I learned there cannot be applied here. You will learn to fight in the forest, but there is no forest here. This is a city.'"[48]

Like von der Weid, Reinaldo Guarany was one of the Setenta exiles released from political prisons after the kidnapping of the Swiss ambassador. He also recalls training members of MAPU, but, as part of the guerrilla National Liberating Action (ALN), he had already started moving away from foquismo to prioritize urban operations. "I oversaw providing urban guerrilla training for the Brazilian comrades who would return from Santiago to Brazil. There were six of them. They all returned to Brazil in 1972."[49] The training took place during the day and consisted of courses in making bombs, tactics, and "a lot of theoretical stuff. We weren't going out on the streets to practice it."

The same kind of training was provided to members of MAPU right after the Tancazo, an attempted coup against Allende that took place on June 29, 1973, less than three months before the September 11 coup. Guarany's Chilean students were roughly twenty to thirty hooded men. "They were expecting me to give them a formula to prevent the coup, but I gave them training on what they should do after the coup. They would say to me, 'But there hasn't been a coup yet.' And I said, 'Man, I don't know how to prevent a coup, I'm sorry.' It was crude. I was fooling them. It was worthless."[50] Guarany claims that many ALN members—himself included—were not convinced that Allende's path to socialism could be effective. "It was a moment of hope, but we never believed in a peaceful process. For me, National Liberating Action is a just a fanciful name, because its true purpose was the destruction of capitalism."[51] ALN instructed him not to interact too closely with Chileans and keep working.

In his first years in Chile, René-Louis de Carvalho also avoided engaging with Chileans. He perceived that to be a pattern among exiles who had been part of prisoner swaps. "We lived in a bubble. Only those who had arrived before us and a small minority became more integrated into the Chilean questions. So, we openly criticized Allende's peaceful path, and the ones who joined groups in Chile chose organizations or small groups that had a different position, like preparing an armed resistance."[52]

The Brazilian exile experience in Chile was far from monolithic, and perceptions of Allende's path to socialism differed. While some wanted a faster and more intense process, others contended that this project should take time. Wilson Barbosa remembers that comparisons between what socialism meant in Chile and Brazil were constant. For him, the major difference was that in Chile political engagement was far more prevalent among the masses, while in Brazil it was a bourgeois activity. "In Brazil, there was no class clash. Only the elites had class consciousness," he stated.[53] For him, however, deciding between fidelity to a political system or to a nation was not an either-or question. Despite all the criticism of the Chilean president, "We knew that the triumph of Allende's Chile would be the debilitation of the Brazilian dictatorship. So, we were internationalists. We were one."[54]

MORE THAN NUMBERS

Two groups of exiles received special attention from the international media. The first one, known as the Quarenta, consisted of forty political prisoners released in June 1970 as a result of negotiations to free the West German

The Setenta, seventy political prisoners exchanged for
Swiss ambassador Giovanni Enrico Bucher.
Source: Arquivo Nacional do Brasil.

ambassador, Ehrenfried von Holleben.[55] They fled to Algeria from Rio de
Janeiro in a civilian airplane. A few minutes after takeoff, President Emílio
Garrastazu Médici signed a decree forbidding them to return. Less than a
year later, in January 1971, another famous group of political activists left
Brazil, this time for Santiago. The Setenta were seventy political prisoners
exchanged for Swiss ambassador Giovanni Enrico Bucher, including Aluízio
Palmar, Ubiratan de Souza, Reinaldo Guarany, Jean Marc von der Weid,
René-Louis de Carvalho, Nancy Mangabeira Unger, and Wilson Barbosa.[56]

The precariousness of their exile experience started even before they
boarded the plane to Santiago. "I was not taken. I was dumped," recalled
Barbosa.[57] "We had no idea where we were headed to. They sent us to Chile,
but it could have been any other place. I left the airplane wearing shoes with
no soles. Police officers had cut them in prison. I had no belt, just a piece of
twine tying my pants. No documents, nothing," he recalled more than forty
years later.

Not knowing their destination, the seventy political prisoners tried to
control their anxiety by playing guessing games. "We are certainly going
to Algeria," Bruno Dauster, another Setenta, reckoned, probably thinking
of the fate of the Quarenta.[58] He pictured the over-nine-hour flight and the
arrival, in January, when temperatures are at around 40°F in North Africa.
He and his colleagues dressed for the winter, even though Rio de Janeiro is,
as a popular saying goes, a "branch of hell" in the first month of the year,
with temperatures frequently over 100°F. The soldiers, however, decided
that there was enough time for one last torture session. They calmly let the
prisoners wear wool socks, wool pants, and sweaters, and when it was time

to leave for the airport, they put the men and women in police cars that had been under the sun since early in the morning. "Can you imagine how it was? They opened them and put us inside. We put our noses in some small holes at the back of the car to breathe through. The hot air burned our nostrils. When we arrived at Galeão [the international airport in Rio de Janeiro], the car stopped and they did not let us go," recalls another Setenta, Marco Maranhão.[59] Jaime Cardoso compared it to "a sardine can under the sun." The prisoners felt sick.[60] At the time, he thought that he had handled the experience relatively well, but later he started to notice that he could not stay in confined spaces. "I have this issue which strangely appeared later on, but it was something that grew on me, and today I suffer from very severe claustrophobia."[61]

René-Louis de Carvalho was the son of two of the most active communists in Brazil.[62] Until he entered the airplane, he remained unsure if he would be freed. "We knew we were going to the airport, but we always had a doubt, you know? What was really going to happen? No one had any confidence. We were a little paranoid too, of course. And then they left us for two hours under the hot sun inside the police van. It was a very tense process, and we didn't really know what was going to happen."[63]

Jean Marc von der Weid, who had been imprisoned at Ilha das Flores from September 1969 to October 1970, remembers that they were then taken to a prison inside the Galeão airbase, the same place where some enemies of the regime were murdered, including Stuart Angel.[64] "The commander of the airbase was Brigadier [João Paulo Moreira] Burnier, one of the worst thugs that the dictatorship produced. A remorseless murderer."[65] Von der Weid was the last one to arrive. When he entered the room, the other sixty-nine guerrilla members burst into applause. "I had no idea that I was that popular. So, I asked my friend, Marcão, the reason for all that joy and he said, 'Well it is not about you. It is just that you are the seventieth to arrive. You are the last one, so we are ready to leave.' After that ego deflation, I asked where we were headed to, and someone answered, 'Chile.'"[66]

Von der Weid sat in the airplane beside Frei Tito, probably the best known of the Setenta. In 1970, after months of torture in the Department of Political and Social Order (DOPS) prison, Frei Tito wrote a letter that became a symbol of the movement for human rights in Brazil. He described in detail his attempt at suicide after deciding that it would be better to die than continue to be subjected to the *pau-de-arara* ("parrot perch"), a system of torture in which the prisoner hangs from his knees on a horizontal pole with hands and feet tied together. In most cases, the victim is naked and submitted to electroshocks to the entire body, including the genitalia. Frei Tito's words of sorrow were published all over the world, and he arrived in Santiago celebrated as an example of courage and resistance.[67]

The group of political exiles finally boarded a plane to Santiago the night of January 13, 1971. They arrived the day after, early in the morning. The Chileans received the Setenta with celebration. Hundreds of young men and women sang songs about love, justice, and democracy upon their arrival. Authorities, police officers, and civilians called them heroes. "We left Brazil treated like enemies; those men trampling us; the media calling us terrorists. When we arrived in Chile, still from the stairs of the airplane, we saw that there were two men representing the socialist government. They called us comrades. We shook hands. 'Compañero, sea bienvenido,' they said, and hugged us. That treatment alone had already softened my heart. After two hugs I was crying," Marco Maranhão remembers.[68]

A few days later, Salvador Allende invited the Setenta for lunch in Valparaíso and asked if they needed any kind of support. "I remember that one of our friends, Mara [Curtiss Alvarenga], asked the president to bring her children who were still in Brazil," recalls Wilson Barbosa.[69] Others asked for jobs, documents, or housing. "But since prison, we knew what was going on in Chile, and we knew that it was not a socialist country. Chile was a capitalist country with a precarious socialist government. I would never ask Allende for any help, and certainly 90 percent of the Brazilian exiles who were at the luncheon did not ask for anything. It was not our government, and he had no obligations to us whatsoever," stated Barbosa.[70]

The debate over citizenship and rights was constant among Brazilian exiles. In their daily lives, they faced several dilemmas regarding nationality and identity. On the one hand, they were not forced to relinquish their Brazilian citizenship; on the other hand, they were not allowed to enter Brazil. They moved to a neighboring nation but could not communicate in their native language. Inhabiting a new national space, they had to create a transnational sphere, one that was part of a process not of voluntary international exchange but rather of a forced transborder interaction. To answer questions as simple as "What is your name?" or "Where were you born?" they had to think carefully. Could they identify themselves as Brazilian exiles? As revolutionaries or enemies of the status quo administration? The response depended on who was asking.

The haunting memory of torture was another part of the forging of this group's identity. As living manifestations of state power, they became inhabitants of a new, forced transnational space forged by violence. Fernando

Gabeira, one of the Quarenta, had been arrested for his participation in the kidnapping of US ambassador Charles Elbrick in 1969. After flying to Algeria, he moved to Chile. For him, the Brazilian diplomatic mission in Santiago was a clear demonstration of a transnational aberration defined more by brutality and ideology than by citizenship and nationhood. He wrote that the Brazilian embassy's refusal to help Brazilians after the 1973 coup was well known.[71] In fact, while many embassies became fortresses to protect Chileans and foreign refugees, the Brazilian embassy closed its doors.[72] For Gabeira, the memory of an idealized home was demolished by the shock at the way the official representatives of the Brazilian government operated. It was also marked by two subsequent experiences of defeat.

> We thought of resistance but ended up being involved in the general confusion created to find solutions to escape the police. The same thing happened with many people in Chile. You say you will resist, you leave to resist, but what you end up doing is running away. I remember writing a letter from the Embassy of Argentina [where Gabeira and other Brazilian exiles had asked for protection after the Chilean coup] to a friend in Rio de Janeiro, telling him that I was alive. I said, "Friend, I just lost my second revolution, and I am on my way to break the record of that García Márquez character who lost twelve or thirteen, I think." I saw too many people dying, entire groups hiding in factories and resisting until the last man fell. But the general movement was one of running away.[73]

When it comes to Gabriel García Márquez's book, however, Gabeira and his comrades were probably more similar to the character of Rebeca, Aureliano Buendía's adopted sister, than to the colonel himself. As she did in *One Hundred Years of Solitude*, they seemed to be walking around carrying the bones of their families in a bag, unsure if they would ever be home again. Uncertainty became a glue that connected them as a group. Their lives were permeated with the construction of a particular space in response to the fact that they were not allowed to share the same rights and experiences in which Brazilian and Chilean citizens were included. In this sense, the community emerged as an affirmation of its own exclusion from national regulations. Erik Swyngedouw contends that systems formed by transnational experiences operate differently from state-based arrangements, which follow a top-down hierarchy of power exerted according to a "command-and-control" set of rules. In the case of Brazilian exiles, relations are established ensuing "horizontal networks and interactive relations between independent but interdependent actors that share a high degree of trust, despite internal conflict and oppositional agendas, within inclusive participatory institutional or organizational associations. These are systems of negotiation and covenant that operate beyond the state, albeit not independently from the state."[74]

The idea of nationalism, then, becomes problematic. If the exiles are transnational per se, the modern concept of nation-state becomes limiting to the discussion of this category.[75] The communitarian character of the group, creating and re-creating an alternative transnational public sphere, is marked by a multiplicity of references that help preserve and revisit traditions, shaping them according to the situation.[76] In the case of the Brazilian exiles, the common citizenship (or lack thereof) did not imply a hermetically sealed community. These exiles mingled with ideologies and projects of a democratic national space in which nationality was no longer preponderant. The process of displacement did not paralyze the displaced, but it made them create a particular community, a tentative novel nation, in which ideas of social equality and democracy became more important than place of birth.

In this sense, Brazilian exiles in Chile inhabited a version of a transnational public sphere, a forcedly forged space.[77] It begins with the rupture of the homeland, which turns into the representation of terror, torture, and fear.[78] A return home, then, becomes an impossibility. However, the pain of the defeat and the incongruence of the authoritarian state in contrast with the ideals of democracy were not left behind after they moved to the socialist nation. The fear (and the reality) of having spies and police officers of their home country following them was accompanied by the discomfort of being outsiders in the new land, where they were neither citizens nor immigrants by choice. Therefore, the body of duties and rights that constitutes nationhood did not apply to the former or to the new place.

The perspective of the exiles offers the possibility to analyze the quotidian side of such an experience, which "involved doubt, uncertainty, distress, emptiness, fear, insanity, death, difficulty with documents, work, study, reconstruction of pathways—in short, a redefinition of identity imposed by day-to-day life."[79] Such reformulation is also the result of connections with exiles from other countries in which authoritarian regimes had taken power, such as Uruguay, Argentina, Paraguay, and Bolivia.[80] Although life in exile was an experience of punishment, intolerance, and nullification of the national experience, it offered the possibility of reinvention and change. It meant not isolation but rather the construction of a new set of connections and solidarity.[81]

Nielsen Pires was raised in a religious family in São Paulo. For him, the ideas connected to socialism and communism only made sense because they echoed a message of social justice and love for humankind, so present in the Young Catholic Students group that he became part of during his adolescence.[82] His activism was deeply connected to his faith, so it was only natural that he later joined the University Catholic Youth. These two lay groups evolved into a socialist political organization, Popular Action (AP), also known as the Christian Left.[83]

It was 1970, a few years after the implementation of Institutional Act no. 5 (AI-5). Two progressive priests, Dom Luciano Mendes de Almeida and Dom Hélder Câmara—the archbishop of Olinda and Recife, who identified as socialist—created a course to teach leadership to some politically engaged young members of the Catholic Church.[84] Pires was among the students, and he went to Rio de Janeiro to attend the classes. On the first day, the military invaded the meeting and arrested several leaders of the Church, including Pires. After an intervention from the Vatican, the officers allowed the ones who were not from Rio de Janeiro to return home and remain in house arrest. From October to December, all that Pires was allowed to do was go to work at Colégio Maria Imaculada, a Catholic school in the São Paulo neighborhood of Paraíso.[85] And yet, he felt both lucky and guilty, knowing that many of his colleagues from Rio de Janeiro were still imprisoned and being tortured.

In 1971, he was talking to a priest near the school when two men approached them. They separated the friends and punched the priest. It seemed like a senseless attack. Pires asked them to stop, and they responded loud and clear: both Pires and the priest should leave Brazil within forty-eight hours, or they would be killed. The priest decided to leave for Panama and promised to contact someone he knew in Chile to support Pires. Pledge kept, Pires arrived soon after in Santiago with documents, a passport, and a $120 student fellowship, enough to pay for a bedroom, and *empanada y caña*—the small beef pies with a glass of wine that were his daily meals for several weeks.[86]

Pires was part of the so-called second generation of Brazilian exiles, who left the country after AI-5.[87] This group was comprised of young activists whose actions were, in many cases, influenced by the movements of resistance that emerged after the 1964 coup d'état.[88] Therefore, at the time when they left the country, many had no established career and had to start from scratch in a new nation, with a new language, without any of the connections they had had in their homeland.

Vera Vital Brasil was also part of this group. She was a top-of-the-class student in the School of Pharmacy at the Federal University of Rio de Janeiro. Coming from the small town of Piquete, in a rural area of São Paulo State, she was attracted by the energy of student activism. She was arrested in December 1969 and taken to one of the most infamous prisons of the dictatorial regime, the Information Operations Detachment—Internal Defense Operations Center (known by its Portuguese abbreviation DOI-CODI). Her then boyfriend, who was also in the student movement, fled to Chile, afraid of also being arrested and sent her the address. She bribed a person in the Brazilian government to receive her passport and followed her boyfriend. "I arrived in Santiago in April 1970. I embraced it as my second home because it represented care after the blow of torture and imprisonment."[89] Vital Brasil faced some challenges, especially because she did not speak Spanish. "It took me a month or so to be able to articulate anything. But I had left a country under censorship to one in which the enthusiasm with Allende's campaign was everywhere. People were writing about Marx and Lenin on the walls. It was a dream."[90] She found a job at a laboratory of clinical analysis and little by little turned trauma into hope.

José Serra also had a steady job while in Chile. The Chilean government hired him to coordinate a literacy campaign for peasants in the southern province of Arauco. The idea was to apply Paulo Freire's method. At the time, the Brazilian educator was also in exile in Chile, and Serra dated his daughter, educator Madalena Freire, who was then finishing high school.[91] Later, he was accepted in an ECLAC program. Although he could not receive a fellowship because he had not been nominated directly by the Brazilian government, ILPES invited him to teach math to his peers.[92]

Journalists José Maria and Teresa Rabêlo recall the exiles in Chile as a very stratified group. They half-jokingly divided them into three major sets, according to income.[93] In the upper level of the pyramid was the "bourgeoisie," composed of those who found jobs in international private companies. Then there was the "middle class," formed by those who worked for unofficial international institutions, the Chilean government, or state-owned companies. Teachers in schools and universities were also part of this group. Finally, the "proletariat" was mostly made up of students, those who had no work permit and no contacts and, for one reason or another, had to rely on the caixinha or "little box" to survive.[94]

The caixinha was a fund used to support those in need with monthly stipends to pay for school tuition, housing, food, or anything urgent.[95] Much of the money was invested in a restaurant in the neighborhood of Providencia, with the objective of generating more revenue to support the exile community. The funds came not only from the profits of the restaurant but also from individuals and institutions—mostly the World Council of Churches—and could also be used for emergency situations.[96] Wilson Barbosa relied on that for six months, the maximum time an exile was allowed to use the help. The caixinha was created and managed by a kind of committee of exiles, many of whom were connected to the exile-founded Brazilian Information Front (Frente Brasileira de Informações), ironically dubbed the "FBI."[97] "It had no party colors. It was for anyone who needed help," attested Barbosa.[98]

Not everyone thought so. Stories about corruption and misappropriation of the funds abounded. Some complained that the money, especially what was destined for a program of scholarships with the aim of stimulating the pursuit of higher education, disproportionly benefited militants from some organizations. The fund was completely off the books and the lack of organization allowed at least one spy to benefit. Jaques de Souza Coimbra was one of the "lumpens," the pejorative term that some exiles used for those who did not take part in any political group. He arrived in Santiago with no visa in April 1970. He asked the Student Federation of the University of Chile for help and was immediately connected to Edmur Fonseca, who, at the time, worked at the Center for the Economic and Social Development of Latin America and would later become a professor and researcher at the Center for Humanistic Studies at the University of Chile. A poet, journalist, and political scientist born in Minas Gerais, Fonseca is described by his peers as a sweet man with a big heart.[99] He put Coimbra in contact with other Brazilian exiles, gave him money, and made sure he became a recipient of the caixinha. In a ten-page report that he wrote to the Intelligence Center of the Ministry of Foreign Affairs, Coimbra mocked the assistance given to him, stating that he participated in meetings in which security and solidarity were debated "with me, a complete stranger, listening to everything."[100] Months later, Coimbra would provide the Brazilian embassy in Santiago with detailed information about the exile community, including addresses, physical descriptions, and accounts of meetings.[101]

Despite the lack of organization and accountability surrounding the caixinha, the restaurant was successful. Journalist Armênio Guedes was part of a "committee of solidarity" dedicated to supporting the recently arrived exiles and worked in the business.[102] "We organized a restaurant where people could eat; refugees paid less but, at the same time, it was a regular restaurant that sold food for dining halls inside factories. We had a lot of activities."[103] He also recalls that the "FBI" coordinated radio shows, publications in newspapers, and other activities to denounce the abuses of the Brazilian regime. Even after the coup of 1973, under the protection of the United Nations, the restaurant continued producing food for refugees in embassies and at the National Stadium. The fact that despite its being known as a political business, its two managers were never arrested by the dictatorship would later arouse suspicion among the exile community, as well as invite accusations of embezzlement and of spying for the Chilean junta.[104]

At the time of his arrival in 1971, however, Wilson Barbosa was unaware of the accusations and felt grateful for the caixinha. If at the airport and in the first days in Santiago he was treated as a celebrity, the myth of a glamorous exile soon collapsed. "Once the freshness was over, in a few months, I had no job, no documents, nothing. I was living in a slum in Macul [a neighborhood in Greater Santiago], and I remember that I would go to Santiago's central market and ask the vendors to spare me some food. As a history professor, I could not work without a document attesting that I had a degree. And the Brazilian consulate would never help me get my documents."[105]

Informal methods of survival, such as the caixinha, were even more important because of the impossibility of relying on official channels. Most of the exiles kept a distance from the Brazilian embassy. It was seen as the "enemy's house."[106] The only time when Ubiramar Peixoto went to the embassy was due to extreme necessity and some naïveté. He had written to his father asking for his academic records. Peixoto had finally been accepted at the University of Chile and would be able to study and get a fellowship. It was a tremendous opportunity for someone who had had no regular job since his arrival in Chile. His father sent the requested materials, but they needed to be stamped at the Brazilian embassy.[107] When Peixoto arrived, staff members of the consular section made him wait for hours, setting up what he compared to "a sort of mental torture chamber." When he was finally invited in, a tall man with a gold-buttoned jacket asked why he wanted to study in such a "shitty" place if Brazil had the best universities in the world. "I kept thinking that he could just kill me, and nobody would find out," Peixoto recalls. He decided to scare the official by lying about his family. "I abruptly said that I was there because my father had a lot of money, grabbed the documents, and left."[108]

Peixoto also depended on the caixinha when he arrived. He had many friends living in Santiago and relied on what he called "Chilean solidarity." As he notes, "My friends recommended me to go take a course in lathe mechanics at the Technical Training Center of the Technological University of Chile, a professional institute that gave us 100 escudos just to be there."[109]

But after the course was over, still unemployed, he realized that the caixinha was his only means of survival.

Nielsen Pires says that he fortunately never had to use the money and did not know how it worked when he was questioned at the National Stadium, where interrogators seemed obsessed with understanding the details of the resource. However, after leaving the stadium, he finally met the person who took care of the caixinha and confirmed that it used to function inside a restaurant in a wealthy neighborhood, not only to generate a source of income, but also to avoid suspicion.[110] "Some say that there was a cell of the Brazilian Communist Party there. The fact is that in the days after the coup, when we were refugees, the person who served the food in embassies was Camacho, the manager of the restaurant. It was all connected."[111] The location of the caixinha and the origin of the money were the most frequently asked questions by Brazilian torturers in the National Stadium according to the Brazilian exiles who were imprisoned there.

For Reinaldo Guarany, the caixinha was "completely naive. It was a totally welfare-based thing that never, ever had resources of great importance. It moved little money." He survived with funds from ALN, indirectly provided by his family. "The day after I was arrested in Brazil, my father and my uncle went to the *aparelho* [hidden location for guerrilla members], contacted ALN, and returned them the weapons and some bags with money. I went to Santiago and erased my family from my mind."

His father, however, didn't. He traveled to Chile looking for his son. The family was in a difficult financial situation. They owned a small pharmacy in the Rio de Janeiro neighborhood of Leme, but police officers parked a car in front of it during business hours, as a form of punishing his family. Costumers stopped showing up. "Despite that, after he found me in Chile, my father started providing me with some money every month, although they had very little for themselves."[112]

Before his father's arrival, however, life in Santiago was rough. "At first, the Chilean government gave us a place to stay at Hogar Pedro Aguirre Cerca, a shelter inside a park where all the Setenta were. Around three or four months later we had to leave, and I went to live with my partner, Dora." Maria Auxiliadora Lara Barcelos, known as Dora, was a medical student connected to VAR-Palmares who was also forced into exile in Chile. She and Guarany moved to a tenement with floors covered with soil. "I had asthma as a child," Guarany recalled. "I had bronchitis, so those nights were hellish for me. I contacted ALN and said, 'Look, I will have to apply what I know best here in Chile. I will carry out armed action to get money, I'm sorry.'"[113]

Differently from what happened in Brazil, according to Guarany, they never robbed banks or Chilean institutions. Their focus was on money changers or "dollar traffickers," as he called them. "They were obviously all linked to the CIA and were there to inject dollars to devalue the Chilean economy. They didn't complain when they were robbed because they had nothing to complain about, right? The dollars they had didn't even exist in the real, open, true economy."[114] The result of this small-scale political burglary was not a large amount of money. Only enough to survive and buy materials.

LETTERS FROM THE OTHER SIDE

During the period of exile, censorship prevented intellectuals from publishing broadly about their experiences. However, in the late 1970s, after the *abertura*—the process that culminated in the end of this ban and, eventually, of dictatorial rule—the subjects of exile themselves responded to this "opening" by producing what would become a foundational part of the historiography of the Brazilian dictatorship. The first wave of works on the subject was published during the civilian-military regime and consisted mostly of firsthand accounts written by exiles.[115] These publications, which included both works of scholarship and testimonial literature, became a central source for researchers, who relied on the memories and perspectives of the exiles to understand the latter's experience abroad. Biographies and testimonies accounted for most of the published works from the late 1970s and over the next two decades. Although they do not include an analysis of the political and social impact of exile in Brazil, they offer perspectives that are not available in official documents.[116]

In 1976, sociologists Pedro Celso Uchôa Cavalcanti and Jovelino Ramos collected interviews, testimonies, manuscripts, and a long narrative of the torture and death of Frei Tito.[117] With the support of three renowned intellectuals who lived in exile—Paulo Freire, Abdias do Nascimento, and Nelson Werneck Sodré—they turned these sources into one of the most influential books of the period. The title, *Memórias do exílio, Brasil 1964–19??*, ended in two question marks to reinforce that, for the exiles, the date when they would be able to go back to Brazil was still undefined.[118] It was the first time that their experience was written as a collective one.

The idea emerged from a group established in Poland, who reflected on how the transnational experience of different groups of Poles informed their understanding of their nation. The authors justified the urgency of the project, stating that "in conditions marked by historical rupture, such as the ones that provoke exile, the collective memory has to be *made* because it demands a conscious effort of recuperation for the national culture."[119] Although the Brazilian exiles seem aware of their influence in the rethinking of Brazilian identity and national policies, they do not address that in the book; at the time, it was too early to define such a role. *Memórias do exílio, Brasil 1964–19??* was published in 1978 in Brazil, two years after its world release and a few months before the approval of the Amnesty Law. The editors requested interviews from exiles in different countries in a letter that asked, "How does this international experience among Brazilians affect your world vision? How does this experience modify the exiles' vision of Brazil? What will be the impact of the exile on Brazilian culture? These questions need to be answered because Brazilian exiles are not outside but inside the history of contemporary Brazil."[120]

The same intellectuals who had published *Memórias do exílio* in 1976 reunited with a group of female exiles to write a book from their perspective.[121] *Memórias das mulheres do exílio* (Memories of women in exile) was an attempt to forge women's collective memories of the period, clearly informed by the flourishing of gender studies at the time.[122] Their objective was directly stated: "Women, like all the other groups that have not been recognized by the historiography, do not have their history registered. That's what generates the sequence of testimonies of the present on the present, the life stories, the oral tradition, an effort of reconstitution."[123] On the cover of the book, the words "das mulheres" (of women) is depicted as forcefully inserted into the rest of the title. This is not by chance. For them, the fact that there were no female authors in the first publication of the series demonstrates that they were not included even in this already peripheral group.[124] Whenever discussions of race or gender were brought to the table they were marginalized by the larger and more urgent preoccupation with ending the dictatorship. Only when a democratic voting system was guaranteed did such debates gain strength.[125]

In the 2000s, a new shift in the historiography of exile began. Once again, the turn followed a trend in the general historiography of Latin America that shed light on the role of the diaspora and transnational studies.[126] The examination of the exile experience emerged as a central topic, not as a marginal part of studies of immigration or dictatorial regimes.[127] Questions of identity became secondary, giving way to discussions of power, nationalism, and displacement. Notably, many scholars favored transnational analysis over national histories, finally offering an interpretation of the political and social impact of exile experiences.

In 1979, with the approval of the Amnesty Law, most of the Brazilian exiles returned home.[128] The transnational experiences they brought with them were essential for the subsequent fight for democratization. The movements for civil rights, demonstrations at universities, and, more broadly, discussions of gender, race, and social relations in the democratic nations where they had lived, including early 1970s Chile, had planted seeds that would blossom into action in the upcoming years, culminating in the first democratic election, in 1985. The movement for universal suffrage and direct elections, Diretas Já, is an example.[129]

In his brief history of citizenship in Brazil—which he traces as beginning in 1822 with independence from Portugal—Brazilian historian José Murillo de Carvalho looks at the Amnesty Law of 1979 as an ambiguous process of redefinition of citizenship because it was "broad, general, and unrestricted," meaning that it included at the same time the exiles and perpetrators of torture, murder, and other crimes committed during the regime.[130] Although it restored political rights to intellectuals and leaders who would later run for public office, it also granted the same freedom to torturers.

The creation of the Brazilian Truth Commission, in 2012, opened new avenues to research into the exile experience. The availability of sources and the testimony of victims of the Brazilian dictatorship allowed scholars to examine not just how this period shaped the lives of those who were expelled from Brazil but also how their experience redefined the way the country addressed the legacy of political violence. Their presence became central to the reconciliation with democracy.[131] As privileged witnesses of the period, able to track the events from both Chilean and Brazilian perspectives, they influenced the political landscapes in the two countries, while also being influenced by them. Later, their bold questioning would result in museums of memory, truth commissions, and other initiatives to preserve the history of regimes that for so long survived by erasing their victims' individual histories. Although both Chile and Brazil are still trying to properly confront their past and the fight for democracy is still in the making, the vocal demands of the exile community over decades were essential for this reckoning. Curiously, the rebuilding of their memories is also broadened by the declassification of documents by intelligence services that had been monitoring their lives, almost as if writing a diary of their community.

3

THE DIPLOMATIC BRANCH
FROM MULTILATERALISM
TO ESPIONAGE

I was deeply aware that I was doing something to contribute
to the Brazilian people. A people who I felt was like my aunt,
cousins, brothers, nephews, friends. A people that I loved.

CABO ANSELMO, DOUBLE AGENT FOR THE MILITARY,
INTERVIEW FOR *RODA VIVA*, TV CULTURA, 2011

Soledad no viviste en soledad
Por eso tu vida no se borra

[Soledad you did not live in solitude
So your life cannot be erased]

MARIO BENEDETTI, "MUERTE DE SOLEDAD BARRETT"

Manoel Pio Corrêa had a long and fruitful career as a diplomat. He was the
Brazilian secretary-general of foreign affairs and served as ambassador to
Uruguay and Argentina, among other prominent positions. His actions and
beliefs, however, could not be further from the traditional expectations of a
negotiator. For him, dialogue and conciliation were not tools to fight communism; weapons and threats were. For this reason, he appointed police officer

Rui Dourado to be his right-hand man.[1] In his autobiography, Pio Corrêa lists three of Dourado's credentials. The first was having "climbed, alone, with a machine gun under his arm, into a dangerous favela and returned with—handcuffed and ignominiously held by one ear, to be seen by the entire slum—a dangerous ruffian, who was hiding there." The second was having instituted a 10 p.m. curfew in the violent neighborhood of Bangu, in Rio de Janeiro. He would play a military song to warn "all rowdies to leave the public areas." Dourado would then take the streets with his "band of police officers and arrest any vagabond he could find to spend a night in jail. Soon, Bangu became a calm neighborhood, more silent than a small rural village." Finally, there was the serendipity of Dourado's being near a bank when "four thieves were leaving the branch. Three died right there, by the door, and the fourth, 100 meters farther." Pio Corrêa's appreciation for violence and war made him the perfect Brazilian ambassador to Uruguay, where João Goulart, Leonel Brizola, and "something like 200 Brazilians had received political asylum, forming a real community, a tough political nucleus."[2]

In Montevideo, Pio Corrêa delineated the creation of the intelligence service of the Ministry of Foreign Affairs, the most important civilian arm of the dictatorship. To fight what he called "subversive agents," he modeled the Brazilian Foreign Office's Intelligence Center (CIEX) on "all of the intelligence services in the world, not only the communist states, which usually keep in other countries two types of agents. The first are the 'legal' residents, meaning the ones who are officially hired as workers for their respective countries—under the cover of diplomatic or consular positions, or as military, commercial, or cultural attachés."[3] In the other category are the "illegal" ones, who have no protection and live clandestine lives. Pio Corrêa oversaw the first group.

A division of the Ministry of Foreign Affairs (also known as Itamaraty for its location in Brasília's Itamaraty Palace), CIEX was created with the objective of closely monitoring the lives of Brazilian exiles in countries of the Southern Cone and tracing their connections with international leftist groups.[4] It was a branch of the Brazilian National Intelligence Service (SNI) and although many have claimed that the employees of Itamaraty remained neutral during the military regime, the existence of CIEX is proof of the deep involvement of diplomats in the government's actions.[5] Moreover, the freedom that CIEX agents enjoyed in Chile during Allende's presidency demonstrates that there was a connection between the Chilean Armed Forces and the Brazilian diplomats in repressing left-wing groups.[6]

Manoel Pio Corrêa founded CIEX in 1966, and it operated until the end of the military government in 1985.[7] Working side by side with the military attaché Colonel Câmara Senna, Pio Corrêa focused his tenure on combating any plans of resistance from former president João Goulart and his brother-in-law, fellow politician Leonel Brizola, who were exiled in Uruguay. The diplomat created a network of surveillance that included professionals from different areas, such as politicians, judges, lawyers, military personnel, businessmen, and even farmers. They were trained in Brazil, but their expertise improved after several trips to Uruguay. The country became the pilot project for the surveillance.[8]

Central to Pio Corrêa's performance as diplomat was his military career. He graduated from the Brazilian War College (ESG), in Rio de Janeiro, an institute of the Brazilian Ministry of Defense dedicated to academic research. His interest in secret investigations had appeared much earlier than the creation of CIEX. In 1959, when he replaced Ambassador Odette de Carvalho e Souza as chief of Itamaraty's Political Department, she handed him an "archive" with documents and notes about foreigners and Brazilian citizens suspected of being connected to "subversive activities" in the 1940s and 1950s.[9] It was "a precious gift," according to Pio Corrêa, who worked hard to expand the records. When he left the department, at the end of the Kubitschek administration (1956–61), he remained suspicious of how the next government would operate. So, he decided to leave the expanded version of the archive with a trusted friend. His anticommunist stances—which could have isolated him during the Quadros and Goulart years—were well received by President Humberto de Alencar Castelo Branco. "I used to conspire against the government, and the victory of the March 31, 1964, revolution represented the coronation of my most cherished hopes," he stated.[10] After becoming the ambassador in Uruguay, Pio Corrêa was promoted again and, as soon as he became secretary-general of Itamaraty, he founded CIEX.

Inspired by the US Central Intelligence Agency (CIA) and the British Secret Intelligence Service, Section 6 (MI6), CIEX first received the official name of Foreign Policy Documentation Advisory. From its creation to 1975, it was housed in Annex I of the Itamaraty Palace, on the fourth floor, in room 410.[11]

CIEX was a rehearsal for the infamous Operation Condor, established in the mid-1970s, with the support of the United States and the active participation of Argentina, Bolivia, Brazil, Chile, Paraguay, and Uruguay. It secretly monitored and repressed political enemies of the governments abroad. The effectiveness of CIEX may explain why Brazil was not as active as other countries in the clandestine political campaign of Operation Condor.[12] Most of the work that could interest Brazil in the Condor years had been guaranteed with CIEX.[13] Its agents followed a "Plan of External Search" with the support of military attachés and of the National Intelligence Service (SNI).[14] They sent most of the reports to the SNI as well as to other intelligence services, including the Army Intelligence Center, Aviation Intelligence Center, Navy Intelligence Center (CENIMAR), and the secretaries of the General Staff of the Armed Forces (EMFA).[15] Documents attesting to the existence of CIEX emerged after the discovery of the so-called Archives of Terror, in Paraguay, a collection of cases of murder, torture, and disappearance during Operation Condor.[16]

Many exiles, however, believed they were being watched much earlier, and many of them denounced it at the time. Besides CIEX, spies from other governmental agencies joined the surveillance, including CENIMAR and EMFA.[17] "The streets were packed with military personnel disguised as exiles," recalls Wilson Barbosa. "The famous Brazilian musician exiled in Chile in 1968, Geraldo Vandré, was always with three 'friends' who, just by looking at them, you could tell were from the military. Their bodies, their scruff . . . Only Vandré, who was very naive, did not notice." He estimates that there were "between ten to twenty of them" in Santiago. "They were the reason why we carried guns. But they never approached me. Except for once when I was in line to buy cigarettes and one of them asked me what brands were available."[18]

Nielsen Pires had a much closer brush with the spies. He remembers being robbed by a man he is certain was one of the disguised Brazilian officers. "I was walking the streets of Santiago at 7:30 a.m. when this very athletic type takes the papers that I was carrying. He did not ask for money or anything. All he took were documents! And he was strong, wearing tennis shoes. He did not look at all like a thief. But all I had were discussions on Karl Mannheim's *Ideology and Utopia*. Nothing to do with the political documents that they probably expected me to be carrying."[19]

The spies sent reports to the Ministry of Foreign Affairs with descriptions of daily events in the lives of Brazilian exiles. They did not elaborate on an analysis of the Chilean political scenario or diplomacy. Former Communist Party president Amarílio Vasconcelos was one of their favorite victims.[20] His meetings with Salvador Allende and other members of the Chilean government were narrated in detailed reports. In one of them, the topic was a series of requests Vasconcelos and other two exiles, Cândido da Costa

Aragão and Oswaldo (whose last name is unknown by the spies), had made to Allende, including the concession of a visa for Miguel Arraes, former governor of Pernambuco, who had been jailed and exiled.[21] In another document, the subject matter is the appointment of Vasconcelos and Aragão to jobs at state-owned companies mediated by "Chilean communist Gustavo Díaz, ex-husband of socialist representative Carmen Lazo."[22] The obsession with their personal lives appears in many reports. One of them quotes a supposed statement by Vasconcelos about Allende's use of sexual stimulants. "If President Aguirre Cerda died due to red wine, President Allende will die due to women."[23] The central question is, How did CIEX spies know in such detail the conversations among government members? For several exiles, the explanation is obvious: moles had infiltrated among them and inside La Moneda Palace.

THE PERFECT DOUBLE AGENT: FROM REVOLUTIONARY TO MOLE

The popularity of the most famous double agent of the Brazilian dictatorship began to build a week before the dictatorship itself. José Anselmo dos Santos, known as Cabo Anselmo, became a celebrity among leftists on March 25, 1964, when he led a group of over 2,000 sergeants and low-ranking military personnel commemorating the second anniversary of the Association of Sailors and Marines (Associação dos Marinheiros e Fuzileiros Navais), an illegal entity that challenged Navy authorities.[24] Cabo Anselmo opened the event categorically questioning the punishment imposed on twelve leaders of the association who had openly supported the "Basic Reforms" proposed by then-president João Goulart. He declared that the group favored the program because it would "free from poverty the exploited people of the countryside and the city, of the ships and barracks."[25]

Of course, this did not sit well with the military. The minister of the Navy, Sílvio Mota, issued an arrest warrant for the leaders of the revolt. Instead of following his orders, however, the marines joined the rebels with the backing of their commander, Rear Admiral Cândido da Costa Aragão, who would later be exiled in Chile and closely monitored by CIEX.[26] The episode, known as the Sailors' Revolt, ended with the resignation of Sílvio Mota and an agreement with the rebels, who were arrested for a few hours and freed after being pardoned by Goulart. This forgiveness was widely contested by high-ranking officials, further aggravating the polarization in the armed forces. Less than a week later, on March 31, a coup removed Goulart from the presidency.[27]

Cabo Anselmo, the most infamous double
agent of the Brazilian dictatorship.
Source: Arquivo Nacional do Brasil.

Close to six decades later, Cabo Anselmo's deep-set eyes were framed by a curtain of white hair. He carried his slim figure to meetings with far-right groups in Brazil, where he engaged with conspiracy theorists about cell phone waves and Marxist indoctrination in schools. In the late 2000s he sued the Brazilian government, arguing that he had been a victim of the dictatorship in the early 1960s, although he continued publicly defending all human rights abuses committed by the regime and said he was nothing but a "stupid boy" at the time of the Sailors' Revolt.[28] The fact that he was a double agent and "shifted from persecuted to persecutor" was decisive for him in losing the judicial fight.[29] A few years earlier, he also took to the courts to be recognized by his baptismal name, after forty-four years having lived without official documents, a result of his clandestine life.[30]

The shift from "persecuted to persecutor" was not a smooth one. After the Sailors' Revolt, Cabo Anselmo was punished by Institutional Act no. 1.[31] He found asylum at the Mexican embassy.[32] Two weeks later, he left the embassy to join groups fighting against the new regime but was arrested the next day. After escaping, in 1966, he hid in Uruguay, where he met João Goulart's brother-in-law, Leonel Brizola. In 1967, he participated in the first Conference of the Latin American Solidarity Organization, held in Havana. The event was foundational for guerrilla movements in Latin America, reinforcing Che Guevara and Régis Debray's project of foquismo.[33] Following this lead, Cabo Anselmo helped create the first group of guerrilla training, called the Popular Revolutionary Vanguard (VPR). In Cuba, he "ate lots of lobster and fish" and was exposed both to Fidelistas and anti-Castro intellectuals.[34] When asked about the Brazilian involvement in the Chilean coup of 1973, he said that, although there were rumors, he could not attest to that. The only instances in which he claims to have witnessed foreign interference were from the left, in attempts to implement the "Castro-Guevarista foquismo in Brazil, from people determined to start a civil war."[35]

In 1970 Cabo Anselmo was still commanding VPR guerrillas in Brazil, when some started to find it suspicious that many people close to him were being arrested or killed. To aggravate the speculation, he was detained in June 1971 and freed days later. The VPR leadership, however, still believed that he was fully committed to communism and the fight against the dictatorship. In October, he went to Chile as if he were just one more exile. Aluízio Palmar remembers that day. There was much gossip and confusion about some celebrity having arrived. It was Cabo Anselmo. "For us, he was a great fellow, a hero. Always fashionable, he seemed to be a fantastic human being, with all the things that he had done while in the Navy. We had no suspicions."[36]

The hesitation about Cabo Anselmo ended up dividing the exile community in Chile. In May 1971, Inês Etienne Romeu was arrested.[37] That same month, Cabo Anselmo was detained in São Paulo. She was taken to Sérgio Fleury, the chief of the Department of Political and Social Order (DOPS).[38] Fleury was known as one of the dictatorship's most violent torturers. Cabo Anselmo claims that he was one of his victims but "was given the opportunity to survive" after being tortured.[39] Inês Etienne Romeu witnessed the privileges directed toward Cabo Anselmo and managed to write a letter to other guerrilla members, stating that the former guerrilla leader was now collaborating with Fleury.[40]

Maria do Carmo Brito, known as "Lia" among clandestine factions, joined multiple organizations until becoming the first woman to run a guerrilla group in Latin America, a revamped version of the VPR, in 1969.[41] She had been one of the Quarenta, the forty political prisoners freed in exchange for German ambassador Ehrenfried von Holleben, in 1970. During her exile in Algeria, she met former guerrilla comrade Ângelo Pezzutti, who became her partner. They moved together to Santiago. Monitoring Brito was one of Cabo Anselmo's main jobs in Chile. He wrote a detailed account of this period to Fleury called the *Relatório de "Paquera"* ("Flirt" report). On the first page he lists the targets of his narrative: Onofre Pinto, Maria do Carmo Brito, and Marcio Moreira Alves, three of the Brazilian exiles in Chile.[42] In what now reads as a macabre diary, he narrates step-by-step the scope of operations and vigilance. They include visits to the Cuban embassy, to the *aparelhos* (places of hiding), and lists of addresses and passwords used by guerrilla members. He also describes the fear of being caught, stating that a Cuban named Julián had asked too many questions and hinted at the fact that Anselmo was a double agent.

MIR militant Angélica Fauné introduced Cabo Anselmo to Maria do Carmo Brito as soon as he arrived in Santiago.[43] Right after, Brito received the letter from Inês Etienne Romeu and denounced Cabo Anselmo to Onofre Pinto, then chief of the VPR in Chile. Aluízio Palmar believes that her claims were not taken seriously because of internal fractures in the guerrilla group—"at that time an organization divided by all sorts of mistrust and intrigue."[44] One of the debates was about whether to hold a conference that had been scheduled over a year before. According to Palmar, there were three factions. First was Onofre Pinto's group, which did not want the conference. They argued for immediate return to Brazil and the resumption of armed actions. Second was the group led by Ângelo Pezzutti, which defended the conference as essential to defining the direction of the organization and demanded that Onofre Pinto be investigated. Third were militants recently arrived from Cuba and North Korea who wanted the conference and, unlike Pezzutti's group, did not accept punishing Onofre Pinto.

Pezzutti, Maria do Carmo Brito's partner, tried to alert Onofre Pinto of Cabo Anselmo's treachery. Pinto not only contested the accusation but allegedly gave the double agent $50,000 to build a place in Pernambuco to house VPR guerrillas who came back from military training.[45] Although most were not as supportive of Cabo Anselmo as Pinto, many exiles felt that their suspicions were not enough to result in action. "These uncertainties came from gossip, so most of us ended up thinking that they were not worth pursuing. What some say is that Onofre Pinto had been arrested and changed sides. And that was the strategy of the Brazilian military: getting people from political groups and shifting them to their side," recalled René de Carvalho.[46]

The alert was only taken seriously when it was too late. On January 8, 1973, VPR members Eudaldo Gomes da Silva, Evaldo Luiz Ferreira de Souza, Jarbas Pereira Marques, José Manoel da Silva, Pauline Philippe Reichstul, and Soledad Barrett Viedna were arrested, tortured, and murdered in a small farm near the capital of the state of Pernambuco, northeast Brazil.[47] The slaughter became known as the "Granja São Bento Massacre."[48]

At the time of her killing, Soledad Barrett Viedna was Cabo Anselmo's partner and was pregnant with his child. That was not enough to prevent Cabo Anselmo from giving the green light to the military and letting them kill her. Soledad Barrett Viedna was born in Paraguay in 1945, the granddaughter of anarchist writer Rafael Barrett. In her house, social justice was part of the conversation around the dinner table. From a very early age she joined demonstrations and political groups, including Asunción's Youth Student Front and the United National Liberation Front.[49] Barrett traveled around the world supporting the communist fight, from Argentina to Moscow and Brazil, where she met José María Ferreira de Araújo, with whom she had a daughter. He returned to Brazil in 1970 but was located by the military and killed. Soledad decided to join the VPR and there met Cabo Anselmo. They became a couple around 1972. Little did she know that he was already a double agent.[50]

Soledad's brother, Jorge Barrett, had recently joined the VPR and became a sort of homing pigeon for the organization, traveling frequently from Chile to Brazil with messages to the militants, including his sister. In the last of his trips, he carried a letter from Onofre Pinto, finally surrendering to the pressure of his peers and alerting the group, in Recife, to leave the area. But Jorge Barrett gave the letter directly to his sister. In love and expecting his child, Soledad showed the letter to Cabo Anselmo. The double agent warned Sérgio Fleury, and the chief of the DOPS immediately ordered the operation that killed Soledad and five other members of the VPR. The massacre destroyed Onofre Pinto's reputation, and he left Chile soon after.[51]

ORDINARY LIVES, STRANGE DEATHS

The lives of double agents did not always feel like a Hollywood movie. Many of them were not as well known as Cabo Anselmo and looked more like George Smiley than James Bond. Even Cabo Anselmo's "Flirt" reports are full of "blank days" and "no replies."[52] After gaining access to part of the CIEX archives, in 2007, the Brazilian newspaper *Correio Braziliense* published a series of stories about the activities of the diplomatic secret service. One listed the names of the most prominent diplomats who were employees at CIEX. Among them was Agildo Sellos de Moura, who worked in Santiago from 1967 to 1971, when he became an adviser to the intelligence service. A year later he was named chief of the Intelligence Security Division (Divisão de Segurança et Informações; DSI). Among diplomats, CIEX workers were perceived as the lowest class of professionals and were nicknamed "garbage men."[53] However, like Sellos de Moura, after working as spies, they were rapidly promoted and advanced in their diplomatic careers.

Some of the moles also relayed impressions of the domestic climate in Chile. Many times, these observations were spurious. In May 1972, a report gathering information from Brazilian asylees and Chilean leftists stated that Allende would do a self-coup and proclaim Chile a socialist republic in the first half of that same month. "According to other rumors," it continues, "Allende will only close the national Congress and, following constitutional measures, will not call elections in the short term."[54] Another report from the same day was not as misguided. It brings an analysis of the support (or lack thereof) for Allende in the Chilean Armed Forces. Gustavo Vidal, a member of the Press Committee of the Chilean Communist Party (Partido Comunista Chileno; PCCh), told the exiles that among tenants and colonels, 85 percent were against the Popular Unity government. In the Navy, 75 percent were against Allende. The Air Force was the only branch still supportive of the Popular Unity government, with only 30 percent against it. A few months later, another report stated that a coup against Allende was nigh. The sources were affiliates of the Popular Unitary Action Movement (MAPU), the PCCh, the Radical Party, and a housekeeper of Genaro Arriagada, a member of the Central Commission of the Christian Democratic Party (Partido Demócrata Cristiano; PDC). She had heard her boss talking about a coup to put Eduardo Frei in power.[55]

A secret document from CIEX mentions the March 31, 1970, edition of the leftist Chilean newspaper *Última Hora*, which announced an upcoming visit of police officer Sérgio Fleury to Chile. According to the newspaper, the torturer's objective in Santiago was to "make contacts with the General Direction of Investigations to prove the existence of a link between Brazilian guerrilla members with the Uruguayan Tupamaros, and also with Chilean leftist groups. The information could then be used to 'justify' agreements of repressive action under CIA control."[56] Fleury's presence in Chile worried the diplomats. Another report from CIEX questions the success of the police officer's trip, pointing out that the fact that the "communist media" knew about it demonstrated the "total lack of security" around the visit.

For the exiles living in Chile, the interference of the Brazilian government created a nation within a nation. It was clear that dictatorships supported each other, and exiles would not be considered citizens by any state of exception. It was also evident that, with the constant monitoring, no matter where they were, they would never be completely safe from the Brazilian authorities.

The realm of arts and culture was one in which the vigilance felt harmless. In the early months of Allende's government, the reports from CIEX described cordial encounters, observed at events such as the Eleventh São Paulo Biennial, in 1971, to which the Chilean government sent an artwork by the collective group of geometric painters Movimiento Forma y Espacio.[57] The Brazilian participation in the annual Santiago International Fair (Feria Internacional de Santiago; FISA), where countries exhibited their technological innovations, continued with the same regularity observed since the early 1960s, when the Chilean National Society of Agriculture (Sociedad Nacional de Agricultura; SNA) created the event. The Chilean government sponsored the 1971 FISA, although Allende did not attend because the president of the SNA had protested agrarian reform and other policies of the Popular Unity government during the president's introductory speech.

Even in the arts, however, there were tense moments. In May 1971, a group of exiles organized the exhibition "Journey of Solidarity with the Brazilian People." Takao Amano, Amarílio Vasconcelos, Amadeu Thiago de Mello, and Edmur Camargo displayed posters about the political situation in Brazil in the lobby of the Catholic University of Chile. Brazilian student

Luis Gonçalves de Oliveira destroyed five of them, screaming that it was an insult to his homeland. He was arrested, but Brazilian ambassador Câmara Canto committed himself to protecting Oliveira at all costs.[58]

Less than a month after the exhibition, one of its curators became a fatal victim of Brazilian transnational espionage. Edmur Péricles Camargo, known as Gauchão, was one of the Setenta. On June 15, 1971, the attaché of the Brazilian Army in Buenos Aires was notified that the "terrorist" would stop in Buenos Aires in his attempt to go from Chile to Montevideo on a LAN/Chile flight. Due to the torture he had endured in Brazil, he was seeking medical treatment with a prominent doctor in Uruguay. However, upon arrival at Ezeiza Airport in Buenos Aires, the Argentinean police arrested him. Less than a week later, a CIEX report to other intelligence agencies stated that Brazilian exiles in Chile had been worried about Camargo's disappearance. According to the Brazilian Truth Commission, he was "arbitrarily arrested by the Argentinean organs of repression, during a flight stopover in Buenos Aires at dawn the next day, and put in a Brazilian Air Force airplane which brought him to Brazil, where he disappeared while in the hands of public agents of the Brazilian military dictatorship." CIEX operations in this case are proof of how the "military dictatorial state completely subverts the function of its relevant diplomatic services, transforming them into the long arm of the law over their own nationals, to imprison and eliminate them."[59] For the truth commission, Camargo's death was an example of how the activity of the Brazilian Foreign Office's Intelligence Center was a precursor to the actions of other intelligence services during the years of Operation Condor.

MULTILATERALISM AND NEGOTIATION

CIEX was not created in a vacuum. The 1964 coup inspired another form of diplomacy, which embraced not only violence and spying but a far more multilateral approach than the alignment with the United States would suggest. Paulo Fagundes Vizentini defines the foreign policy of the military period as the "second phase of multilateralization." The first phase started in the 1950s, with the governments of Getúlio Vargas and Juscelino Kubitschek followed by the unsuccessful attempt to put in practice an "independent foreign policy" during the administrations of Jânio Quadros and João Goulart. With the civilian-military dictatorship, the multilateralist project became effective and dominant, initiating bold attempts to create new connections and alliances in regional and global systems while at the same time maintaining old relationships, thus circumventing exclusive allegiance to the United States.[60]

The first minister of foreign affairs of this era was Vasco Leitão da Cunha, who remained in charge until January 1966. He prepared the terrain for multilateralism, tearing down the "independent" policy of the Goulart administration. The means for that was the implementation of the theory of "concentric circles," which stipulated different objectives for relations in Latin America, with the United States, and in the Western Hemisphere. During one of the first events of his tenure—the closing of the UN Conference on Trade and Development (UNCTAD) on June 16, 1964—Leitão da Cunha defended the need for "collective economic security," a responsibility shared by "developed and developing nations." An irony of the meeting was that Brazil started by promoting its independent foreign policy and ended with the "course correction" of the new administration. The opening ceremony took place on March 24, just a week before the coup. The country's representative was João Goulart's chancellor, João Augusto de Araújo Castro, who echoed the independent foreign policy, declaring that the "underdeveloped countries" called for independence: "This Conference is not an isolated event but a moment in a historical process in which the consciousness of the underdeveloped countries was more and more attuned to the solution of their problems by their own means, thereby giving to those solutions a genuine character that could not be imported from abroad."[61]

The discourse of the Brazilian dictatorship's representative at the same conference, in June, brought few collisions with such proposals. The emphasis on bipolarity and alignment with the United States seemed merely a way of opposing the Goulart government. At the heart of the speech were words already aligned with multilateralism that would characterize the foreign policy of the dictatorial regime, including the accountability of developed nations: "Development is not an objective to be sought separately by rich and poor but one that, quite on the contrary, is a common goal of both developed and developing countries in the accomplishment of which responsibilities and burdens must be shared jointly and severally. There is interdependence of interests and coresponsibility in the solutions."[62]

Juracy Magalhães, who had been appointed Brazil's ambassador to the United States in 1964, took over the Ministry of Justice in 1965 and, later, replaced Vasco Leitão da Cunha as minister of foreign affairs between 1966 and 1967. Magalhães made clear in his inaugural speech that he owed no allegiance to other nations, stating that the cultural connections with the West, despite being the foundation of Brazilian foreign policy, did not represent "a mortgage of any kind capable of stalling its step in achieving the greater objective, which is the uncompromising defense of the national interests."[63]

The new minister went on, flirting with the common "cultural tradition" that Brazil shared with Western Europe, arguing for a "friendly coexistence" with Eastern Europe, and a "broad cooperation" with what he called "Afro-Asians." Latin America received more attention, as it was identified as the region in which "our history develops, and our future is generated. Integrating ourselves into the world through and with Latin America is one of the central objectives of our foreign policy."[64] Such integration, however, was still seen through the prism of East-West bipolarity, leaving aside the North-South antagonism.[65]

In this context, Latin America was instrumental to the full development of multilateralism. The country's aspirations to become a powerhouse of its own included an interventionist diplomacy, in which anticommunism was the main theme. Historian Luiz Alberto Moniz Bandeira affirms that Médici created a unique military diplomacy that was essential "for the success and the consolidation of the coups in Bolivia (1971), Uruguay (1971–73) and Chile (1973)."[66] Such a policy implied intervention, covert or not, that did not occur under the guidance of the United States. They were independent security policies that aimed at authoritarian nationalism in the region.

This authoritarian nationalism must not be interpreted as a populist vision or mistaken for an independent foreign policy. Historian José Honório Rodrigues summarized it as a mixture of "patriotism, the struggle for economic freedom and against imperialism, in its form of economic exploitation, the defense of national interests and aspirations, the tendency toward neutralism and against international tutelage, and, in extreme forms, the feeling of anti-Americanism."[67] Chile represented an important consumer market and a place for collaboration and innovation. Nevertheless, Juracy Magalhães's focus on Chile was due not only to its economic importance but also to its role as a harbor for enemies of the regime.

THE SECOND BRANCH

The Brazilian government's intention of undermining and eventually removing Allende was not hidden; it went beyond secret meetings and was well known even to members of the socialist government. The US ambassador to Chile, Edward Korry, blamed Brazil directly in a 1981 article in the *Los Angeles Times*, declaring, "The CIA did not overthrow Allende, no matter what the Democratic Party would have us believe. It played almost no role. The actual technical and psychological support came from the military government of

Brazil, a regime that had been helped to power by the Johnson Administration in 1965."[68]

In 1985, while Chile was still under Augusto Pinochet's rule and Brazil had elected its first civilian president in over twenty years, Nathaniel Davis published an insider's account of the years before the Chilean coup. He was the US ambassador in Santiago at the time and coined the expression "Brazil Connection" to explain the Brazilian influence in the process through which Chile became a dictatorship.[69] The first branch of the operation, Davis argues, was the Brazilian business sector.[70]

Davis also notes Marlise Simons's story in the *Washington Post*, full of interviews with right-wing Brazilian businessmen who admitted having helped the coup in Chile. One of them declared that "the private sector played a crucial role in the preparation of both interventions, and the Brazilian businessmen who plotted the overthrow of the left-leaning administration of President João Goulart in 1964 were the same people who advised the Chilean Right on how to deal with Marxist President Allende."[71]

The second branch of the Brazilian support of the coup, according to Davis, was the Brazilian ambassador. The former US diplomat narrates a meeting in which Antônio Cândido da Câmara Canto's role was explicit: "At lunch with me in late March 1973 he made a series of leading suggestions (which I turned aside), trying to draw me into cooperative planning, interembassy coordination, and joint efforts looking toward the Allende government's demise. Later I noticed that the reminiscences of leading coup planners like General Arellano reflected a special tie of consideration for the Brazilian ambassador, manifested even in the frenetic days before September 11. All in all, there is no real doubt in my mind that allegations of a Brazilian connection are true."[72]

In an interview with a Brazilian newspaper at the time of the book release, Davis offered that he did not remember the names of Brazilian businessmen involved in the conspiracy, except for Câmara Canto, who "was very subtle."[73] In another story, Brazilian diplomats denied Davis's allegations. One of them, who refused to be identified, treated it as business as usual, suggesting some level of support, as "the Brazilian government opened a line of credit of $20 million for the Chilean government, so that they could buy buses."[74]

The lines of credit to which the Brazilian diplomat referred were also confirmed by the recently declassified documents from the Brazilian government. The EMFA and Foreign Affairs Ministry reports show that those credit sources were offered for the purchase of items as varied as automobiles and meat.[75] The reason for the Brazilian government to boost lines of credit during the Allende government was clear.[76] The strategy allowed the country to continue exporting to the Chilean government, one of the most important consumers of Brazilian goods, and at the same time turned Chile into a debtor.[77] Whenever a company canceled one of the exports to Chile for financial reasons, the Brazilian embassy intervened, demanding that the Central Bank of Brazil investigate what had gone wrong.[78] The country never stopped presenting its products at the Santiago International Fair (FISA) during the entire Popular Unity administration. The Chilean president himself visited the Brazilian booth at the FISA, in which entrepreneurs proudly showed new technological developments.[79] These events were so important to the Brazilian economy that in 1972, when Allende decided to cancel the UN Conference on Trade and Development due to disagreements with the Chilean National Society of Agriculture, the Brazilian government suggested the construction of its own exhibit site 300 feet from the UNCTAD headquarters.[80]

Despite this business partnership, Allende embodied Brazil's worst fears. The country worried as much about the deterioration of the Chilean economy as it did about the expansion of communism. For Câmara Canto, the solution to the impasse was Allende's removal. In a telegram to the Brazilian government about the 1973 parliamentary elections, he stated that the only way to guarantee "democratic and free elections in Chile, on March 4, is the army."[81] After Popular Unity emerged victorious, Câmara Canto raised the hypothesis of fraud. In May, he wrote to the Brazilian government warning of the possibility of a civil war. He repeated the alert in June, referring also to a likely coup d'état.[82] A month before the overthrow of Allende, in August, he wrote that the situation in the country was calamitous. "There is no fuel, no buses, no trucks to transport all kinds of commodities, no conversation between the government and the opposition, in sum, no cabinet."[83]

Soon after the 1973 coup, Chilean military authorities recognized Câmara Canto's importance and paid homage to his support. Near a small church, the Capilla Sagrada Familia de Nazareth, located in the metro Santiago community of Pedro Aguirre Cerda, a bucolic little street was named after Antônio Cândido da Câmara Canto in 1977. It was the year of his death. In Brazil, similar tributes took place. It is hard for current inhabitants of the Chilean street to understand why a Brazilian diplomat deserved such distinction. An ambassador to Chile from 1968 to 1975, Câmara Canto was no regular officer. A ferocious anticommunist, he dedicated three years of his mandate to weakening the presidency of Salvador Allende, and two others to supporting his close friend, Augusto Pinochet.

Brazilian ambassador Antônio Cândido da Câmara Canto reading a speech.
Source: Arquivo Nacional do Brasil.

Tall, robust, and with a strong southern accent, Câmara Canto was a man full of convictions. In April 1969, he coordinated the Commission of Summary Investigation, a McCarthyist-style group designated by the Brazilian Ministry of Foreign Affairs to expel communists from its staff. It would become the biggest purge in Brazilian diplomatic history, resulting in the annulment of forty-four mandates. Of them, however, only four were for political reasons. Câmara Canto decided to use the opportunity to get rid of bohemians and homosexuals. "Aguantas una verdad? [Can you handle the truth?]," he would ask the defendants in Spanish. One of the dismissed employees, who had no connections with the Communist Party whatsoever, asked why he had lost his job. The answer the Brazilian paper *Jornal do Brasil* did not dare to write fully: "You were fired because you are (unpublishable word, designating homosexual)."[84] Also among the victims of the commission was the nonconformist poet, musician, and diplomat Vinícius de Moraes, lyricist of the song "The Girl from Ipanema." Rumor has it that when he heard that Itamaraty would fire homosexuals and bohemians, he rushed to announce, "I'm an alcoholic!"[85]

Among Câmara Canto's closest friends in Santiago was Sergio Arellano Starck, who led the "Caravan of Death," a helicopter-borne killing squad under Augusto Pinochet, which resulted in the murder of "at least 75" civilians.[86] Starck was one of the most prominent supporters of the Chilean coup, and so were other intimate friends of Câmara Canto, such as Gustavo Leigh (a general who represented the Air Force in the 1973 Chilean coup d'état), José Toribio Merino (one of the four members of the military junta from 1973 to 1990), and Herman Brady (minister of defense during the Pinochet regime).[87]

According to the ambassador, opposing the Allende government caused him a great deal of harm. He described his life in Chile as miserable. Luiz José Torres Marques, who detailed the Brazilian ambassador's plans in case of Allende's electoral victory in the 1970 elections, was shocked by the diplomat's routine. "The ambassador and his family live cloistered in their house, inside the embassy, and, in case they have to leave because of work obligations, the embassy secretaries and Brazilian military attachés give them some coverage, working as if they were police officers." The reason for such fear was the "frequent threats he suffers from national subversive elements and from Brazilians who have been refugees in Chile since the March 1964 revolution." Torres Marques finished his report urging the Brazilian government to reinforce security in the embassy, asserting that the mood in Chile was mounting against Brazilian representatives. "I was advised to wear civilian clothes for my own safety."[88] When September 11, 1973, arrived, however, Câmara Canto would feel free to identify himself not only as a member of the Brazilian dictatorship but also as a major contributor to the coup.

4

MONEY TALKS

THE TRANSNATIONAL ORGANIC ELITES

> The rhythmic pounding of empty pots and pans by thousands
> of Chilean women last week had the sound of war drums.

NEW YORK TIMES, MAY 12, 1971

> For a long time, for defending economic liberalism,
> I was considered a reckless heretic. World events
> have promoted me to responsible prophet.

ROBERTO CAMPOS

The Brazilian military was not the only sector of the country unsettled by
the Allende administration. As was the case in the 1964 coup that overthrew
João Goulart, the action to disturb the socialist government in Chile came
from a combined effort with civilians, especially the business sector.[1] In 1961,
the world was introduced to the ideas of the Alliance for Progress, which
heavily influenced Brazilians whose fear of communism had intensified
with the Cuban Revolution.[2] First, the economic program established by
John F. Kennedy furnished these groups with some of the mottos that would
define their political agenda. It was not the promise of "home, jobs and land,
health and schools" that attracted them but the commitment to economic

modernization.[3] In the following years, the connection went beyond an ideological influence and grew into considerable financial support of politicians antagonistic to Goulart.

The other major source of inspiration for Brazilian conservatives was *Mater et magistra*, the 1961 encyclical of Pope John XXIII on "Christianity and Social Progress." It proposed a revamping of Pope Leo XII's *Rerum novarum*—also known as Rights and Duties of Capital and Labor. Pope John XXIII stressed that the 1891 encyclical was a product of the Industrial Revolution, and therefore required a makeover that responded to a new way of thinking about work, businesses, and the role of the state. Especially attractive was his defense of private property, "including that of productive goods," which was classified as "a natural right which the state cannot suppress."[4]

This chapter unveils the many ideas—religious, political, and economic—used as frameworks by the Institute for Social Studies and Research (IPES) and the Institute for Democratic Action (IBAD), the two Brazilian think tanks that served as models for Chilean entities that would later be fundamental to the removal of Salvador Allende. These included the fascist group Patria y Libertad and business entities like the Federation of Chilean Industry (SOFOFA).[5] It also looks at the Council of the Americas, the Atlantic Community Development Group for Latin America (ADELA), and other transnational groups that embraced the fight for liberalism as a way of strengthening the business sector in the region.

Chilean and Brazilian entrepreneurs played a major role in weakening the socialist leader. First, IBAD and IPES showed Chilean institutions that would be vital to the 1973 coup how to be "groups of action," ones whose objectives went far beyond economic and political theories. They wanted to shape public opinion.[6] In a special feature, *Reader's Digest* praised IPES for "staying on the job—sponsoring courses to train democratic leaders, especially from the middle and lower classes, and developing ways to keep the public alert and enlightened."[7] The effort was based on the Brazilian Campaign of Women for Democracy (CAMDE), created by IPES, through which the anti-Allende El Poder Feminino organized the "march of the empty pots," an enormous demonstration in the streets of Santiago that significantly harmed the government's popularity.[8] Second, businessmen and institutions offered financial and logistical support. Chileans who fled to Brazil right after Salvador Allende's election in 1970 secured jobs in multinational corporations, established friendships and commercial enterprises, and found role models in some of the "architects of the 1964 Brazilian coup."[9] They created the Private Institute for Socioeconomic Research (Instituto Privado de Investigaciones Económico-Sociales; IPIES) modeled after IPES.[10] In addition to the propaganda against the socialist government, the two institutes also organized classes and seminars in self-defense and guerrilla strategies.[11]

This chapter also investigates the contribution of Brazilian liberal economists Roberto Campos and Otávio Gouveia de Bulhões in the shaping of *pinochetista* policies. Their influence—especially in support of a laissez-faire approach to the economy—was tremendous and helped shape the ideas of the dictators' advisers, known as the "Chicago Boys."[12] Campos and Bulhões introduced the Government Economic Action Program (PAEG) less than four months after the 1964 coup.[13] The main objective was to fight inflation, and the recipe was strikingly similar to what the Chicago Boys would propose in "El ladrillo" (The brick), their tome of economic policies: increased foreign investment, tax and financial reform, cuts in public spending.[14] PAEG was short-lived, and despite having claimed that Chile was not the perfect laboratory for capitalism, Campos only saw his ideas flourishing when they were implemented in the neighbor's house.[15]

IPES AND IBAD

Although its origins date back to the Juscelino Kubitschek years—when high inflation and the president's populist prose triggered alarm in the business community—the Institute for Social Studies and Research (IPES) was not officially created until November 29, 1961. Its founders proclaimed it a bastion of morality and a savior of the Brazilian economy, threatened by the specter of communism. At the time, a large swathe of the elite was unhappy with the administration of then-president João Goulart, with whom US industrialists had been dissatisfied from the very beginning.[16] High inflation, the perception that the government lacked sound economic policies, and the preoccupation with the spread of Marxism in Brazil inspired businessmen to create the institute as a think tank to develop ways of opposing the president.[17]

At first, it was based in Rio de Janeiro and had the participation of groups from São Paulo. But in a few months, IPES had collaborators in several states. The main focus was to connect right-wing movements with the mission of combating the "growth of Soviet communism in the Western hemisphere."[18] To that end, they collected information on thousands of "suspicious people" around Brazil. In its early years, IPES was directed by General Golbery do Couto e Silva, a professor at the Brazilian War College (ESG) and one of the main theorists of the Brazilian National Security Doctrine. Later, Golbery would help create the Brazilian National Intelligence Service and act as its head from 1964 to 1967. From 1974 to 1981, he served as chief of staff to presidents Ernesto Geisel and João Figueiredo.[19] For some, this role immortalized Golbery do Couto e Silva as a crucial figure in the democratization of the country.[20] For most, however, he was the "mastermind behind the military coup that toppled President João Goulart in 1964."[21]

Golbery do Couto e Silva was in his thirties when, in 1944, he traveled to the United States to join a trainee program at the US Army garrison at Fort Leavenworth, in Kansas. This was when he fleshed out the idea that a country's development would only be possible through national security. To get there, the state should work side by side with businesspeople, the military, and the socioeconomic elite. He contended that these groups shared the same objective: development, to which a strong centralized power was instrumental, even if that negatively impacted democracy. These propositions would later become the core of the Brazilian National Security Doctrine, which was used to justify the violence of the authoritarian regime.

Under Couto e Silva's leadership, IPES invested heavily in anticommunist propaganda. The tone was unconcealed: Goulart was connected to socialism, a regime in which people were to be exploited and could be sent to concentration camps for long periods.[22] In short movies filled with images of workers and students, it summoned Brazilians to join the movement in search of a "new concept of democracy" and the halt of communism.[23] The institute also supported politicians who opposed the Goulart administration and financed groups hostile to his policies, such as the Working Circles in Rio de Janeiro and São Paulo, the Brazilian Confederation of Christian Workers, the Campaign of Women for Democracy, the Women's Civic Union of São Paulo, and the Alumni Association of the Brazilian War College.[24]

IPES's declared objective was "defending personal and corporate freedom, threatened by the dormant socialization plan of the João Goulart government," by "improving the civic and democratic consciousness of the people."[25] In practice, this meant disseminating publications and rumors about the links between the president and the Communist Party, including data suggesting that the economic crisis was more severe than it was in reality.[26] The urge to moralize society went hand in hand with the belief that the young population was prone to communism and needed to be educated about its danger. This notion was the topic of a series of fourteen newspaper articles by journalist Sonia Seganfreddo, who accused the National Union of Students of subversion. IPES also promoted classes and conferences, published books, reports, and even released a series of fourteen movies on

O QUE É O IPÊS

Inspirados nos princípios básicos desses dois grandes documentos, definidores e afirmativos da Democracia, e aceitando as teses, premissas e indicações nêles contidos é que nos reunimos, cônscios de nossa responsabilidade na vida pública do país, empresários e democratas para o progresso, na constituição do Instituto de Pesquisas e Estudos Sociais (IPÊS).

Em agôsto de 1961 os países da América, entre êles o Brasil, elaboraram um documento - A Ata da Aliança para o Progresso - conhecida como declaração de Punta del Este que se pode qualificar como um instrumento perfeito para a concretização, em nosso Hemisfério, dos princípios contidos na Encíclica "Mater et Magistra".

Para ver, julgar e agir constituímos o IPÊS

An Institute for Social Studies and Research flyer
attempts to answer "What is IPES?"
Source: Arquivo Nacional do Brasil.

"democratic indoctrination."[27] The civilian-military regime celebrated such efforts with a presidential decree stating that IPES was a group of "public utility."[28]

IPES reached well beyond Brazil's borders. The anticommunist think tank also advised Chilean businessmen on how to "prepare the ground" for the military overthrow of President Salvador Allende.[29] The recipe was the same one that the CIA had used in its "spoiling operations" and that IPES had applied to Brazilian deposed leader João Goulart: creating a sense of severe economic crisis among the population, connecting the president to the "cruelties" of communism, and organizing institutions to protest against the government.

The monitoring of Communist Party members and sympathizers within the government was also part of the playbook applied in Brazil and exported to Chile. According to Glycon de Paiva, director of IPES from 1962 to 1964, the institute spent between $200,000 and $300,000 per year gathering information and distributing it to key military officers.[30] Paiva described the structure of the monitoring as a large entrepreneurship, occupying thirteen rooms on the twenty-seventh floor of a massive building on Rio de Janeiro's Avenida Central. A plethora of recording devices taped conversations on 3,000 phone numbers in the city.[31] This was the work of the most important "group of study and action" at IPES: the Conjuncture Survey Group.[32] It monitored not only individuals but also any relevant political event, creating reports with detailed evaluations of the political and economic situation and delineating responses. These intelligence operations would not only serve as a model but would also be directly shared with the plotters of the coup in Chile.[33]

One of the most prominent of these conspirators was Orlando Sáenz Rojas, president of the prestigious SOFOFA, a major force behind the coup in 1973. He states that the masterminding of September 11 came from Brazil. "They gave us substantial logistic help, they sent us all of these economic reports, where we could find crucial information for our organization."[34] According to Sáenz Rojas, all the money used to support the coup came from abroad. SOFOFA instituted centers to coordinate the financial logistics in Europe; New York; Monterrey, Mexico; as well as a smaller center in Argentina.

The interest of IPES in supporting anticommunist groups in Chile, such as SOFOFA, was part of a commitment to an integrated capitalism, in which a centralized organization was as important as the internationalization of the financial-industrial market. The forging of the Atlantic Community Development Group for Latin America is a major manifestation of this undertaking.

Founded in 1962, ADELA was responsible for accessing the potential of markets on behalf of multinational corporations, using local partners to develop a friendly environment for financial transactions. The group, made up of 240 companies from 23 countries, somehow usurped a role previously limited to government in Latin America. Many of the companies connected to the US-sponsored ADELA and International Finance Corporation supported the opposition to João Goulart in Brazil.[35]

Such connections, combined with the fact that IPES was maintained not only by Brazilian businessmen but largely by foreign capital, raises an inevitable question: What was the nature of the Brazilian involvement in anticommunist enterprises in other nations? Were they lone wolves or mere pawns of the United States in the game of large corporations?[36] The *Washington Post* published a story in January 1974 that argued for the first hypothesis. Less than a year after the overthrow of Allende, journalist Marlise Simons investigated the ties between IPES leadership and the coup in Chile and affirmed that "the coup that brought Brazil's armed forces to power in March 1964, appears to have been used as a model for the Chilean military coup. The private sector played a crucial role in the preparation of both interventions, and the Brazilian businessmen who plotted the overthrow of President João Goulart in 1964 were the same people who advised the Chilean Right on how to deal with Marxist President Allende."[37]

Simons talked to members of the institute who confirmed that they had played an important role not only in the Brazilian coup but also in the Chilean one.[38] Glycon de Paiva, vice president of IPES during its embryonic phase (1961–67), was one of the interviewees.[39] The mining engineer had held a series of prominent positions in Brazilian politics, including being president of the National Bank for Economic and Social Development (Banco Nacional de Desenvolvimento Econômico; BNDE)—currently known as the National Bank for Economic and Social Development (Banco Nacional de Desenvolvimento Econômico e Social)—from 1955 to 1956.[40]

One of the founders of IPES, Paiva advised Chilean businessmen on "how to 'prepare the ground' for the military overthrow of President Salvador Allende." He stated that after Allende's inauguration, these entrepreneurs sought his advice and he colloquially explained that "the recipe exists, and you can bake the cake any time. We saw how it worked in Brazil, and now again in Chile." Paiva confirmed that such interventions require a great deal of resources but stated that it was all well invested. "The money businessmen spent against the Left is not just an investment; it is an insurance policy," he concluded.[41]

Another central character in Simons's narrative is Aristóteles Drummond. He was a young employee at the private bank Banco Nacional and one of the founders of the IPES branch in Minas Gerais. He was also a journalist and denied having talked to the *Washington Post* reporter. The story, he claimed, was a "novel."[42] According to the *Post*, Paiva and Drummond traveled to Chile twice, "taking money 'for political actions' to a right-wing anti-Allende organization."[43] He confirmed that he traveled to Chile, but claimed that the visit was part of the research for the story "Uma Cuba no Pacífico [A Cuba in the Pacific]," published by *Diários Associados* (Associated Dailies), a group of conservative communication media outlets founded in the 1920s by polemical media mogul Assis Chateaubriand.[44] Drummond confirmed that Simons contacted him but denied having talked to her. He said that he was shocked to see the article in the *Washington Post*. "I went to Chile between the direct and indirect elections. So, I didn't participate in the rescue of democracy, order, and freedom in Chile, but I would have done anything that didn't involve violence. I repeat, I did not participate [in the events described in Simons's article] but I would have participated, and I am an admirer of President Pinochet's economic policies. For me, he was a benefactor for his country and history will recognize that later."[45]

Like IPES, the Brazilian Institute for Democratic Action (IBAD) was created in reaction to João Goulart's presidency with the objective of saving Brazilian democracy.[46] While IPES invested heavily in propaganda, IBAD concentrated much of its activity on alliances with anticommunist paramilitary groups, such as the Anticommunist Movement, created by Aristóteles Drummond, and the Democratic Military Liberation Crusade.[47]

Founded in 1959 with major support from the CIA, IBAD was responsible for collecting and distributing funds to anti-Goulart politicians in the elections of 1962.[48] The group divided its activities into two central areas: influencing the elections was the job of the Popular Democratic Action (Ação Democrática Popular; ADEP), whereas Vendas Promotion SA worked as an advertising agency.[49] IBAD was connected to the CIA branch in Rio de Janeiro. Its director was Ivan Hasslocher, a supporter of the fascist movement Integralismo and a CIA officer for Brazil, Bolivia, and Ecuador.[50] The group intensified its actions after João Goulart's inauguration.[51]

IPES and IBAD were such powerful forces in Brazilian politics that they were capable of impacting elections results, generating outrage among candidates defeated in the polls. In 1963, the Brazilian Congress set up a parliamentary inquiry commission (*comissão parlamentar de inquérito*; CPI) to investigate a list of politicians suspected of having received funds from these institutions, presided over by Member of Congress Ulysses Guimarães. After long deliberations and collections of testimonies, the commission concluded that multinational companies such as Texaco, Esso, Coca-Cola, Bayer, and IBM were connected to IPES and IBAD, and colluded to influence the outcome of the 1962 elections. Nobody was punished.[52]

Aristóteles Drummond claims that neither IPES nor IBAD had direct influence on the 1973 coup in Chile. His first reasoning is that, at that point, both institutions were already demobilized. IPES officially closed its operations in São Paulo in 1970 and two years later in Rio de Janeiro. IBAD had already disappeared from the public eye in the 1960s.[53] Second, Drummond argues that they had no real interest in what was happening in Chile. He contends that at this time businesspeople were focused on domestic issues, paying close attention to the nationalization of companies, which had the support of military sectors. "The so-called Right is very practical and rational and, of course, we were all happy about Allende's fall, but that had no consequences for Brazil whatsoever. After all, the two countries do not share a border; they were still implementing their own revolution; and there were no common economic interests."[54]

Could it be the case that Brazilian businesspeople suddenly lost interest in what happened in Chile, even though the country had been a key economic partner for centuries? This seems unlikely. The two governments and their industrialists profited from the trade between Chile and Brazil. Successful commercial partnerships meant more money, and money talked even louder when added to the disgust with the new president. While Chile lost traditional trade partners, commerce with Brazil increased after the election of Salvador Allende, and the smaller neighbor remained instrumental for the Brazilian economy. Chile continued to be of economic and strategic importance to Brazilian entrepreneurs. In comparison to 1968 and 1969, exports to Chile remained stable, and imports increased from $26 million to almost $33 million.[55] Established in 1963, Chile's subsidiary of the largest public bank in Brazil, Banco do Brasil, remained protected from any interference from the Chilean government. This does not mean, however, that these groups were unconcerned with the situation in Chile and unwilling to intervene. On the contrary. It stands to reason that the more the statization of private companies advanced, the more alarmed the business community in Brazil became.

The efforts to derail the Allende government went beyond monetary and logistics operations. Brazilians also offered the framework for movements that were instrumental to the fall of the socialist leader. The infamous Chilean women's movement responsible for the March of the Empty Pots was inspired by the Campaign of Women for Democracy (CAMDE), created by IPES in 1962.[56] The capacity to spark political conversation was one of the institute's greatest talents. CAMDE was created shortly before the 1962 elections by Golbery do Couto e Silva, Glycon de Paiva, and Leovigildo Balestiero, a Franciscan vicar from Rio de Janeiro.[57] Religion was a major attraction to the women who engaged in the movement. For the ones who attended the meeting where CAMDE's objectives were delineated, communism was connected to atheism; therefore, fighting against it meant fighting for the Church.[58] The movement also resisted birth control and divorce—which was only legalized in Brazil in 1977.[59]

In the beginning, the objective was to use the female figure as a symbol of popular will. With women as its face the movement seemed to echo what most Brazilians wanted, including hindering the appointment of Francisco San Tiago Dantas as Goulart's prime minister.[60] It worked. In June 1962, Goulart nominated Dantas for the job after Tancredo Neves's resignation, but Congress did not approve the appointment. CAMDE expanded, eventually culminating in the largest of the Marches of the Family with God for Freedom, which brought nearly a million people to the streets of Rio de Janeiro on March 13, 1964. The group was characteristically anticommunist, elitist, and Catholic.[61] It embraced the public-private dynamics and reaffirmed the home as the proper female territory in Brazil.

It was not a coincidence, then, that kitchen utensils became weapons to oppose the Allende government.[62] On the first day of December 1971, about 5,000 women took to the streets of Santiago in a *cacerolazo*, a form of protest that consisted of beating empty pots and pans.[63] The message was twofold: the emptiness of the pans referred to food shortages and rising prices; at the same time, the object symbolized the domestic sphere, connected to women. The March of the Empty Pots marked the birth of the Chilean women's organization El Poder Feminino, which became vital in the weakening of Allende. Many other demonstrations, including the March for Freedom, would follow.[64]

As was the case in Brazil, female public protests were a crucial part of showing discontent with leftist ideals. The March of the Empty Pots followed the blueprint of the Marches of the Family with God for Freedom.[65] IPES's then–vice president, Glycon de Paiva, recalled that women's participation in the anti-Allende movement was a central part of his conversation with Chileans. "We taught Chileans how to use their women against the Marxists. We ourselves created a large and successful women's movement, the Campaign of Women for Democracy, and Chile copied it."[66]

The marches in Chile were also connected to bourgeois women.[67] However, the idea that upper-class women made up the entirety of the crowd that took to the streets in both countries is a myth. Similar to what happened in Brazil, the movement also included working-class women.[68] While some connected dissatisfaction with the government to the fear of the weakening of the family structure, others said that the left-wing government did little for them.[69] The Popular Unity government talked about creating more jobs for women and amplifying access to birth control, but not much was done in practice.[70] El Poder Feminino brought together women from different social classes and political parties, including members of the National, Radical, and Independent Parties.[71]

The playbook of Brazilian businesspeople in opposing Goulart also highlighted the need to expand the sense of crisis beyond women. It reads chillingly similar to the "Scare Campaign" promoted before the 1964 presidential dispute in Chile, in which Eduardo Frei—in an alliance between the Christian Democratic Party and the rightist Partido Nacional—defeated Salvador Allende. With the help of foreign capital and the US government, the propaganda offensive was substantially directed toward women with the objective of reaching out to the entire society, connecting the preservation of family to anticommunism.[72] The *gremios empresariales* were instrumental supporters of women's organizations in Chile.

This kind of business guild—or community of practice—had, for decades, represented a huge political force in the country, often associated with right-wing groups.[73] They were a powerful influence in creating an environment of crisis.[74] The population was alarmed by frequent strikes, organized by the *gremios*. They were instrumental, for instance, in the truck owners strike of October 1972, the Paro de Octubre.[75] The movement had the support of the CIA and of the Confederation of Truck Owners (Sindicato de Dueños de Camiones; SIDUCAM), headed by León Vilarín.[76] He was also one of the leaders of the fascist group Patria y Libertad. SIDUCAM connected more than 160 unions, composed of over 40,000 truckers. It also received the support of Chilean "organic elites," especially of Orlando Sáenz's SOFOFA.[77]

SOFOFA ET AL.: TRANSNATIONAL FORMS OF LIBERALISM

Historian Tatiana Poggi interprets the removal of Allende and the building of the dictatorship in Chile as a *projeto de classe*, a project with the objective of supporting the interests of one specific group: the Chilean industry and business class.[78] In that sense, the Chilean coup, which followed the playbook established by Brazil with the help of the United States, also replicated the will of businesspeople. René Dreifuss argues that the engagement of the "transnational organic elites" with liberal economic theorists was a form of maintaining class privileges.[79] Dreifuss coins the term "organic elite" in the context of IPES and IBAD to refer to the solid union between intellectuals and business elites.[80] Expanding Antonio Gramsci's concept of the "organic intellectual," Dreifuss includes in the Brazilian "organic elite" businesspeople, managers, and thinkers involved with the strategic planning and implementation of a hegemonic political class action.[81] If in Brazil these "organic elites" found in IPES and IBAD a structure to put in motion such a project, in Chile, SOFOFA and the Latin American Industrial Association (AILA) were the engine.

In 1971, while the Chilean business sector fumed against the hundreds of company expropriations, the powerful Federation of Chilean Industry (SOFOFA) and AILA were directed by the same person: Orlando Sáenz Rojas. AILA was founded in April 1962, the same year when the Atlantic Community Development Group for Latin America (ADELA) was created. SOFOFA had been established almost a century earlier, in 1883, with the objective of strengthening Chilean industry. It included virtually all the industrialists in the country. It was one of the most powerful guilds in Chile, and, as an agent of the interests of Chilean industrialists, it followed their international ambitions.

The Brazilian National Confederation of Industry (Confederação Nacional da Indústria; CNI) opposed the nomination of a Chilean to lead AILA, although it was the country's turn in the rotation system of the institution: Venezuela had come before and Argentina would be next.[82] CNI's president, Thomás Pompeu de Souza Brasil Netto, thought it could be dangerous to allow someone from Chile to take the position while a Marxist commanded the country.[83] Orlando Sáenz Rojas flew to Brazil to convince him otherwise. After landing, he boarded a taxi to CNI's central office. The driver asked where he was headed. Sáenz Rojas gave the full address. The driver replied, "Oh, Three Powers Square." Confused, Sáenz read the directions aloud and the driver replied that a military base, a US consulate, and the CNI were on the same square, which explained the nickname.[84]

Upon his arrival, Sáenz noticed some resistance from Thomás Pompeu and relied on his friend—and future minister of the economy of Brazil from 1974 to 1979—Mario Henrique Simonsen to vouch for him and convince Pompeu to relent. Sáenz dramatically narrated the situation of Chilean industrialists, portraying it as a "complete disaster" that demanded action. His main preoccupation was that as soon as Allende took power, he would start expropriating companies. Sáenz made it clear that he sided with the Brazilian dictatorship, and added that the leaders of Popular Unity, like all Marxists, did not understand that "capital is the blood that feeds the lungs. There is no development in any society without it." His conspicuous metaphors convinced Pompeu of Sáenz's trustworthiness and of the urgent need to remove Allende. He not only gained Pompeu's support of his candidacy for AILA's presidency but also won the promise of "unconditional aid" in the fight against the socialist president.[85] Five decades after the meeting, Sáenz still remembered that Pompeu used a white telephone and interrupted the conversation frequently to call the minister of the economy, Delfim Netto. At other times, he used a black telephone, which connected him directly to then-president Emílio Garrastazu Médici. That year, Brazil had the largest delegation at AILA's conference, the Assembly of Industrial Companies of the Countries of the Latin American Free Trade Association. According to Sáenz, it was the only time when the number of foreigners was larger than that of local industrialists.

As president of AILA, Sáenz was a dominant figure in the Latin American business community. As the leader of SOFOFA, he became one of the most influential figures in Chilean politics. He recalls a meeting with Salvador Allende, a few months before the coup, arranged by then commander-in-chief of the Chilean army, General Carlos Prats. According to Sáenz, the conversation started off tense, with the socialist president aggressively accusing Sáenz of conspiring to remove him from power. Sáenz threatened to immediately end the meeting. Allende then adopted a conciliatory tone and blamed the crisis on his own inability to implement better economic policies. He challenged Sáenz to state how many companies had been expropriated, to which Sáenz replied, "Eight hundred thirty-six, President."[86] Allende tried to compromise and offered to give Sáenz a list of 100 companies that should continue as state-owned and return all the others to the hands of the former owners in exchange for Sáenz's support. First, Sáenz said that he would have to discuss the proposal with SOFOFA's council. Then he added that, in his opinion, it was not feasible. "I have been in this position for three years; you know very well that I am a businessman and not a politician, but if I have learned something about politics, it is that you never agree with a defeated person. And you [Allende] are defeated." When Sáenz was about to leave the room, Allende tossed one more question, referring to the family who owned the conservative newspaper *El Mercurio*: "Do you think the military is going to carry out a coup to save the Edwards's fortune?" to which Sáenz replied, "No, President, they are not going to raise an uprising to save the Edwards. They will do it to save Chile."[87]

SOFOFA's methodology to stir the population against the government counted on powerful allies: unions and guilds. The wave of strikes took Chileans by surprise and exacerbated an already tense situation. In 1970, 75 percent of the Chilean population lived in cities. Industrial belts surrounding Santiago were tremendously influential.[88] According to Sáenz, financial support came not only from the CIA but also from ranking members of SOFOFA who sent funds to striking truck owners without having to ask for the support of any foreign group. The money was distributed in the months preceding the coup, with each trucker receiving roughly $2,000 per week, a small fortune considering the value of the dollar on the black market.[89]

SOFOFA was one of the many business organizations connected to fascist group Patria y Libertad, also supported by the National Society of Agriculture, the Association of Metallurgical Industries, the Chilean Chamber of Construction, the Union of Owners of Commercial Establishments, the Union of Farmers, the Confederation of Truck Owners, the National Front of Private Activity, and the Association of Industrialists of Valparaíso.[90] All were powerful industrialists who connected to the fascist group with the intention of destabilizing the socialist government.

Brazilian businesspeople also actively supported Patria y Libertad. Between 1972 and 1973, they sent weapons and ammunitions to Valparaíso from the port of Santos, in the Brazilian state of São Paulo. The ordnance was hidden in boxes of agricultural products imported by then–Chilean senator Pedro Ibañez Ojeda and had as its final destination the Chilean paramilitary group.[91] Bolivian dictator Hugo Banzer Suárez was also involved in the export of weaponry to the Chilean Far Right, allowing North American and Brazilian businessmen to smuggle arms into bases on Bolivian territory. In addition to the "political affinities" there was a quid pro quo: "The general wanted to sell oil to Brazil and, since 1938, Brazil wanted to control Bolivia's reserves of natural gas."[92]

The preoccupation of US businesspeople with Salvador Allende started to grow much earlier than that, during the 1964 Chilean presidential election. The prospect of a socialist candidate winning the presidency mobilized business leaders who feared that land reform and the nationalization of key industries—including copper mines—would impact US investments in Chile. The United States actively supported Allende's opponent, Eduardo Frei, whose campaign received at least $20 million—about $8 per voter—through the US Agency for International Development and covert money from the Business Group for Latin America.[93] Much of this sum was transferred to Catholic organizations connected to Frei's Christian Democratic Party. Frei won the elections with 56 percent of the vote.

A year earlier, in 1963, President John Kennedy had asked David Rockefeller, then president of Chase Manhattan Bank, to create the Business Group for Latin America as part of the fight against Fidel Castro and the spread of communism in the region. Its executive committee included the heads of all US corporations connected to the copper industry in Chile, such as Charles Jay Parkinson, board chairman of Anaconda, and Harold Sydney Geneen, head of International Telephone and Telegraph (ITT).[94] In 1965, the Business Group for Latin America merged with the American Council of the Americas to form the Council of the Americas (COA), which defines itself as a group of influential business organizations with a "common commitment to economic and social development, open markets, the rule of law, and democracy throughout the Western Hemisphere."[95]

During his presidency (1964–70), Frei was a member of COA and actively promoted its goals of economic integration and free trade in the region. Friendly with the United States, he also argued that economic cooperation should go further, and worked to strengthen ties with Latin American countries. This agenda was the main topic of his 1966 speech to COA, in which he called for a "new era of cooperation" in the region.[96] He suggested the creation of a Latin American common market to facilitate the flow of capital, goods, and services across national borders.[97] Although it reflected the will to reduce dependence on the United States, the speech also echoed the Alliance for Progress's goals of taking responsibility for combating poverty and social inequality through economic growth and development.

The solid relationship that Frei built with COA was shattered by Allende's victory in the 1970 elections. Less than a month after his win, members of the group met to discuss approaches to diplomacy, the economy, military forces, and public appearances, as well as the Peace Corps.[98] It was strongly suggested that the group include Brazil and Argentina in seeking an international boycott of the Chilean economy.[99]

BEFORE THE CHICAGO BOYS: BOB FIELDS
AND OTÁVIO GOUVEIA DE BULHÕES

At the beginning of 1973, Orlando Sáenz Rojas received an invitation to give a lecture in Argentina. Requests of this sort were common, and it did not come as a surprise. However, on his way to the event he realized that the plane was headed somewhere else. He arrived at the small airport of Campo de Marte, in São Paulo, to find out that the lecture was to a group of Brazilian military people. The only other civilian present was Roberto Campos. The economist and former minister of planning seemed crestfallen and despairing about the future of Brazil and Chile relations. Sáenz believed that Brazil had always been the ideal place to develop a capitalist government project, given its huge consumer market. Campos responded that, to the contrary, this project had not worked and his Government Economic Action Program (PAEG) had become the cause of the country's economic failure. Chile, in contrast, was too small for a perfect capitalist model. "If I lived in Chile," Campos told Sáenz, "I would also be a socialist."[100]

Jokes aside, the differences between Chilean and Brazilian dictatorial economic policies have contributed to the lack of research about the influence of Brazilian thinkers in Chile's economy. However, this commonsensical view ignores the fact that two Brazilians convincingly introduced free market ideas to the Chilean right wing much earlier than the Chicago Boys.[101] The IPES Boys were Roberto Campos, who would later become minister of planning for the first dictatorial administration, and Otávio Gouveia de Bulhões, minister of finance in the same period. They were the only two liberals to have cabinet positions linked to economic policies in an otherwise protectionist dictatorship.

Campos's relationship with Chile started much earlier. In 1949, fresh from completing his doctoral studies at the Sorbonne in Paris, he moved to Santiago to be part of the recently created Economic Commission for Latin America and the Caribbean (ECLAC). Although he did not shape the ECLAC worldview at the time, casting himself in the role of observer, Campos saw that period as fundamental to his shift from a structuralist and

Brazilian dictator Humberto Castelo Branco (*lower row, center*) and his
ministers. Juracy Magalhães is at the far right, in the lower row. Otávio Gouveia
de Bulhões is the third from the left in the second row. In the top row, future
president of Brazil Ernesto Geisel is at the far left, beside Roberto Campos.
*Source: Centro de Pesquisa e Documentação de História
Contemporânea do Brasil / Fundação Getulio Vargas.*

Keynesian agenda to the embrace of neoliberal policies that would later
define his career.[102]

In 1953, as director of the National Bank for Economic Development
(BNDE), Campos went back to Chile to research ECLAC's "integral planning
[*planejamento integral*]" and try to understand the applicability to Brazil of the
thesis that a dominant primary-export sector leads to low technical progress,
deterioration of terms of trade, and a peripheral condition. Although Campos
never adhered to the doctrine of import substitution or followed ECLAC's
theories of inelasticities of agricultural supply and exports, at this point he
still believed that the commission could offer insightful ideas. He claimed

that his interest in ECLAC's methodology "mixed intellectual curiosity and pragmatic skepticism. I was correct in my intuition. The methodology of ECLAC was never successfully applied in Latin America. The Chilean (under Salvador Allende) and Peruvian (under General Velasco Alvarado) experiments, which came closest to the ECLAC model, were resounding failures. General planning was illusory without socialist authoritarianism. And socialist authoritarianism proved over the years to be a mixture of political tyranny and economic inefficiency."[103]

Campos was the first economic director of the National Bank for Economic and Social Development and had Glycon de Paiva as technical director—the same man who had talked to the *Washington Post* about having advised and supported Chilean businessmen in the overthrow of Allende.[104] Campos recalls a visit to Santiago in January 1953 "to request ECLAC's technical assistance for Brazil's planning, explicitly stating Raúl Prebisch's desire to have Celso Furtado as ECLAC's group leader." Campos criticized ECLAC's methodology, claiming not to believe in the government's ability to "rationally coordinate the market" and strongly rebuffing the economic policy of the Allende government.[105]

Campos was critical of commercial blocs and reacted skeptically to the formation of "an Andean bloc, not only to accommodate medium-sized and small countries fearful of the three great powers—Brazil, Argentina, and Mexico—but also to affirm a supposedly democratic axis formed by Eduardo Frei's Chile, Fernando Belaunde's Peru, Lleras Restrepo's Colombia, and Raul Leoni's Venezuela against the supposedly authoritarian axis formed by Brazil and Argentina."[106]

Campos's appreciation of a liberal economic approach intensified during his time as Brazilian ambassador to the United States. He started almost as soon as John F. Kennedy began his presidential term, in 1961, under the assumption that Latin America was among the most vulnerable areas in the world to the spread of communism.[107] It was the time of the Alliance for Progress and the apex of the Cold War. A champion of entrepreneurship and the free market, Campos was so in tune with US economic policy that he was nicknamed Bob Fields, the English translation of his name. He was a central figure in negotiations between the Brazilian and US governments on the statization of Companhia Rio-Grandense de Telephones, a subsidiary of the North American company International Telephone and Telegraph, in February 1962. While Leonel Brizola, João Goulart's closest ally, defended the interests of the Brazilian government, Campos adopted a moderate tone, advocating for ITT.

In fact, Campos attributes the invitation to become minister of planning in the first administration of the Brazilian dictatorship to his affinity with the United States. Campos met Castelo Branco in Washington in March 1951 during the Fourth Meeting of Consultation of Ministers of Foreign Affairs of America. The central theme of the gathering was the Korean War. Campos "sought critically to evaluate the areas of coincidence and conflict between the interests of Brazil and the United States," which coincided with Castelo Branco's vision of a foreign policy aligned with the United States.[108] After the coup of 1964, official relations between Brazil and the northern giant immediately became stronger. The United States extended a large loan to the new government, and the support continued for years to come. Between 1964 and 1970, Brazil received $2 billion in US aid, ranking third behind Vietnam and India.[109]

Campos's appointment to the Ministry of Planning also received the important support of two old friends. Glycon Paiva, at this point a central figure at IPES, and Julio de Mesquita Filho, editor and owner of the newspaper *O Estado de S. Paulo*, spread good words about the economist.[110] Jorge de Mello Flores, IPES legislative coordinator, added Campos's name to a list of potential candidates for three ministries: Foreign Affairs, Economy, and Planning (the third was still to be created). According to Campos, several military officials expressed surprise at his suggestion, mentioning the stigma of "surrenderer" that the press attributed to Campos. Mello Flores minimized the critics, reminding them that Campos had once been called a communist, which could not be further from the truth.

Campos and Otávio Gouveia de Bulhões were the golden boys of liberalism in mid-twentieth-century Brazil. They were behind the ideals that turned IPES, IBAD, and the ESG into the unbreakable triangle of economic thinking among the Brazilian business elite. The more aggressive proposals to fight inflation, which were at the heart of their Government Economic Action Program, paired well with the hatred of João Goulart's policies. Campos recalled that what some considered to be the early productivity of the dictatorial regime was the result of years of work by IPES leaders, especially its Groups of Study and Doctrine (Grupos de Estudo e Doutrina). Under the supervision of José Garrido Torres, the group prepared the text of legislation on various topics, such as land and administrative reforms, taxes, banking, and antimonopoly laws.[111] For Campos, these reforms would be the foundation of modernized Brazilian capitalism. Some of their economic measures were extremely unpopular. However, under an authoritarian regime, they needed no justifications to implement them.

Once Campos and Bulhões became powerful ministers, IPES experienced a tension. On the one hand, the think tank struggled with the absence of its most famous sons. On the other, its influence expanded tremendously after 1964, precisely because of the higher positions of its leaders. In addition to Campos's and Bulhões's roles as ministers, Golbery do Couto e Silva became the chief of the SNI, one of the most prestigious ranks in the dictatorial structure; Paulo Assis Riberito was now the president of the Brazilian Institute of Agrarian Reform; José Garrido Torres became president of the BNDE; and Glycon de Paiva was made a member of the National Council of the Economy. There were more than a dozen IPES associates in the upper echelon of the new government.[112]

Humberto Castelo Branco's administration allowed IPES fellows to put into practice most of the institute's ideas. Campos and Bulhões introduced the PAEG in July 1964 and determined that it would have a limited duration: from November 1964 to March 1967. The objective was to contain inflation and accelerate growth during this period. To get there, they proposed a financial policy to reduce the governmental cash deficit by cutting spending and privatizing state-owned companies. In terms of an international economic policy, the program included an exchange rate and foreign trade policy aimed at diversifying supply and encouraging exports. Finally, the wage policy should allow for the "synchronization of the fight against inflation."[113]

During his tenure as minister of planning of Brazil and later, during Pinochet's dictatorship, Campos made several trips to Chile, where he met with businessmen and members of the country's right-wing movements. The left-leaning Chilean press saw in Campos an alarming indication of the ties between Brazilian businessmen and the opposition to the Allende government. In November 1971, when Campos no longer held a cabinet position, the newspaper *Última Hora* described with concern the trip of the former Brazilian minister of planning to Santiago. According to the publication, Campos was "quietly in touch with the right wing of Chile" and was "the right person to establish high-level contacts between Chileans and the Brazilian Right."[114] In describing the story to the Brazilian government, ambassador Antônio Cândido da Câmara Canto noted that the article was "obviously distorted," since Campos's relations with capitalists from the Americas simply "accentuated" the economic ties between the two countries.[115]

In Chile, Campos witnessed the materialization of ambitions that he could only dream of putting into practice in Brazil. After the 1973 coup d'état, the Pinochet government entrusted its economic policies to the Chicago Boys, who drew on the teachings of Milton Friedman and Arnold Harberger from the Department of Economics at the University of Chicago, from which most of them had graduated.[116] The central tenet of their economic strategy was to encourage the free operation of the private sector, which would become its most important element; prices would be self-regulating, as a consequence of competition among corporations; government expenditures would be reduced so that control of inflation could finally be possible. Milton Friedman, sounding like a proud professor, used the nickname in his memoirs to say that in 1975, "when inflation was still raging and a global recession triggered a depression in Chile, General Pinochet addressed the 'Chicago Boys' . . . and appointed several of them to positions of power in the government."[117]

The neoliberal model implemented by the Chicago Boys focused on the seven modernizations, a series of reforms officially announced in 1979—although many of them had begun to be adopted as soon as Augusto Pinochet took power. A decade later, the Washington consensus would recommend such measures as the recipe against foreign debt: fiscal discipline with dramatic cuts in public spending, tax reform, financial and trade liberalization, increase in direct foreign investment, privatization, deregulation, and protection of property rights.[118] The labor reform indexed wages to past inflation while severely limiting the right to strike and collective bargaining.[119]

WHAT DID NOT WORK IN BRAZIL
COULD WORK ELSEWHERE

In accepting their ministerial positions, Bulhões and Campos warned President Castelo Branco that the measures necessary to contain a "country disorganized by inflation" could affect his popularity. They claimed that it would be necessary to put "the house in order" before leading the country to economic acceleration, and that "the results are slow; often the early stages of the fight against inflation results in higher inflation, the need to set prices out of phase, especially in the public sector. It is necessary to cut budgets, limiting credit, and it should not be ruled out that there could be a period of recession." Twenty days after the Brazilian coup d'état, Castelo Branco gave them the green light, underscoring the powers of a dictatorship: "Perhaps you underestimate me. I have no electoral concern."[120]

When Artur da Costa e Silva became president, in 1967, Campos and Bulhões lost power. The measures of the IPES Boys were far too unpopular with society in general and businessmen in particular. If Castelo Branco could afford to use authoritarianism to implement such measures, Costa e Silva did not think it was worth it. There is yet another difference between the IPES Boys and the Chicago Boys: the former were under a rotating authoritarian leadership, while the latter dealt with one long-lasting dictator. The unpopularity of the Chicago Boys with economists in South America who favored the planning and control of the economy by the federal government—policies antagonistic to those proposed by the Pinochet team—did not influence the dictator enough to make him change course. The Chicago Boys had carte blanche to advocate for "widespread deregulation, privatizations, and other free market policies for tightly controlled economies."[121]

In Brazil, the weakening of the IPES Boys was abrupt and can be seen in the number of cabinet positions they held in the Costa e Silva administration: zero. The period between 1969 and 1974, while Antonio Delfim Netto was the Brazilian minister of finance, is considered one of the fastest periods of economic growth in the country's history. The "Economic Miracle," in which spending and state intervention increased, assured Delfim Netto of enough popularity to enjoy a long and stable political career that included five consecutive terms as representative for the state of São Paulo.[122] The positive economic figures of this period are attributed to the investment of federal taxes in infrastructure. As a complement to these administrative changes, the bank Caixa Econômica Federal and the Casa da Moeda (Brazilian Mint) became public companies. The Interministerial Price Council began regulating prices in all sectors of the Brazilian economy. The protectionist economic policies that defined the Brazilian civilian-military regime continued to be robust.

Henceforth, after Delfim Netto's departure from the Ministry of Finance in 1974, Brazilian dictatorial economic policy followed the same steps, increasingly distancing itself from the style of the IPES Boys and the Chicago Boys. However, instead of creating a vacuum, the process that had detached Bulhões and Campos from state power forced the Brazilian "organic elite" to aim beyond the nation's borders. After the creation of IPES and IBAD, transnational groups with similar economic visions multiplied in the region. ADELA, AILA, and the Inter-American Council for Commerce and Production continued working to protect the interests of foreign capital in Latin America.

The Brazilian organic elites and intellectuals, such as Campos and Bulhões, had already adapted US-style liberal policies to the Southern Cone. The Government Economic Action Program did not achieve all its objectives in Brazil, but Chile seemed to be fertile soil for the same policies. Analyzing the first six years of the Pinochet regime, Arturo Valenzuela concluded that, "in Chile, the institutions of the state were so closely intertwined with the political system, the political parties, and the efforts to bring about socialism, that a policy of laissez-faire seemed logical in meeting the overall goals of the military to crush the Left, demobilize society, and dramatically change the Chilean polity."[123] Furthermore, state-owned companies were linked to the national budget, something that was not as preponderant in Brazil.

The wave of nationalizations driven by the Brazilian civilian-military dictatorship would become emblematic of this period. Indeed, it is one reason why many today consider the Brazilian and Chilean models to be opposites. Campos and Bulhões, however, had always objected to national-izations. Campos famously disdained what he called the three great "isms": communism, fascism, and, "most enduring of all, nationalism."[124] From the oil and nuclear industries to the telecommunications sector, during the dic-tatorial period various activities previously undertaken by the private sector were absorbed by the Brazilian government, almost always in a monopolistic fashion.[125] The former minister of planning associated such policies with Brezhnevian socialism.[126]

The devaluation of private companies was, for Campos, the main ex-planation for the economic failure of the Allende administration. In 1964, however, before referring to what he called the death of nationalism, Campos stated that "a certain type of nationalism, in a particular historical context, can contribute to the process of sparking development." He added, classify-ing this type of nationalism as "appropriate nationalism (often practiced by me), which tries to compel foreign investors to nationalize faster, or to leave in the territory in which they operate a greater proportion of the fruits of the investment." Campos concluded his critique of the three great "isms" with a prognosis for the late twentieth century: "In the first quarter of this century, we have avenged the socialist utopia. In the second there was the birth, pas-sion, and death of Nazi-fascism. In the third, capitalism and communism would fight in the Cold War. In the last quarter of the century, the old 'isms' will increasingly give way to liberalism."[127]

The transnational capital developed ways of influencing local politics, incorporating ideas of efficiency into the core of Brazilian capitalism. In this process, the role of intellectuals was decisive. They represented the elite as a class on its way to "become" the state itself.[128] IBAD and IPES achieved a level of homogeneity (in the Gramscian sense) that led them to become more than just influential groups; in 1964, its members became government lead-ers.[129] Nothing was more natural, then, than expanding influence to other territories in the Americas, including Chile. Gramsci's idea that most of the population finds a consensus that is actually a mere acceptance of the imposition of a dominant group is apt here, especially when one considers that the state apparatus of coercive power during the dictatorship increasingly naturalized its authoritarian nature. Its methods were, therefore, applicable to any imposed regime, including Chile and the South American dictatorships during the Cold War. Gramsci's definition of organic intellectuals, who can form the foundation of a political organization, is the source of Dreifuss's definition of the Brazilian organic elite, represented, for example, by Roberto Campos and Gouveia de Bulhões. It is not by chance that Campos called Dreifuss's classic book "a detailed, albeit prejudiced and ideologically distorted, description of the activities of IPES."[130]

Campos celebrated the Chicago Boys when he remembered, with relief, the years after Allende's death. He had feared that Allende's suicide would result in the crystallization of a "myth." He predicted that alive Allende "would only be a case of lack of objectivity and rudimentary economic truths. Dead, he could become a symbol of the restless pursuit of a 'third way.' Fortunately, the Chilean military developed reasonable economic efficiency and, helped by the international situation adverse to socialism, put an end to the myth."[131]

5

BEFORE CONDOR
THE UNITED STATES AND
BRAZIL PLAN THE 1973 COUP

Ellos aquí trajeron los fusiles repletos
de pólvora, ellos mandaron el acerbo exterminio

[They brought here rifles full
of powder, they ordered bitter extermination]

PABLO NERUDA, "LOS ENEMIGOS," 1950

The Allende administration was not blind to attempts to interfere in the
socialist government. On March 23, 1971, the Chilean ambassador to Brazil,
Raul Rettig, wrote a chilling, long, and strictly confidential letter to the Department of Coordination and Analysis about an alarming plan. He started
mildly, mentioning the frequent attempts by Brazilian authorities to weaken
Allende, including the suggestion to move the third meeting of the UN Conference on Trade and Development (UNCTAD) to Mexico City. Later in the
letter, however, Rettig confirmed that the neighboring government went as
far as trying to recruit guerrillas to be trained in the Andes with the objective
of overthrowing the president.[1]

Rettig also described the reaction of Brazilian minister of foreign affairs
Mário Gibson Barbosa to the intention of opening a Chilean consulate in
Rio de Janeiro. Barbosa ordered a confidential investigation of the consular

service. On that occasion, one of the Brazilians in charge of the inquiry told a Chilean diplomat that "at this point, for Itamaraty, Chile is one more country on the other side of the 'Iron Curtain'; one even more dangerous, however, because it is in our continent; therefore, I have to, despite my regret, investigate meticulously all the references to your personnel, including the salaries."[2]

Although Rettig connected such instructions not only to Barbosa, but especially to the military—more specifically, to the National Intelligence Service (SNI)—he contended that the Armed Forces had not mentioned Chile in the press in months. The ambassador added that, in February, a member of the Chilean Army recounted that a Brazilian Army general had approached a Chilean journalist to organize a movement of armed resistance to the Chilean government. The military man offered money and support to form urban guerrillas and fight against the "red danger."[3] The journalist was a close friend of the Brazilian general and a supporter of defeated right-wing presidential candidate Jorge Alessandri.

Rettig had more to report. A Brazilian lawyer told a diplomat who worked in the Chilean embassy that there was a room in the Ministry of the Army, in Rio de Janeiro, with a scale model of the Andes, including Chile's entire border with Argentina, Bolivia, and Peru. Working with the model, groups of Brazilian military men discussed the best areas and tactics to establish an anticommunist guerrilla group to be trained in the Chilean Andes.[4] The military team would be ready to attack in case an intervention became necessary. The Brazilian Army would be responsible for instructions and training, helping to teach combat and survival techniques. However, it determined that the guerrilla fight must be conducted by civilians, not soldiers, and by foreigners, especially Chileans. Brazilians should not be directly involved.

The Chilean diplomat received authorization to travel to Rio de Janeiro and gather more information. In the Chilean consulate in Rio, he met again with the attorney, who confirmed that he had a close contact who was a military man working for the Intelligence Service of the Army. The attorney refused to reveal the name of his source but stated that he was a leftist who seemed outraged about the Brazilian military efforts to interfere in Chile. The military man confirmed what the Chilean government had already guessed: secret agents of the Brazilian Army had entered Chile with tourist visas and infiltrated groups of exiles to gather information. Two of the spies had mingled among the group of Brazilian exiles known as the Setenta, but the military informant could not name them.

The Chilean diplomats were also informed that the Brazilian Army had been seeking Chilean volunteers to help "undertake a war adventure" in Chile. These individuals would become guerrillas *in loco* to train in the Andes and fight against Allende. A group of students at Santiago's Pontificia Universidad Católica de Chile who founded the right-wing publication *Fiducia* in 1962 was in charge of making connections with the Brazilian military. They would later create the Chilean Society for the Defense of Tradition, Family, and Property.[5] In the beginning, the group opposed agrarian reform and other progressive ideas of Eduardo Frei's government only to later shift its objectives to "promote a real crusade against all forms of communism and collectivism—among which were included the Christian Democrats and a significant number of members of the Catholic clergy—in order to protect property and certain values that they considered to be linked to the most essential of Chilean and Christian traditions."[6]

Rettig had to reconcile this new information about conspiracies with the will to maintain Brazil as a strong commercial partner. In June 1971, in one of his long economic reports about possible avenues of cooperation, the ambassador warned of what he called a "diplomatic rush," in which Brazil was finalizing agreements with several nations in the region, and suggested that Chile keep an active position in attracting investments.[7] Just a few months earlier, he had alerted the Chilean leadership that the Brazilian Armed Forces had "apparently sent to Chile several secret agents disguised as tourists, with the mission of sourcing information about areas where a guerrilla movement could operate."[8]

VARIOUS STRATEGIES, ONE ENEMY

While the Brazilian government made plans to forcefully remove Allende from power, Chilean leaders intensified a campaign against the socialist. Almost a year into the UP administration, former president Eduardo Frei joined in the attacks. CIEX spies reported to Brazilian authorities that the Christian Democrat leader accused the Chilean Communist Party (PCCh) of conducting a campaign to destroy the opposition and, consequently, democracy in Chile. For Frei, the PCCh imposed its methods and rules, applying a tactic that communists have used in every country under their tyranny, as it was "interesting for them to hurt the prestige of any person who is an obstacle to the implementation of its fatal dictatorship." The CIEX report also contended that Allende supporters had started a violent movement to spread lies and hate against right-wing parties, creating a climate of restlessness in an attempt to justify an upcoming economic crisis. "The blame would be put on the 'seditious,' the conspirers, and the saboteurs of the 'center-right.'"[9]

The military plans of action aligned with a diplomatic shift in Brazil. It was the time of "responsible pragmatism," a foreign policy that replaced alignment with the United States with a multipolar and regional approach. The focus was on the economic needs of Brazil, and that entailed a neutral stance on Middle Eastern affairs, the recognition of the governments of China, Angola, and Mozambique, and a closer relationship with the rest of Latin America and with Europe.[10] In the process of designing this tense new engagement with the United States, Chile served as a point of agreement. While the Brazilian project of building nuclear reactors, for instance, resulted in dispute with the most powerful nation in the world, the fight against Allende offered a constant source of dialogue, partnership, and friendly negotiations. Richard Nixon and Emílio Garrastazu Médici were both certain that they commanded strong nations and were responsible for ending the spread of communism in Latin America. Therefore, it is not surprising that they worked autonomously and cooperatively to weaken the Left in Chile and overthrow the government of Salvador Allende.[11]

The United States counted on the expansion of the Brazilian government's role to destabilize Chile domestically. In 1972, the CIA affirmed that the South American giant would have a substantial responsibility in the area, "seeking to fill whatever vacuum the U.S. leaves behind. It is unlikely that Brazil will intervene openly in its neighbors' internal affairs, but the regime will not be above using the threat of intervention or tools of diplomacy and covert action to oppose leftist regimes, or keep friendly governments in office, or to help place them there in countries such as Bolivia and Uruguay. While some countries may seek Brazil's protection, others may work together to withstand pressures from the emerging giant."[12]

Brazil looked forward to occupying whatever spaces the United States left in the region and worked independently to fight communism in the Southern Cone.[13] The role of the largest nation in South America, however, has been overshadowed by the support of the United States. It is widely accepted that US actions were fundamental to the overthrow of Allende.[14] The economic crisis and lack of money for investments during the socialist presidency resulted not only from mistakes by the socialist administration but also from maneuvers by US officials. As early as 1970 the White House succeeded in preventing the Inter-American Development Bank from lending money to Chile.[15] From 1970 to 1973 the CIA kept contact with the Chilean military with the official justification of gathering intelligence. However, the connection "meant that the United States sustained communication with the group most likely to take power from President Salvador Allende."[16]

Brazil's actions nevertheless remain mostly cloaked. The lack of archival sources is only one of the reasons. There is also a tendency to overlook the role of less powerful nations, to think that there is always a great foreign power to determine the direction of "small" countries, and to categorize the interregional approach as secondary. The links connecting the United States, Chile, and Brazil, however, allow us not only to understand the facts and forces that led to the September 11 coup, but also to reevaluate the US role in the dictatorships of Chile and Brazil. The actions of the northern giant were not the only reason for the overthrow of Allende. They were part of a much broader articulation that included a local Cold War dynamic in which Brazil sometimes figured as an independent player and at other times as an important US partner against the spread of communism.

Salvador Allende was aware of the Brazilian efforts and looked for help from his allies in the Southern Cone. In 1971, he met with then de facto Argentine president, Alejandro Lanusse, in the northern Chile region of Antofagasta, and asked about the risk of a Brazilian armed intervention in Uruguay in case of a victory by General Liber Seregni. Lanusse, in a "short and dry" answer, stated that Argentina would not allow such a thing.[17] At this point, Brazil and the United States had been articulating direct and indirect ways of interfering in Uruguay, Argentina, and Chile.

Most of the time, the two countries acted in secret. In a 1974 press conference about the pardoning of Richard Nixon, President Gerald R. Ford was faced with an unexpected question: Would his government continue interfering in foreign administrations, as it had with Allende? He stated that there had been "no involvement in any way whatsoever" and blamed the Chilean president for trying to destroy opposition media and political parties when he took power a few years earlier. The United States had only acted to preserve these, according to Ford.[18] A year later, the Senate Select Committee to Study Governmental Operations with Respect to Intelligence Activities, known as the Church Committee, confirmed that it had found no evidence that the United States had been *directly* involved in the 1973 coup in Chile. However, it accused the CIA of supporting an attempted coup in 1970, maintaining years of policies against Allende, and collaborating with the Chilean military that would later plot the 1973 coup.[19]

As much disagreement as there is about the nature of direct US involvement, there is no question of the many ways the country acted to rule out the possibility of a Marxist government dominating Chile at the height of the Cold War.[20] In 1972, Salvador Allende denounced in a speech to the United Nations the "financial-economic blockade" of which his country was a victim.[21] He claimed that before his inauguration, Chile had received almost $80 million in loans from organizations such as the World Bank and the Inter-American Development Bank, a sum that was dramatically reduced during his administration. He was a victim of a "sneaky and double-crossing attack," which was not an open aggression but had had damaging consequences.[22]

It remains a challenge to pinpoint the intensity of different forms of support—direct or indirect—and how decisive they were. It is hard to measure the impact, for instance, of spoiling operations—and even money—on public opinion. Which shifts happened because of US interference and which were due to domestic factors? Much international support is secretive in nature; after all, no big corporation wants to showcase in its budget donations with the intent to topple sovereign governments. Measuring influence in retrospect is an inglorious task, and quantifying how certain groups and ideas served as templates for coups and policies is Sisyphean. Finally, much of this involvement was in the form of "Track Two" diplomacy, with actions of businesspeople and nonofficial institutions.[23] Nonetheless, it is impossible to ignore the prominent role of Brazilian and US leaders in overthrowing Allende's government.

MÉDICI AND NIXON

Besides the results of the diplomatic approach of "responsible pragmatism," which posed challenges given Brazil's historically subservient position, the partnership raised even more concerns for the United States. After the passage of Institutional Act no. 5 (AI-5), the world—and especially public opinion in the United States—was no longer blind to the violence perpetrated by the Brazilian government. It was a turning point that brought questioning among members of the US government and criticism from the public. A few days after AI-5's approval, Jack Kubisch, a Brazil specialist from the Department of State, wrote a memo in which he recognized that human rights "have already suffered to some extent and remain under serious threat."[24] Despite the acknowledgment, relations between the countries remained cordial. In 1972, Secretary of the Treasury John Connally traveled to South America. The summary of his visit to Brazil, sent to President Nixon, stated that Connally "had a long and particularly warm meeting with President

Emílio Garrastazu Médici and Richard Nixon meet in Washington in 1971.
Source: Richard Nixon Presidential Library and Museum.

Médici who recalled with pleasure his conversations with you last December. Médici reaffirmed Brazil's policies with respect to Cuba, indicated his enthusiastic support for your initiatives in the international arena, and promised Brazil's support for the US efforts to restructure the international monetary and trading system."[25]

The conversations Emílio Garrastazu Médici "recalled with pleasure" took place during the Brazilian president's visit to the United States. Uncharismatic and authoritarian, Médici is considered by many to be the most repressive of the Brazilian military leaders. His reputation for being assertive and arrogant preceded his public appearances. Although aligned with US interests, he did not seek Nixon's blessing. He considered himself the ruler of a powerful nation of his own.[26]

The trip offered the conservative media a thread of positive stories to tell, in not only Brazil but also the entire Southern Cone. The Chilean magazine *Qué Pasa* published a cover story about Médici's trip to America. Titled "Brazil Will Speak in Washington as a World Power," the story applauded Brazilian economic success and ignored any mention of torture or censorship.[27] It was a considerable shift from the previous months, when several newspaper articles denouncing abuses of human rights stained the image of the Brazilian government abroad. The negative press began simultaneously with the start of a new strategy by Brazilian leftist groups to denounce the dictatorship and gain prominence: the kidnapping of international authorities in exchange for political prisoners.

In 1969, the guerrilla groups National Liberating Action (ALN) and October 8 Revolutionary Movement (MR-8) abducted US ambassador Charles Elbrick in Rio de Janeiro.[28] In March 1970, the Popular Revolutionary Vanguard (VPR) kidnapped the general consul of Japan, Nobuo Ozuchi, in São Paulo.[29] In June of that same year, the VPR and ALN pulled the German ambassador Ehrenfried von Holleben from his car in Rio. He was freed five days later, in exchange for forty political prisoners.[30] The Brazilian government reacted violently, with more imprisonment and punishment. While the local media was under censorship and accused the rebels of being terrorists, Chilean leftist networks supported the guerrilla groups and called for demonstrations against Emílio Garrastazu Médici.[31] The climate of criticism would not end soon.

Médici, however, relied on numbers to boost morale. During his government, the Brazilian economy had achieved impressive growth—on average, 11.1 percent per year from 1968 to 1973. The population was moving from rural to urban areas, and the middle class had grown considerably. Exports rose from 4.1 percent (1964–67) to 24.6 percent (1968–73) and imports from 2.7 percent to 27.5 percent per year, during the same interval. The country seemed headed toward an active international policy.[32] It was in this climate that Richard Nixon invited Médici to visit the United States in December 1971.

They agreed on a three-day tour, from December 7 to 9. The strong economic momentum led Médici to decide that it was time to seek Nixon's endorsement. The open support of the US president would impress his military colleagues, the press, and influence Brazilian public opinion. It would also legitimize a regime suffering from accusations of torture and violence.[33] Demonstrations against the Brazilian regime were widespread. During Médici's stay in Washington, a group of Brazilian exiles and US intellectuals carried a large poster, readable from the White House, that demanded, "Stop U.S. Dollar Complicity with Brazilian Torture."[34] While visiting the Organization of American States (OAS), Médici was once again challenged when a protester, who had entered the meeting pretending to be a journalist, stood up and screamed in Portuguese, "Long live free Brazil—stop tortures!"[35]

Just a few months before Médici's visit, the *Washington Post* published a one-page article about Marcos Arruda, who lived in the United States, in forced exile. It recounted in detail a story "based largely on one man's account of his arrest, nine-month imprisonment and torture at the hands of the Brazilian military government." The newspaper added that the Brazilian embassy in Washington refused to comment on the accusations, saying that it "lacked direct information about it."[36] The article had wide repercussions.

The narrative started by describing the day of May 11, 1970, when officers arrested Arruda. They subjected him to interrogations and torture for several months. His mother, Lina Penna Sattamini, was a naturalized US citizen, living in the United States since 1958 and working as an interpreter for the US Agency for International Development. She received a letter from her mother explaining that after twenty-four days waiting for news, she had finally learned that Arruda had been arrested. "My son had been tortured so badly that he had been taken to a hospital, where they thought that he was going to die." Sattamini traveled to Brazil to be reunited with her son. He had been under arrest for almost three months when the family was allowed to see him for the first time. After the encounter, Sattamini wrote a letter to the minister of justice of the Médici government: "Respected Minister, my son is an invalid! His left leg is paralyzed, and he can't move it. His right eyelid is almost shut, and the left is half-open. He suffers convulsions of the thorax, swallows only with great difficulty, and pronounces his 'r's doubled, as the French do."[37]

Arruda was released on February 1, 1971. Using her influence as a US State Department employee, his mother was able to help him obtain a visa. Arruda resisted at first. But after three months, while he was still recovering, he found out that a case was being presented against him at the Military Supreme Court, accusing him of subversion. "I would be arrested again and would have to wait for the judgment in prison. At this moment, my family, my comrades, and I decided I had to leave the country. Much against my will, because I was very critical of U.S. policies, we decided that it was time to go."[38]

Emílio Garrastazu Médici was determined not to bother with stories of Brazilian exiles and other political enemies based in the United States—or, at least, not to demonstrate that he did. On the night of his arrival, Nixon offered him a dinner in the State Dining Room at the White House. It was almost 10:00 p.m. when the US president proposed a toast. He looked at the Brazilian leader, who listened carefully to the translator, and declared, "Working with you as the leader of that country—because we know that as Brazil goes, so will go the rest of that Latin American Continent—the United States and Brazil, friends and allies in the past, and as this dinner tonight reaffirms, strong and close personal and official friends today, we shall work together for a greater future for your people, for our people, and for all the people of the American family, for which we have a special place in our hearts."[39]

The day after, a self-assured Médici entered Nixon's office at the White House. Through an interpreter, the Brazilian president said that his "visit and his welcome had been far above anything he had expected." He continued, making it clear they were equals by saying jocularly that the "word had gotten around that he had hit it off well with the President, that they had become friends, and that was why people were asking for him to intercede with the President," to which Nixon replied that they had indeed "established a close and friendly relationship."[40]

The "close friends" went on talking about Cuba and what a great coincidence it was that neither wanted any kind of relations with the communist island. Then Nixon suggested that they open a secret line of communication, to which diplomats and their respective ministries of foreign affairs would not have access. Nixon said that he would name National Security Adviser Henry Kissinger to be the one responsible for the channel; Médici pointed to Mário Gibson Barbosa, who had been handling a number of matters secretly, in a special file where everything was handwritten, so that "not even typists had knowledge of them." After talking about the situation in Bolivia and stressing the difficulty they had "in dealing with the Latin Americanists," Nixon asked what Médici thought of the situation in Chile. Médici then made it clear that "Allende would be overthrown for very much the same reasons that Goulart had been overthrown in Brazil."[41]

The conversation between Médici and Nixon on that cold morning of December 9, 1971, shows that the cooperation between Brazil and the United States to overthrow Allende was direct and lengthy. Just a year after Allende's inauguration, the US president talked openly about a coup d'état, asking Médici if he thought that the "Chilean Armed Forces were capable of overthrowing Allende." The Brazilian dictator replied "that he felt that they were, adding that Brazil was exchanging many officers with the Chileans, and made clear that Brazil was working towards this end." Nixon then stated it was important that the two countries work together and offered his help. "If money were required or other discreet aid, we might be able to make it available. This should be held in the greatest confidence. But we must try and prevent new Allendes and Castros and try where possible to revert these trends."[42] Médici declared that he was happy to see that their positions were so close.

On December 20, 1971, only a few days after Médici left Washington, Nixon met with British prime minister Edward Heath in Bermuda. Brazil was one of the topics of conversation. The two leaders mentioned the country's important role in South America, and Nixon made it clear that he meant what he had said to Médici. When asked about Cuba, he stated that Fidel Castro was "too radical even for Allende and the Peruvians. Our position is supported by Brazil, which is after all the key to the future." And he added, "The Brazilians helped rig the Uruguayan election. Chile is another case—the Left is in trouble. There are forces at work which we are not discouraging."[43] The US leader's reliance on the Brazilians was not sudden. It came from decades of collaboration, including in the coup that instituted the dictatorship in 1964.

THE START OF COOPERATION: THE BRAZILIAN COUP

Ease is not a quality one usually associates with a military coup; but it is probably the best way to describe what happened in Brazil on March 31, 1964. A group of soldiers marched into Rio de Janeiro. That same day, the presidency was declared vacant. President João Goulart did not try to resist. On April 1 he traveled to Brasília, then to Porto Alegre, and finally to exile in Uruguay. He would never again return to Brazil until his body was buried there, in 1976. Just a few days after the coup, the national Congress appointed General Humberto de Alencar Castelo Branco as president. He promised to call elections soon, but Brazilians would not see this happen for more than twenty years.[44] Washington immediately recognized the new government, declaring it part of the democratic forces emerging in Latin America, against the dangers of communism.

Right after the coup, when João Goulart was still in Brazil, Lyndon B. Johnson sent a telegram to the president of the Brazilian Congress, Ranieri Mazzilli, who had temporarily assumed the Brazilian presidency: "Please accept my warmest good wishes on your installation as President of the United States of Brazil. The American people have watched with anxiety the political and economic difficulties through which your great nation has been passing and have admired the resolute will of the Brazilian community to resolve these difficulties within a framework of constitutional democracy and without civil strife. . . . I look forward to the continued strengthening of those relations and to our intensified cooperation in the interests of economic progress and social justice for all and of hemispheric and world peace."[45]

On April 9, the Brazilian military junta signed the first of a series of institutional acts, an invention of the regime that did not exist in the Brazilian Constitution. Institutional Act no. 1 called the coup a "revolution" and denied political rights to any citizen who opposed the regime.[46] The new government canceled the mandates of senators, representatives, and governors. The act also determined that the country would have indirect elections, meaning that Congress would choose the Brazilian president. The constitution was suspended for six months. A large part of the population celebrated the "revolution," including businessmen, press outlets, members of the Catholic Church, and politicians such as the governors of the state of Guanabara (today's Rio de Janeiro), Carlos Lacerda, and of São Paulo, Ademar de Barros.

During the Goulart administration the US government had reduced foreign aid, alleging that Brazil was becoming hostile. As soon as Castelo Branco took office, however, relations grew strong. The United States extended a large loan to the new government, which received $2 billion from 1964 to 1970 and ranked third, behind Vietnam and India, as a recipient of US aid.[47] In response, the military president adopted a policy of alignment with the United States.[48] In his memoirs, Gibson Barbosa came to criticize what he called the "Manichaean dichotomy of the Cold War," defined as the "need for Brazil's alignment (obviously with the United States)," which had its height in the Brazilian military intervention in the Dominican Republic in 1965.[49] In April of that year, at the request of Washington, Brazil officially declared it would help the United States intervening in the Caribbean country to prevent it from turning into a "new Cuba."[50] The commanding officer and most of the 2,500 Latin American troops who were deployed in the OAS operation came from Brazil.[51] Relations between the two countries grew closer and the United States continued celebrating the fact that "the armed forces brilliantly stopped communism from taking over Brazil."[52]

In the late 1960s, preoccupation with Chile required the return of the Brazil-US alliance. Supporters of Salvador Allende started organizing his presidential bid motivated by the impression that Eduardo Frei's policies were too timid. Frei, who had defeated Allende in 1964, introduced a series of measures to tackle poverty, including agrarian reform and housing programs.[53] The creation of the Ministry of Housing and Urbanism in 1965, is still considered a turning point in Chile's housing policies. The severe rainy season of that year made it necessary to build alternatives for the homeless. The government launched Operación Sitio—first as a temporary measure and later as one of the biggest housing projects of the country's history.[54] Chilean citizens could apply for loans and buy small parcels of land with access to water and electricity.

The rapid pace of migration from rural areas and the increase in population, however, created an urgency that made many perceive Frei's process of "Chileanization" to be too slow. If the construction of affordable houses took a long time, the solution was to occupy areas of Santiago and other urban centers. In March 1967, the Revolutionary Left Movement (MIR) supported the taking of Herminda de la Victoria, the first in a series of over 400 land occupations. The government was under pressure: peasants asked for more rights, while sectors of the middle class demanded the nationalization of the copper industry.[55]

Allende promised that implementing a socialist government would expedite and expand Frei's boldest measures. "La via chilena al socialismo [the Chilean path to socialism]" included deep changes in Chile's economic structure, such as the nationalization of industries and of the country's most important resource, copper. It also rejected monopolies—foreign or national. Popular Unity vowed to break up large land properties and promote a wider agrarian reform.[56]

When the day of the elections arrived, it was impossible to predict who would win. The United States had decided to not officially back any candidate but rather to secretly "wage 'spoiling' operations against the Popular Unity coalition which supported the Marxist candidate, Salvador Allende." The CIA spent from $800,000 to $1 million on the campaign, equating Allende's presidential bid "with violence and repression."[57] On September 4, 1970, the socialist won 36.29 percent of the votes. Second place went to Jorge Alessandri, from the National Party, who received 35.76 percent, and in third place was the Christian Democratic Party's Radomiro Tomic, with 27.95 percent.[58] Allende therefore won a plurality, not a majority, and the Chilean Constitution determined that in such cases, the Senate should appoint one of the two leading candidates to rule the country.[59]

The decision of Congress in favor of the socialist leader was not only based on numbers. On October 25, the killing of General René Schneider, commander-in-chief of the army and a ferocious opponent of any armed intervention to block Allende's constitutional election, turned public opinion in favor of Allende.[60] The military also despised the violence of the assassination, which was the result of a plot orchestrated by the CIA.[61] Commotion filled the country and Congress named Salvador Allende president after he signed the Statute of Constitutional Guarantees proposed by the Christian Democrats, in which he promised to preserve the democratic regime.[62] On November 3, he was finally inaugurated president of Chile. More than a simple victory, his confirmation was a reaction to US intervention.[63] The socialist project was now a reality that enjoyed the support of the population and the tolerance of the military. Nevertheless, the US government's fear of a new Cuba was greater than ever.[64]

FIDEL CASTRO AND THE END OF NEGOTIATIONS

As soon as Allende was inaugurated, the Brazilian government began to demand that allied nations reduce Chile's role in the international system. On January 21, 1971, Murillo Vasco do Valle Silva, chief of the General Staff of the Armed Forces, sent a letter to President Médici recommending the removal of Chile from the Inter-American Defense Board, founded in 1942 to offer military support to OAS member states. Comparing the situation to what had occurred in 1961, when the United States requested the withdrawal of the Cuban delegation from the institution, Valle Silva argued that "the socialist program in development by president Salvador Allende, in Chile, although not openly declaring accordance to Marxist-Leninist principles, tends to create disharmony and distrust in agencies where measures of protection from communist ideological infiltration on the American continent are debated."[65] The presence of Chile, therefore, was a menace to these protections.

Allende's fragility in the international arena was accentuated in 1971, when Fidel Castro arrived to what the Cuban Communist Party called "a symbolic encounter of two historical processes."[66] The journalist and diplomat José Rodríguez Elizondo defined it differently, stating that Castro had sabotaged the Popular Unity administration. "First, there are no syllogisms for complex situations. Second, the illuminated ones always try to drag along their friends, even if it is to their death. And third, the illuminated ones cannot have friends, only followers."[67]

It started on a warmer than usual summer evening in Santiago. The customary smooth breeze of the Chilean capital in November was replaced with a heat wave, a harbinger of the upcoming weeks. It was hard to tell, however, if this was the result of unpredictable weather phenomena or of the movement of more than 1 million people squeezing together on the sidewalks of the Chilean capital to see the much-expected guest. Castro epitomized the

Chileans take to the streets to welcome Cuban leader Fidel Castro.
Source: Colección Museo Histórico Nacional de Chile.

international fears and domestic fragilities of the time. On the first anniversary of the Allende government, the president announced to a crowd gathered for the celebrations at the National Stadium that the Cuban leader would arrive in a few days. Although the Chilean administration invited him for a ten-day visit, El Comandante never confirmed how long he intended to stay.

The Brazilian government kept track of every new piece of information about the meeting. The preoccupation with relations between Chile and Cuba had started much earlier. On the day of Allende's inauguration, the Brazilian ambassador in Santiago, Antônio Cândido da Câmara Canto, wrote a few lines about the socialist's opinion on Chile's participation in the OAS and dedicated more than half of his telegram to Cuba. The ambassador informed the Brazilian government about Allende's intentions to establish closer relations with Cuba, quoting Allende as declaring it to be "a right that belongs to Chile, and which the country will develop with dignity, in accordance with a sovereign nation. He added that he would do it unilaterally, without requesting OAS authorization." Câmara Canto also contended that a group of thirty representatives of the Cuban government would attend the inauguration ceremony, in what "will be the first contact between the country and the new Chilean president."[68]

Apprehension grew as rumors about the upcoming trip began to spread. On November 1, 1971, a CIEX report stated that there was no certain date for Fidel's appearance.[69] On November 9, finally aware that Castro would arrive a day later, at 5 p.m., Câmara Canto mentioned the Chilean minister of foreign affairs, Aníbal Palma, who had complained about an infamous campaign from minority groups to create chaos amid Castro's visit. The Cubans, Palma stated, were brethren who, just like the Chileans, had implemented their own "path to liberation and national dignity." Câmara Canto described details of the supposed ten-day visit, in which Castro would be accompanied by the ministers of mining and education, "both members of the Cuban Communist Party Central Committee, two members of the political committee of the Communist Party, and the Cuban ambassador to Santiago."[70]

Castro arrived on November 10, 1971, in Antofagasta. Two days later, Câmara Canto described the landing of a "gigantic Ilyushin, from the Soviet enterprise 'Aeroflot,' under protection of the strictest security scheme ever seen in Chile."[71] During the following days, the Brazilian ambassador comprehensively reported every step of the Cuban leader. On November 12, he communicated the arrival of the former presidential candidate and secretary of the French Socialist Party, François Mitterrand, and the mayor of Marseille, Gaston Deferre, for a one-week visit to "examine the current Chilean political experience."[72] On November 14, Câmara Canto detailed Castro's four-hour-long speech at a university in Antofagasta and compared the Cuban leader to a Mexican comic film actor. "In some moments, I got the impression of hearing Cantinflas. In any case, to the present mass of people, obsessed and clearly leftist, the speech of the 'Caribbean Hyena,' so-called by *La Prensa* and *Tribuna*, was a truly revolutionary lesson," conceded the ambassador.[73]

At the end of the first week of the visit, Câmara Canto drafted an extensive report on the political consequences of the encounter between the two leaders. "For Allende, Fidel's visit is, up to this moment at least, a great success. That is because the commander of the Sierra Maestra is acting in Chilean territory more like a politician from Popular Unity than as a foreign chief-of-state." Câmara Canto seemed impressed with the fact that Castro was able to "eclipse" the figure of Che Guevara, who used to be pointed to as the "spiritual guide of all the leftist Latin American movements." His charismatic presence was a "contribution from the Prime Minister to Allende, since it is known that MIR has been impatient, its secretary-general at loggerheads with the UP, and its guerrillas promoting violent actions in the south of the country. Any mention of Guevara's name during Fidel's visit would intensify the demonstrations in favor of the armed path and, up until this moment, Allende points to the Chilean path."[74]

This accurate observation, seen at first as Castro's contribution to Allende, would turn into what some scholars consider to be the beginning of the

Fidel Castro and Salvador Allende in Punta Arenas, during the
Cuban leader's visit to Chile, in November 1971.
Source: Colección Museo Histórico Nacional de Chile.

collapse of the Chilean path to socialism.[75] Historian Alberto Aggio contends that there were two phases in this process. At first, Castro's magnetic figure overshadowed the Chilean president.[76] Embodying the communism sought by the far-left movements in Chile, he stole all attention away from Allende at a moment when the government was celebrating its popularity and the positive results of the municipal elections. Side by side with one of the most charismatic young leaders of the time, Allende looked like "the uncle of the hero."[77] Later on, when Fidel decided to stay in the country for much longer than anyone could have predicted, he took on the appearance of an inconvenient guest, his charming looks fading away, the novelty of his visit wearing off; he was a visitor who had forgotten to bring good manners along with his luggage. On November 19, Câmara Canto observed that Fidel was no longer on the front page of the Chilean newspapers, and that the crisis of the universities was the main topic, "even in leftist publications." He also highlighted that Castro, when answering a member of the Socialist Youth, stated that "there is no revolution happening in Chile, but a revolutionary process."[78]

Castro stayed for twenty-three days, visiting more than a dozen cities, including Santiago, Antofagasta, Santa Cruz, and Puerto Montt. He went to factories, houses, the Chiquicamata copper mine, the carbon mine in Lota, and several university campuses. At Concepción University, thousands of supporters came to listen to one of his famously long speeches. But Castro did not focus only on the perils of imperialism and the international conjuncture. He also mentioned Chilean domestic issues and created an embarrassment by severely criticizing the Uruguayan government. The Chilean administration was forced to declare that it did not share the opinion of the Cuban prime minister.[79]

While Salvador Allende tried to profit from the result of the municipal elections to control the demands of the radical leftists and the opposition, Castro talked about a more radical Marxist approach, contending that "to unite and wage the struggle, it is not necessary to get everyone to agree on everything."[80] While Allende insisted on a conciliatory tone to convince workers to avoid strikes, Castro criticized them for behaving as if, after nationalization, they owned the factories. He declared that "saltpeter belongs to all Chileans, the textile industry belongs to all Chileans, copper belongs to all Chileans, and all the natural resources of the nation belong to the entire nation, because this is what determines the will and the duty of the workers of all the Chilean people."[81] While Allende's advisers tried to find solutions for an unprecedented crisis at the University of Santiago, Castro responded that "when a revolutionary process is begun, when a revolutionary crisis is produced, the struggles and battles become tremendously acute."[82]

Historian Lubna Z. Qureshi suggests that the Allende administration was a victim of its own moderation. Amid the Cold War, the socialist government was an enemy of the United States and Brazil, but at the same time, it was not radical enough to gain the same financial and military aid that Cuba and the Soviet Union offered to other socialist countries. Chile was "too fragile to support any movement of national liberation" and did not get Castro's assistance. On the day of the coup, fewer than 150 Cuban agents were in Chile, while Castro dispatched 36,000 troops to Angola in 1975.[83] Castro's visit to Chile forced him to reevaluate Cuba's foreign policies and attempts to take his promises of revolution worldwide.[84]

For historian Tanya Harmer, the Chilean coup was not the result of Washington-Moscow tensions but of the dispute among Cuba, Chile, the United States, and Brazil. In South America the Cold War was not a bipolar but a multidimensional conflict, in which Cuba and other countries from the region played decisive roles. Harmer also highlights the level of attention that the Brazilian press paid to Chile in the aftermath of Allende's election. Knowing of the ties between the censored media and the civilian-military government, she suggests that the climate of concern present on the front pages of newspapers could have reflected the same feelings in the upper echelons of the administration. Although the CIA campaign to spread fear and alarm contributed to this, the Brazilian government also worked to frustrate Allende, as can be seen in the tone of Câmara Canto's reports, in the media coverage, and in the investigation of Brazilian intelligence agents into specificities of Allende's governmental structure.[85]

Castro was still in Chile when the opposition to Allende culminated in the March of the Empty Pots, a large demonstration in which thousands of people marched to La Moneda Palace beating pots to protest the government.[86] The movement for a plebiscite on whether Allende should remain in power gained strength. The divisions among Chileans intensified. The fragility of the Popular Unity administration was patent.[87]

Allende had no option other than to react boldly. "A fascist germ is mobilizing certain sectors of our youth, especially in the universities," he said during a farewell event to Fidel Castro on December 2, 1971. As if he had a premonition of what Emílio Garrastazu Médici would say a few days later, while talking to Richard Nixon at the White House, Allende compared himself to the deposed Brazilian president João Goulart. "The events are similar to those experienced in Brazil during the Goulart government." And he continued, once again presaging what was soon to come, "I am not a martyr. . . . I will leave La Moneda only when I have fulfilled the task entrusted to me by the people. Only by riddling me with bullets can they stop me from fulfilling the people's program."[88]

6
THE CHILEAN SEPTEMBER 11

Dime si es justo, soldado,
con tanta sangre ¿Quién gana?

[Tell me if it's right, soldier,
with so much blood who wins?]

VÍCTOR JARA, "CANCIÓN DEL SOLDADO"

After a long day visiting patients, Otto Brockes spent the night of September 10, 1973, organizing resistance groups to a possible coup d'état in Chile. They discussed how to defend themselves and where to go in case of a military insurgency. There was no time to overthink. A comrade was categorical: it will happen tomorrow. The Brazilian physician returned home to the distant neighborhood of Macul, hoping that the Chilean military would prove them wrong. Brockes had not eaten anything and found the refrigerator empty. He went to bed hungry. The next day, he woke up and noticed that there was no public transportation in the area. He jumped in a truck and then walked to downtown Santiago, where he was supposed to meet his peers in a factory. As soon as he arrived, a Brazilian comrade told him that the coup was taking place.[1]

The leaders of the group divided up the men and women who were present into safe houses and sent Brockes to the home of a prominent communist. When he arrived, still hungry, the wife complained. They had very little food for themselves, yet her husband had brought guests. The older son lectured her about the sacrifices that the revolution required. Brockes felt embarrassed. He decided to take a chance and go back home. When he got there, starving and tired, he found the same empty refrigerator. He started reading a document that a Trotskyist friend had given him and fell asleep.

"Nationality?" screamed the soldier, standing over the bed.

Brockes woke up immediately and replied, "Brazilian."

"Can I see your documents?"

And when the doctor turned to find his ID card, he felt the blow to his back. The acute pain blended with a feeling of despair and disgust. "They did not have the guts to attack me looking at my face, but when I turned, they hit me and put me on my knees. They beat me from that moment on, until the end of night, nonstop. They broke my ribs, my head got huge, swollen. I was butchered inside my home. I fainted once, twice, and they continued beating me, while I was completely covered in blood."[2]

The soldiers then asked about the enemies of the newly imposed government. Where were they? Was he one of them? Where were the weapons? In a flash, Brockes thought of his mother, his friends who had died at the hands of Brazilian torturers, the lives he had saved working as a doctor. "This is the wrong approach," he told himself. "I am making them kill me. I can pretend without telling them anything." So, he denied being a guerrilla fighter and told the soldiers he was a doctor who had arrived in Chile as a tourist, hoping that they might see the stamp in his passport from a month earlier, when he had been to Brazil. "Cállate, perro [shut up, dog]," one of them answered. Another officer, however, looked at his documents and commented, "But it does say doctor here . . ." They began to calm down.

Suddenly a carabinero found a room where one of Brockes's comrades kept fake documents, pictures, and equipment used to falsify passports. Ironically, that saved his life. "They thought I was a big boss; some high-profile person and they concluded it would look good if they took me to the Ministry of Defense and bragged about having arrested me. I fainted again and when I woke up, I was already being dragged down the street. My feet had no more nails; I was practically naked at this point. They threw me into a bus, and sat on my head, laughing."[3]

The police officers took him to a station of the Carabineros de Chile, the Chilean national police force, where officers interrogated and tortured him again. "At that point, I hadn't eaten anything for almost two days. They offered me water. I pretended, but of course I did not drink. It could be poisoned." Then, the soldiers took him to a police department on General Mackenna Avenue, where other political prisoners were. He was thrown into a cell with several Chileans. At some point, a very courteous police officer said he was sorry for all the rudeness, which was "not in tune with the politeness of the Chilean people" and introduced him to a Brazilian woman. "The officer told me that she had been raped several times and added, 'You are both in terrible condition. Please, talk to her and maybe you can cheer her up a little bit,'" recalls Brockes. He recognized her immediately, but she did not recognize him. His face was disfigured from the beatings. Brockes had examined her child a week earlier. He held her shoulders and said, "It is me, the Brazilian doctor." She hugged him and let out a howl of pain. He never learned her name and never saw her again.

Brockes was one of the many exiles and thousands of people who suffered at the hands of the state in that violent September in Chile. In some cases, their previous experience with other dictatorships helped them create ways of surviving their ordeal. The Brazilian citizens in this transnational experience of torture and violence are the main narrators of this chapter. At the National Stadium and at international embassies, they were central in structuring movements of resistance. They were also key witnesses of the influence of the Brazilian civilian-military regime in the 1973 coup, since they were among the few people who could identify Brazilian officers inside the National Stadium. They could understand and describe the lessons in torture that these military men gave to their Chilean counterparts. This chapter will also investigate how the connections between the Brazilian government and the Chilean strategists of the coup played out at the National Stadium. The ideas and practices of the dictatorship in Brazil were replicated and the support continued in the installation of a similar regime in Chile.

A FEW MONTHS BEFORE: PLOTTING
WITH THE ARMED FORCES

Brazilian exiles had long worried about a coup in Chile. One of them, Cândido da Costa Aragão, met with Salvador Allende in March 1973 to share his concerns. The Chilean president replied with irony: "There is no problem because in this country gorillas are castrated when they are born."[4] They did not know that they were being watched at that very moment. Spies from the Brazilian Foreign Office's Intelligence Center (CIEX) soon reported the conversation to the Brazilian government. Two months later, CIEX informed the diplomats that a Chilean military movement with the objective of overthrowing the Allende government would likely take place between May 13 and 19. They added that the Navy and Air Force were ready to act. However, there was still no agreement with the Army about the formation of a central military command.[5]

The Brazilian spies could have been referring to the Tancazo, a failed but still frightening attempted coup.[6] On June 29, Colonel Roberto Souper learned that the conspiracy to overthrow Allende had been discovered and he would be relieved of his command. Souper crossed the streets of Santiago with eighty soldiers, six tanks, and ten other armored vehicles. They circled the La Moneda presidential palace and the building of the Ministry of Defense and opened fire. General Carlos Prats, then commander-in-chief of the army, suffocated the rebellion in less than three hours. For some Brazilian exiles, who had been hearing about the threat of a coup for months, the short life of the Tancazo came as a breath of hope. "Our impression was that it was possible to prevent the coup, but we also felt that it would take some sort of military fight. So, we were already talking about international brigades," remembers Jean Marc von der Weid, who at the time was leading Popular Action from Switzerland, where he then lived in exile. Von der Weid had arrived in Chile with the Setenta, but moved to his country of citizenship a few months later and only returned to Chile two other times before the coup—the first, around the time of the Tancazo; the second, in September 1973. "I could have not picked a worse time. I had arrived in Chile on September 1, when there was still some optimism because the Tancazo had been defeated, so workers were organizing in factories, arming themselves. But we could already feel that things had gone awry."[7]

The Tancazo, organized by Patria y Libertad, was a prelude to the successful coup of September 11. A report from CIEX stated that the Chilean Communist Party was divided about what the reaction should be to a potential coup d'état organized by "Generals Urbina, Pinochet, Brady, and Pickering, among others" to keep Allende in the presidency and to "nominate technicians and military people to the government."[8] A "self-coup" to keep Allende in power never materialized. Brazilian authorities, however, soon learned that "trustworthy and well-situated sources considered it to be possible for them to finally see an outcome in the next days, which could culminate in the fall of the Allende government."[9] Food shortages and high inflation contributed to the climate of insecurity. Both conservative groups with their empty pans and leftist organizations, tired of waiting for the socialist promise to be fulfilled, marched against Salvador Allende.

The Chilean right wing looked at the success of the Brazilian dictatorship as a source of protection and inspiration. On the morning of August 2, 1973, some of highest profile members of the Chilean military met at the air base El Bosque, in Santiago, to debate strategic matters. What admirals, generals, and commanders of the Allende Armed Forces discussed, though, was not the state of the country. They assessed how "the measures adopted by the Brazilian military during the revolution of March 31, 1964, could be useful in Chile."[10] Brazilian government leaders spread the information about the meeting to their intelligence services in a report that remained secret for almost four decades after the Chilean coup d'état.

It seemed like a serpent's nest, full of members of the Allende administration who would become the highest echelon of the Pinochet regime. General César Ruiz, who had been commander-in-chief of the Chilean Air Force since 1970, was among the participants. A week after the meeting in El Bosque, Ruiz was nominated as Allende's minister of public works and transportation. He resigned only nine days later, unable to control the truck drivers' strike. He also stepped down as commander-in-chief of the Chilean Air Force, upon Allende's demand. Being unemployed, however, was not a concern for him. The perspective of a change in leadership was also the promise of new professional endeavors. In October 1973, less than a month after the coup, the dictatorial government nominated him dean of the University of Chile, where he remained until 1974. He was later appointed Chilean ambassador to Japan.

At the meeting in El Bosque, Ruiz stated that Chile was "on the razor's edge" and the spirit of rebellion had permeated all the armed forces of the country. In the case of a military insurgency, he assured his peers that all the garrisons in Chile were ready to act as soon as they were given word, and that the Santiago garrison was committed to the rebellion, except for the Infantry School, which was nevertheless very close to supporting the revolt.

Ernesto Jobet, commandant of the First Naval Zone, was also in El Bosque, representing José Toribio Merino, then commander of the Chilean main combat fleet. Merino would lead the Navy branch for virtually the entire period of the military junta, until 1990. Also attending the meeting were Commander Ernesto Huber Von Appen, director of the Naval Aviation, and "several other" officials of the Chilean Air Force and Navy. The group praised the interview of General Alfredo Canales on July 31, in which he talked about the creation of a new party, the Junta Unificadora Nacionalista, with the objective of "promoting a great national development to overthrow Marxism and give Chileans peace, order, and a sense of authority." The interview was considered an ultimatum for the Allende government and a call to action to the Chilean Armed Forces. The Brazilian informant who wrote to the government stated that this approval seemed to confirm the impression that the military was finally motivated to intervene against Allende.[11]

After being briefed about the meeting, Admiral José Toribio Merino decided that it was urgent to prevent the political context in South America from spoiling the coup. He needed to confirm that the Peruvian dictator, Juan Velasco Alvarado, would not take advantage of the possible fragility of the Chilean military to advance into the territory of Tarapacá. Rumors were spreading in the Southern Cone that Alvarado was seeking to recover the area lost in the War of the Pacific in the late nineteenth century. Looking for guarantees that the region was ready for a new government in Chile and would not interfere, Merino turned to Brazil. The admiral, who would become the president of the Government Junta of Chile from 1974 to 1990, was a close friend of Brazilian ambassador Antônio Cândido da Câmara Canto.

Reaching the Brazilian authorities to mediate talks with Peruvian leaders, however, was a delicate process. It had to remain secret; otherwise, the plot to overthrow Allende would be ruined. Merino asked former naval officer Roberto Kelly to fly to Brazil and meet in person with members of the government. Calling or sending a letter would be too risky. Although he trusted Kelly deeply, Merino avoided telling him about the full reasons for the trip. When he arrived in Brasília, not yet sure about what the objective of his visit was, he faced intense questioning. A few hours later, lost and unsure if he would be able to deliver what his boss wanted, Kelly received a mysterious and anonymous phone call. On the other side of the line, a muffled voice ordered him to go back to Chile immediately and tell Merino not to worry because "Peru will not go."[12] Merino assured the other leaders of the military that external forces would not hurt their plans. It was the green light they needed to go ahead with the coup.

A FEW DAYS BEFORE: THE EMBASSY AS ALCOVE

Four days before the coup, on September 7, the Brazilian embassy in Santiago received a select group of people to celebrate Brazilian Independence Day.[13] It was an annual tradition, but in 1973 it served as the perfect cover for a meeting to set the last details about the overthrow of Salvador Allende. Members of the Chilean Navy, Air Force, Army, and the Carabineros—the Chilean national police force—were typical guests of the traditional celebration. This time around, however, Ambassador Câmara Canto reserved a special room for them, where the actions that would take place in the next few days could be privately discussed.

The military junta established right after the coup had four leaders, one from each military branch. Câmara Canto was nicknamed the "fifth member," given his importance in the process.[14] On September 8, he wrote a telegram detailing the Independence Day event to Brazilian authorities. Enthusiastic, he bragged that "around 800 people attended," and he highlighted the participation of some of the most prominent supporters of the coup, including "several members of the Army, Air Force, and Carabineros," and the president of the Chilean Supreme Court, Minister Enrique Urrutia, who would later give Augusto Pinochet his presidential sash.[15]

There were also some faithful prominent figures of the Allende government in attendance. They were part of the ambassador's attempt to project a public facade of tolerance between Brazil and the Popular Unity administration. One of them was the minister of defense and deputy minister of foreign affairs, Orlando Letelier. A few days later he would become the first member of the Allende government to be arrested by the new regime. Letelier then went into exile in the United States, where the Chilean secret police assassinated him in 1976.[16] The president of the Chilean Central Bank, Hugo Fazio, also attended the gathering. He was a former director of the Chilean Communist Party and would later be forced into exile in the Soviet Union for most of the duration of the Pinochet regime. This effort to project an image of forbearance, an essential tool of diplomacy, was fundamental in the days that preceded the bombing of La Moneda. It not only allowed the Brazilian government to deny for decades its participation in the events of September 11, but it also gave the Chilean military a refuge. From Câmara Canto and CIEX agents, they knew they could expect support in the form of ideas, financial resources, and information on the internal affairs of the Allende government, extracted with the help of spies infiltrating groups of exiles.

The bombing of La Moneda Palace and the overthrow of Salvador Allende were the pinnacle of a plot that had been almost a decade in the making. As we have seen in the preceding chapters, the Brazilian dictatorship had been planning to react to an Allende presidency many years before it became a reality. With the support of the ambassador and information from moles who had infiltrated groups of exiles in Santiago, Brazilian leaders were able to predict the stages that led to the installation of the Pinochet regime and ensure that it had strong support. On September 11, a long and urgent telegram arrived at the Brazilian Ministry of Foreign Affairs in Brasília, in which Câmara Canto described the long lines to buy bread in the upper-class neighborhoods of Santiago. The violent reactions of consumers resulted in "conflicts with store owners and, many times, in clashes with the police," he wrote. He went on to cite an emotional editorial in the newspaper *La Tercera*: "The lack of bread makes everyday life bitter and harder. It sums up the long and narrow land of lines that Chile has become. . . . Nothing can be more humiliating to a people than suffering from hunger, in any of its forms. This is what is beginning to happen in Chile. There is no doubt that the population could have endured better the process we are living in if it hadn't started to attack something sacred: the right to exist and eat. What is going on does not create fervor, but hopelessness; it does not produce revolution, but desperation."[17]

Later that same day, another telegram from Câmara Canto arrived at the Ministry of Foreign Relations. It was about the strike of transportation workers.[18] After that, the communication became more difficult. The coup had started.

THE DAY OF THE COUP

Around 9 a.m. on September 11, 1973, soldiers hurled the first bombs at La Moneda, where Salvador Allende tried to keep his promise to resist until death. At noon, Hawker Hunter fighter jets bombed the presidential palace. The smoke covered Santiago. For the Brazilian exiles, it felt like a repetition of what they had witnessed almost a decade earlier, in their home country. Nancy Mangabeira Unger compared that Tuesday to a Hollywood movie. She hid from the police inside a closet in the bedroom of a newborn. A comrade's baby was sleeping calmly in the crib when the officers arrived. They had been searching homes and businesses, trying to find enemies of the new military government. The order was clear: to kill. The policemen entered, looked over everything, but did not search inside the closet.[19]

Wilson Barbosa survived despite his uncomfortable proximity to the enemy. His wife was a student at Chile's Latin American College of Social Sciences. The day of the coup, the daughter of one of the most renowned professors at the university invited them to her father's birthday party. On the one hand, the idea of going out was scary. On the other, the promise of a few drinks in a place of celebration was a much-needed escape. After a few minutes at the party, Barbosa noticed one large and three small trucks parking on the sidewalk. Several armed men dressed in black entered the gathering. The professor's nephew was an army captain and loudly inquired, pointing to Barbosa, what "subversive elements" were doing in the house. At that point, the newly imposed government had already declared all foreigners to be suspicious and demanded that they present themselves to a police station. The professor ordered his nephew to keep quiet and insisted that they were his guests and students, and therefore should not be bothered. Barbosa never forgot the discomfort of those moments. "We had to shake hands with the captain. So, you eat those birthday sweets with difficulty, you drink that little champagne with a dry mouth, then you go back home and caress your .38 revolver, which is the only thing that remains." He said that all he could think of was shooting. "A defeat is a defeat, comrade. The problem is that it was one defeat after another, you see? This is hard to swallow. It happens, once, twice, three, four, five times, organizations being defeated, you being arrested, massacred, you go into exile, you are humiliated by these guys. . . . It comes to a point when you either become the state or you go take care of your own life."[20]

Ubiramar Peixoto compared the coup d'état to losing a mother for a second time. He had decided to leave Brazil only after realizing that he would otherwise be killed. Peixoto had been following Salvador Allende since 1958, more than a decade before he was elected president of Chile. Immediately after arriving in Santiago, he engaged with leftist groups. He was still a member of the Brazilian Communist Party and worked to connect it with its Chilean counterpart and similar movements. Peixoto considered himself to be a guerrilla person, a part of Allende's path to socialism, just like any Chilean citizen. "So that defeat hurt me really bad."[21]

Fernando Gabeira felt a similar anguish. Images of the Brazilian guerrilla group MR-8 continued flashing in his mind during that strange September day. He was, once again, experiencing defeat. Along with Allende, the dream of a socialist nation and the hope of taking part in a leftist revolution also died. "It was the beginning of an exile inside the exile; this time, longer and even more painful because we knew that military dictatorships were circling the wagons on the entire continent. In the best-case scenario, we would suffer a lot."[22] After the coup, he moved to Sweden where he worked as a journalist, train conductor, and wrote a script for Swedish television about the death of Salvador Allende.[23]

The Amnesty International report on the Chilean coup highlights the "atmosphere of extreme xenophobia" that dominated the country in the days after September 11.[24] One of the leaflets distributed at the time was emphatic: "The actions carried out by the armed forces and police only pursue the good of Chile and Chileans, and therefore they have the support of civilians. No compassion will exist for the foreign extremists who have come to kill Chileans. Citizen: remain alert to find them and denounce them to the nearest military authority.'"[25]

Brazilian exile René-Louis de Carvalho remembers that the prejudice against foreigners also came from radio broadcasts. After the coup there were nonstop advertisements blaming them for "bringing evil to the country."[26] The Chilean leftists had been under foreign influence, the messages suggested, and therefore were not the only culprits. Denouncing foreigners became an act of patriotism.[27] Aluízio Palmar experienced this firsthand. He emphasizes, however, that the climate of animosity had started before September 11 and felt like a prelude to what was about to happen. He remembers trying to buy a shirt and a wallet the week before the coup. The owner of the store refused to sell him anything, stating that he was an *extranjero* (foreigner), one of those "disgusting lefties." He left empty-handed, aware that his days in Chile were numbered.[28]

After the Tancazo, Reinaldo Guarany felt that the coup was a matter of time. He was not surprised when, on September 11, a neighbor with connections to the Chilean military approached him and begged him to disappear. According to her, it was well known that their apartment was a haven for guerrilleros. He left and ended up being arrested after police officers suspected that he was a foreigner. He recalled the conversation with one of the military men in the police station, who accepted a bribe to let him go. "He approached me and said I was crazy not to surrender because the guys were fascists. I asked: 'And what about you?' He said that he was a soldier, and I bought my life for one hundred dollars. I paid and he told me to leave and never mention passing by him if I was caught later." When Guarany arrived home, he found his partner, Maria Auxiliadora Lara Barcelos, in a panic, having thought he was dead. They decided to run away and, after days sleeping in different places, found protection at the Embassy of Mexico.

Eliete Ferrer had arrived in Chile in August and was still living temporarily with her then-partner, Luiz Carlos Guimarães, in Reinaldo Guarany's apartment. They heard the radio announcements and decided to rush to another place, where another friend, Jaime Cardoso, lived. On their way there, they passed by La Moneda and saw the bombardment. Terror was in the air. One of the radio messages stated that any foreigner caught with a gun would be killed. Jaime asked Eliete, a talented artist, to hide his gun behind the bathroom tile. "I did a perfect work with plaster. I think unless the owner renovated the apartment, they probably have no idea that it is there up to this day."[29] The more than twenty soldiers who invaded the living room screaming "Hands up!" did not find it either. Still, they arrested Cardoso and took the women back to Guarany's apartment.

Brazilian exile Nielsen Pires was a few blocks from the presidential palace of La Moneda when military jets cut across the sky with a force he had only seen in the movies. Tanks crossed the great avenues where free men used to walk. The *alamedas* were forbidding. Pires had seen a similar scenario a decade earlier, in Brazil. However, this time he decided that he was not going to hide. He tried to live normally—or as close as possible to it—in the days following the coup. There were moments when he dared to believe that he had been spared. These were, however, rare instances. His gut instinct told him a different story.

On September 15, the Saturday after the coup, he tried to silence his intuition for a few hours and allowed himself to think that he was not going to be captured. He decided to follow his weekend ritual. After waking up, he drank a glass of milk, ate a small piece of bread, got dressed, walked a few blocks, and boarded the first bus to the wealthy neighborhood where his girlfriend, Sara, lived. At the time they could not imagine that they would eventually marry and have a family of their own. Had the young couple believed in signs of fate, they would probably have given up then. After lunch with her family, Sara drove Nielsen back to his apartment. There, he gathered and gave to her the $300 he had been saving for the past two years, his old transistor radio, and ten of his favorite LPs. He told her to go back home and stop by his apartment the next day. If he were not there, she would know he had been killed or arrested. Running away was not an option this time around.[30]

When officers entered his apartment at 3 a.m., he knew what to expect. "They pushed me with the barrel of a machine gun. I woke up when they screamed, 'Where are the guns? Where is the money?'" The soldiers were accompanied by several men who looked like civilians. They occupied both the room and his mind. There was no space for thinking of anything else as he endured a long series of punches. The soldiers looked at him furiously, as if he were responsible for all the years of economic and political crisis. They searched the apartment and concluded that there was nothing compromising—no radio, no money. His roommate, however, a Panamanian student, had left behind several books on Marxist economics. That was enough. Still bleeding, Pires started to recover consciousness and the first thing he thought of was the voice of Sara's father inviting him to stay in their house. In their upper-class neighborhood, most of the residents supported the coup, so surely he would be safe. "I refused [her father's offer] precisely because I had done nothing wrong, and I was legally in the country. I trusted all would be fine." A few hours later, he became one more prisoner at the National Stadium.[31]

René de Carvalho lived with a Chilean friend. The constant radio advertisements asking Chileans to denounce foreigners made him decide to move to the house of Brazilian students who were not engaged with any guerrilla group and only sympathized with leftist ideals. He felt safe enough to bring a fake passport. The next day, the police invaded the house, following the report of a neighbor. The fake document led police officers to frame him as a foreign agent. "First, they put us in a truck and on our way to the Carabineros police station we watched them pick up their other victims. There was no torture, but we were tied up in a way I had never seen before, not even in a movie. We looked like mummies because of all the ropes. I think it was the next day that they put us in another truck, this time without the ropes, just with handcuffs, and they took us to the National Stadium."[32]

Carvalho was a dual citizen of Brazil and France, and, for this reason, he thinks he was not tortured. "I immediately said that I was French, which was my key to survival. Then the colonel took me aside, put a gun to my forehead and said, 'Sing the French national anthem.' I sang, he hit me a few times and threw me in the National Stadium." Carvalho remained there for roughly a week, until French diplomats rescued their citizens. "I know that for many it was a traumatic experience, but my life was a little different because my parents were members of the Communist Party. So, since I was four years old, I lived in hiding. I had a reclusive life, the paranoia at home was intense. Until a few years ago, I would walk looking over my shoulder to see if I was being followed. But anyway, you end up internalizing and normalizing it, right?"[33]

BRAZILIANS KILLED IN CHILE

According to the Brazilian Truth Commission, six Brazilians were killed by the Chilean dictatorship.[34] The first, Nilton Rosa da Silva, died on June 15, 1973, a couple of weeks before the Tancazo and three months before the coup.[35] Mining workers and truck drivers went on strike with the support of fascist group Patria y Libertad, which threatened to destroy the Committee of the Socialist Party. Thousands of people demonstrated against the far-right organization, among them Silva. A group of right-wing people surrounded and shot him. He was twenty-four. Silva had moved to Chile in 1971 after realizing that the dictatorship's police were aware of his involvement in the Brazilian students movement (Movimento Estudantil). His death was widely covered in the Chilean press but ignored in Brazil.[36]

"The problem of statistics," as Amnesty International calls it, complicates the estimates of the number of Brazilian victims of the Chilean coup d'état. According to Amnesty, "many thousands" of refugees and visitors were imprisoned or expelled.[37] It is hard to determine precisely the number of

Brazilians exiled in the country at the time. Citing the newspaper *Le Monde*, the report estimates that there were around 1,200. The Brazilian Truth Commission recognizes that the true number is still unknown, and acknowledges that some consider it to be "hundreds, others thousands, who had moved to Chile during the three years of the Popular Unity government to escape repression in Brazil—some with the intent of staying there; others on their way to other countries—or to witness or participate in the innovative political experience that Chile was undergoing at that time."[38]

The first challenge is identifying all the exiles who were arrested in several different police stations, barracks, or places such as houses and stadiums that were turned into prisons and torture centers in the days and months following September 11. The second difficulty is deciphering the incomplete records, full of typos and other errors. Some of the prisoners refused to be identified. The Committee Carlos de Ré for Truth and Justice (Comitê Carlos de Ré da Verdade e Justiça; CCR) in the state of Rio Grande do Sul has compiled one of the most recent lists, which was sent to the National Stadium National Memory Corporation for Former Political Prisoners and to Chile's Museum of Memory and Human Rights.[39] It comprises names of 123 Brazilians who were arrested and 6 who were killed by the Pinochet regime. The CCR does not consider this to be a final version of the register and notes that the document continues to evolve. Former exiles usually update it with names of friends who are not on the official lists. The International Committee of the Red Cross estimates that in the early days of the dictatorial regime in Chile, more than 7,000 people were arrested and taken to the National Stadium. Between 200 and 300 of them were foreigners.[40] According to Manuel Contreras, the former National Intelligence Directorate chief, eighty-eight Brazilians, seventy-three men and fifteen women, were arrested at the stadium, the main center of murder and torture in the first year after the coup.[41]

It was there that the Brazilian Wânio José de Mattos died. For other victims of the dictatorship, his death was considered the result of the actions—and neglect—of the Chilean and Brazilian governments. Born in Piratuba, in the state of Santa Catarina, Mattos was a police officer and a member of the guerrilla group Popular Revolutionary Vanguard (VPR). The civilian-military dictatorship arrested him in Brazil on April 24, 1970, and expelled him from the military police. A year later, he was sent to Chile as one of the Setenta. His wife, Maria das Dores, and his daughter, Roberta, followed him. Roberta's birth certificate listed her father as "unknown," a strategic decision of her mother that allowed them to travel without being questioned by the regime.

Mattos taught at the University of Santiago Law School and led a relatively ordinary life until the coup. September 11 forever removed any sense of normalcy from his family's lives.[42]

Mattos, Maria das Dores, and Roberta, who was two years old at the time, were taken to the National Stadium. Later, the officers separated the girl from her parents. Roberta told the Truth Commission of the State of São Paulo that this event traumatized her for life. She still remembers crying from hunger. After a few days, the Red Cross managed to transfer her and Maria das Dores to the French embassy. They finally left Chile and remained in Paris until the approval of the Amnesty Law in Brazil in 1979. At that point, they still had no news of Mattos.

Otto Brockes witnessed the events prior to Mattos's death. He remembers that the former police officer was desperate and talked nonstop about his wife and daughter, stating that he needed to run away to find them; otherwise, they would die in the stadium.[43] Together, the other exiles listened and tried to distract him by suggesting escape strategies. They all knew, however, that it was impossible to run away from the stadium. There were armed guards, walls, and behind those walls, more armed guards with machine guns. Still, Mattos wouldn't let go of the idea of breaking free.

As a doctor, Brockes worried a great deal about the conditions in the stadium. Most of the political prisoners had intestinal problems because they did not have enough to eat. "We would spend twenty days without defecating because we did not eat, there was nothing in our bellies. I asked the guards to bring us some oranges peels, so that we could eat and make the intestines work," recalls Brockes. But the request was never answered. According to Brockes, Wânio José de Mattos suffered from chronic constipation because of a lack of liquid and fiber ingestion. As the days passed, his condition worsened, and his body looked deformed. Brockes examined him and concluded that he had acute abdominal blockage, which required surgery. He wrote a report and, with the document in hand, decided to take Mattos to the Chilean military doctors who worked in the stadium. It was late at night and trying to reach the officers at this hour was particularly dangerous. As soon as the two prisoners approached the first group of soldiers, they were told to put both hands behind their head. They then guided Brockes and Mattos in the dark with weapons pressed against their necks. When they arrived at the improvised doctor's office, Brockes introduced himself as a fellow medical practitioner and described the gravity of Mattos's situation. The military physician told Brockes that once the Brazilian doctor had entered the stadium, he had lost all of his credentials. He was just a prisoner. The two exiles were sent back to their corner of the stadium.

As the hours passed, Mattos's condition became more precarious. "I was then able to talk to a Chilean minister who had been arrested. I don't remember how, but I remember he found a way to have the doctors see Mattos again. I took him there, but the problem was already too serious. From when I diagnosed him to when they sent him back, three days had passed. It was terrible, a horrible suffering. Mattos stayed there and I came back."[44] After a few days, Brockes heard that an official report stated that the doctors had tried to perform surgery on him, but Mattos did not survive.

Many years after the coup, Mattos's family was still trying to find out what had happened to him in the stadium. They spent years with no information about the circumstances of his death. In 1992, after the end of the Pinochet regime and with the creation of the Rettig Commission to investigate torture, disappearances, and murder during the dictatorial period, the Chilean government finally confirmed his death, caused by peritonitis inside the National Stadium.[45] The Brazilian Ministry of Foreign Affairs, however, had had the information much earlier. On December 31, 1973, it received a report about Mattos's death, stating that he had died on October 16 of that year. Attached to the document was Mattos's death certificate, which the diplomats decided to keep secret: "The notice, no. 583/DIS/COMZAE-4, from the Ministry of the Air Force, from November 21, 1973, states that CISA [the Aviation Information Center; Centro de Informações da Aeronaútica] confirmed that, according to information from several different sources, the following Brazilians were killed in Chile, during the Revolution of 09/11/1973 that took place in that country."[46] The list includes Mattos's name. Another document from the Ministry of the Air Force acknowledges that it had received an anonymous letter on March 22, 1974, communicating the death of the "Brazilian patriot victim of fascism in Chile." The letter stated that Wânio José de Mattos had been arrested with his wife and their two-year-old daughter, his body later abandoned in the same street where the family had been imprisoned, and found by a neighbor. It concludes, "The people do not forget their heroes."[47]

Mattos was the only Brazilian known to have died inside the National Stadium. However, he was not the only one to die by the hands of the Chilean military. Born in Cáceres, in the state of Mato Grosso, Jane Vanini moved to São Paulo in 1966 to study social sciences at the University of São Paulo. She joined the student movement and, in 1969, the National Liberation

Action (ALN), with her then-husband, journalist Sérgio Capozzi.[48] Fearing persecution by the authorities, they moved to Uruguay and Cuba in 1970, where they joined the Brazilian Popular Liberation Movement (Movimento de Libertação Popular; MOLIPO), a dissident group from ALN.[49] In Cuba, they received guerrilla training and Vanini worked at Radio Havana.[50] They came back to Brazil and lived a clandestine life, having joined a guerrilla group near the city of Araguaína, in today's state of Tocantins. After the arrest of several of MOLIPO's leaders, they decided to leave the country again, this time for Chile. Vanini quickly connected to the Revolutionary Left Movement (MIR) and started writing for the leftist publication *Punto Final* under a new name, Gabriela Hernández. After separating from Capozzi, she started a relationship with prominent Chilean journalist Pepe Carrasco. After the coup of September 11, Vanini had to go into hiding yet again. The couple moved from Santiago to Concepción.

On December 6, 1974, Carrasco did not return home at noon, as he always did. Vanini immediately realized that he had been arrested and contacted the MIR leadership with a rescue plan too bold for them. They locked her in a bathroom, fearing that she would try alone to fight the officers of Pinochet's political police, who soon arrived. The National Intelligence Directorate was fierce, but so was Vanini. She escaped and went back home. Carrasco resisted hours of torture until, imagining that Vanini had had enough time to run away, he gave them their home address. Vanini was confronted by the officers and fought back for four hours. She was shot and killed, leaving only a note for Carrasco asking for forgiveness: "It was my last attempt to save you."[51] Carrasco was only able to inform Vanini's family of her death when he wrote them from prison in 1975. In 1993, as a result of the Chilean Truth Commission's efforts, the Chilean government acknowledged its responsibility for Vanini's death.[52] After decades of oblivion, the Brazilian Truth Commission's work to unearth details of Vanini's life and death resulted in her ascension to heroic status.[53] She was remembered in a play, academic works, movies, and poems, such as this one by Héctor Sandoval Torres, titled after Vanini's nom de guerre:

CANTO A GABRIELA

Jane flor urbana
Gabriela Rosa Latinoamericana.
Las balas que rompieron tus alas
No eran balas chilenas
No eran balas proletarias

Eran balas Made in USA
Balas Norteamericanas
eran balas mercenarias.
No es verdad y que lo sepan los que luchan
que morías por el amor de un compañero,
eso es desconocer tu condición revolucionaria.
No volastes a Cuba ni volastes a Chile
para buscarte desesperada un novio.
Discípula consciente de Marighella
de la Acción Liberadora Nacional Militante
y del Movimiento de Liberación Popular insurgente[54]

[Jane urban flower
Gabriela Rosa Latinoamericana.
The bullets that shattered your wings
Weren't Chilean bullets
They weren't proletarian bullets
They were Made in USA bullets
North American bullets
mercenary bullets.
It's not true, and may those who struggle know,
that you died for the love of a compañero,
this would be to misunderstand your revolutionary nature.
You didn't fly to Cuba or to Chile
to desperately seek a sweetheart.
Conscious disciple of Marighella
of National Militant Liberating Action
and of the insurgent Movement for Popular Liberation]

Also in 1993, the Chilean government confirmed the killing of Túlio Roberto Cardoso Quintiliano, although the circumstances of his death were not explained. Quintiliano was an engineer and while in Chile attended the meetings of a group called Departure Point (Ponto de Partida), where politically engaged people discussed the Brazilian dictatorship and the future of Latin America. According to the Chilean Truth Commission, he and his partner were arrested on September 12, 1973, and taken to the Military School (Escuela Militar). Both were interrogated.[55] She was freed the same day, but Quintiliano has been considered a missing person ever since.

Quintiliano's family opened a judicial inquiry to find out details of the events surrounding his death. The result was a report conceding that after being taken to the military school, he was transferred to Regimiento Tacna. The commander in charge of this center of detention sent a statement to the president of the court of appeals informing them that he had not ordered the transfer of Quintiliano to any other unit under his command. "The work of the diplomatic representatives of his country in Chile also did not focus on finding information about his fate," states the report, which concludes that the commission "is absolutely sure of the responsibility of the agents of the state, which kept him arrested, producing therefore a violation of his human rights especially because it was confirmed that the victim had been imprisoned, and not freed as suggested at some point."[56]

In the first days of the Chilean dictatorship, the military killed two other Brazilians. Luiz Carlos de Almeida had studied physics at the University of São Paulo and attended meetings against the Brazilian dictatorship even before he joined the Communist Workers Party. After finding out that the police had ordered his arrest, Almeida decided it would be safer to join other friends in exile and moved to Chile. He lived with a couple of exiles: Luiz Carlos Vieira and Carmen Fischer. On September 14, 1973, carabineros invaded their house and arrested the two men.

Carmen Fischer was then married to Vieira and her 1993 testimony was part of a judicial process in the Santiago Court of Appeals investigating the circumstances of Almeida's death.[57] She said that the officers who invaded the house took their books and files with documents about their activity in Brazil, which the three friends used to call a "political archive." The two men were taken to a police station and, later, to the Estadio Nacional. Their time there would be brief. After being tortured, they were put into a police car with a third prisoner, a Uruguayan man, and taken to the banks of the Mapocho River.[58] When they arrived, the officers shot the Uruguayan and Almeida, who was then twenty-five years old. Vieira was also shot three times and was the last of them to be washed away by the water currents. A group of Chileans from a church found him near the shore and saved his life. Vieira and Fischer went into exile in Sweden, where Vieira still lives.

The other Brazilian killed, Nelson de Souza Kohl, was also a member of the Communist Workers Party and attended the University of São Paulo, where he studied communications. In Santiago, he taught private English classes and worked as a translator. According to his wife, Elaine Maria Beraldo Laune, they never engaged in political activities while in Chile.[59] She recalls that on September 15, 1973, a large group of police officers entered their house and inspected every room, even breaking the bathtub in search of weapons. She watched through the window when Kohl was taken to a military car. It was the last time they looked at each other. Beraldo Laune also stated that, after conducting their own investigation, his family was able to find a death certificate from October 19, 1973, signed by Doctor Alfredo Vargas—the infamous director of the Santiago Forensics, who also signed Salvador Allende's and several other death certificates in the days following the coup d'état. Kohl died on September 16, with the "causa mortis" listed as wounds due to bullet perforations in the thorax and abdomen. More recently, the Brazilian Truth Commission also unveiled a certificate stating that Kohl's body had been cremated on January 4, 1974, at the Recoleta Cemetery.[60]

Although not officially listed as one of the six Brazilians killed by the Chilean government, people close to medical student Maria Auxiliadora Lara Barcelos, known as Dora, consider that she was also a victim of that dictatorship.[61] In Brazil, she was a member of the guerrilla Palmares Armed Revolutionary Vanguard (VAR-Palmares).[62] The Brazilian military police arrested her in November 1969. While dancing to the sound of very loud percussive music, around fifteen soldiers beat her, screaming that they wanted to deform her face.[63] She was then put naked on the wet floor and tortured with electrical shocks. In 1971, Barcelos had gone into exile in Chile, one of the seventy political prisoners exchanged for the Swiss ambassador kidnapped in Brazil. In Santiago, she returned to medical school.

Barcelos's partner, Reinaldo Guarany, recalls that they had a unique relationship during their exile in Santiago. While the ALN leadership forbade him from engaging with Chilean society, she worked at a hospital and continued pursuing a degree. "We did not share everything. We would go to the movies, but Dora had a life that was only hers. I did not read her letters and she did not read mine. We were a couple, living together, but as if we were two separate entities."[64]

Following the 1973 coup, they again had to move. After a period at the Mexican embassy, she went to Belgium and West Germany, where she had the support of Amnesty International. Barcelos again returned to school. And one more time, after a few months, her immigration status was questioned. The renewal of her passport was denied pending the official acceptance of her process of asylum. Guarany states that she was psychologically fragile due to all these problems and that she never recovered from the torture she suffered in Brazil.[65] Maria Auxiliadora Barcelos committed suicide by throwing herself in front of a train at the Charlottenburg subway station, in Berlin. She was thirty-one years old.

Solange Bastos woke up and turned on the radio, as she used to do every morning. On September 11, what she heard was Salvador Allende's last speech. Solange and her friends began to destroy documents that could connect them to leftist organizations. "The toilet clogged because we all rushed to do it at the same time." Three days passed, and the concern was about getting news of their comrades. "I had the illusion that I could leave legally. I had a bundle of documents showing that I was a student, school documents, receipts for piano lessons, proof that I did book translations. And off I went to present myself to the authorities. 'Foreigner? Irregular situation? Inside,' they said. I didn't open my mouth, and that was that."[66]

Then rumors began that the detainees would be taken to the National Stadium and that no one left that place alive. Bastos, however, deals well with crisis. Her personality would later help her in a long career as a reporter. Covering emergencies, from shootouts to fires and even plane crashes, she keeps her cool. After being arrested, instead of worrying, she slept in the crowded cell. On the morning of September 17, she was sent to the National Stadium. "I remember that when I got off the bus, I was so scared that my knees were trembling. But I told myself: you must concentrate so they don't notice that you are shaking. I could not give them that satisfaction." Being one of the few women in the stadium has its particularities. "Among eight thousand, maybe ten thousand prisoners, I remember there being at most eighty-something women. They later concentrated us in the pool's dressing room. They made a clear, sexist distinction."[67]

In many cases, the distinction was also present in the way soldiers tortured their victims. The Chilean National Commission on Political Prison and Torture, active between 2003 and 2004, collected testimony from 3,399 women. Most of them reported they had been sexually abused, and at least 316 were raped.[68]

After their partners were arrested at Jaime Cardoso's apartment, Eliete Ferrer and two friends were taken to their former address. They did not have the keys. One of the military men took a chain with a bunch of keys and tried several, until he opened the door. They instructed the three women to go to different rooms and take their clothes off. "I was put in a room with a soldier and the captain was with one of my friends in the living room. What saved us was that she simulated having fainted and the captain told everyone to stop and leave. When people talk about shaking with fear, this really exists.

You can't stand up. They left and said we could not leave. We knew they had the keys and could come back at any time. We slept hugging each other."[69]

Nowadays, Ferrer is one of the most vocal exiles. Still, during our conversation, she had to stop several times. "It is very hard to talk about this and for many years I could not. My mouth up to this day gets dry. I have never returned to Chile and never will." In 2023, when the Brazilian government sent representatives to Santiago for the events of the fiftieth anniversary of the coup with more than 100 exiles, she refused to participate.

Her then-partner, Luiz Carlos Guimarães, was first imprisoned at the Estadio de Chile, a smaller and, according to Amnesty International, worse version of the National Stadium.[70] There, the soldiers forced him and other prisoners to watch torture sessions and made a habit of shooting detainees randomly.[71] During the five days he was there, he ingested no food and only a few sips of water. Some prisoners fainted and then were punished for this "crime." Guimarães was then transferred to the National Stadium, where the officers locked him with some other 200 prisoners in an area close to the bleachers and set apart with a big iron fence. At that point, Guimarães only carried a small case with his asthma medicine. He had entered Chile with a fake passport under a fake name. At the first opportunity he collected items that could connect him to his birth identity and threw them in a toilet full of feces.

A day later, there were almost 400 people in that same space, twice as many as the night before. Every new prisoner went through the same process upon arrival. In the stadium's velodrome, they had to face the wall and put their hands apart on it, while the soldiers beat them with their weapons. "Where are the guns? What is your terrorist organization?" they asked. Guimarães watched the groups go to the velodrome and come back, reduced to almost half. "Where are the others? We asked ourselves. But we didn't dare say a word because we knew the answer would soon come in a silent, hard, and painful way."[72]

Guimarães confirmed the participation of at least five Brazilian officers of the Department of Internal Operations (Departamento de Informações de Operações; DOI), in the torture of prisoners at the National Stadium. The DOI was the main agency for political repression in the Brazilian dictatorship. "They interrogated and tortured the Brazilians who were arrested there. The chief of the team, Captain Mike, an official of the Brazilian Navy, gave instructions in person to the Chilean officers on the already famous method of pau-de-arara."[73] The incorporation of Brazilian practices of interrogation by other regimes in the region was known. Amnesty International recognized that torture was by and large common practice during the questioning of political prisoners, and that confessions extracted using violence were accepted as evidence by multiple military tribunals, including in Chile. In a report, the organization summarized that "torture has been carried out by, among others, members of those intelligence services whose actions are the sole responsibility of the junta."[74] What they did not know was that Brazilian officers were responsible not only for carrying out the torture but also for teaching techniques to Chileans.

Captain Mike recognized Guimarães in the line to be interrogated. He had ordered the torture of the now-exiled man a few months earlier, when he was still a political prisoner in Brazil. "This time you won't escape me," he said menacingly.[75] At that time, the newly installed Chilean government was refusing most embassies' requests to enter the National Stadium. The UN High Commission for Refugees (UNHCR) was also unable to reach foreign citizens, and some of its staff were threatened.[76] For Guimarães, those were the hardest days. He considers that he only started feeling safe when he told his story to the UNHCR, the Red Cross, and the World Council of Churches. He then became one of the many political prisoners in Chile who went into exile in Sweden.

Osni Geraldo Gomes still lives in Sweden and still feels the effects of his time as a prisoner at the National Stadium. In an emotional video sent to the Brazilian Truth Commission in 2014, he narrated those moments. "I was questioned and tortured by Brazilian police officers in Santiago de Chile, at the National Stadium, in 1973," he begins his testimony.[77] According to his sister, this was the first time he was able to talk about the events that had taken place forty years earlier. Gomes said he was not tortured at the stadium until the arrival, in October, of the Brazilian officials. They divided the Brazilian exiles into small groups and kept them in interrogation rooms, facing the wall for hours. The Chilean soldiers were responsible for the interrogation, but they followed the Brazilians' lead, reading from small pieces of paper with detailed instructions, which the officers handed out to their counterparts. He was in the same group as Guimarães, who was at the time identified as Pedro Paulo de Souza, the name on his fake documents.

Osni Gomes was arrested under the name of Edson Campos. He immediately recognized the officers as Brazilians because they were phenotypically different from the Chileans. "One was tall, light, almost blond, the other was a mulatto and the third one with a physical appearance sort of common but, both physically and by the way he dressed, he didn't look like any regular

Chilean citizen. And mulattos were practically nonexistent there at this time, especially among police officers and military." The three Brazilian officers put him on a pau-de-arara—a Brazilian invention until that time unknown to the Chilean military in which the prisoner hangs from his knees with hand and feet tied together—then submitted him to electric shocks all over his body, including his penis and anus. They used a machine that increased the strength of the shock as the torture progressed "until the point when it becomes impossible to speak. In the beginning, they ask, Do you want to talk? Do you want to answer? But then it becomes impossible to react. And they stop at the moment when the shock is unbearable. They checked my throat regularly, I imagine, to see how I was physically." Meanwhile, the Brazilian officers abandoned protocol and asked him directly, in Portuguese, about his connections in Brazil. A group of Chilean military personnel observed the torture. Gomes remembers hearing one of them say to the others, "You see, these guys are professionals. Pay attention to them." Gomes entered the room after breakfast and did not leave until the end of the day. "I spent the night isolated with Guimarães and he told me he knew the blond man, who had been the person who tortured him in Rio de Janeiro."[78]

Otto Brockes says that, after the beatings in the first days, he was not physically tortured again during the four months he was held prisoner at the National Stadium. However, there was no food or water, and the prisoners heard shootings all day long. He remembers that "after several days there, other Brazilians started to arrive. There was a commission inside the stadium, so we asked a man who was a major in the army, or something like that, if he knew that there were Brazilian police officers among the torturers. He said, 'No. But I will check.' The day after, he had a bullet in his head. They said that he committed suicide."[79] Brockes was interrogated several times, always by Chilean soldiers. The Brazilians stayed nearby, giving instructions to their peers. His impression was that their role was to teach, to demonstrate how to do it because the Chileans did not know the techniques. The Brazilian soldiers changed the routine of how the interrogations were conducted. Brockes remembers having seen at least three Brazilian officers, always dressed as civilians. They avoided speaking loudly or in Portuguese. Most of the time, they whispered instructions to their Chilean counterparts, as if they wanted to hide the fact that they were Brazilians. During the torture sessions, they tended to give instructions and avoid direct involvement.

When he met Osni Gomes for the first time, Brockes had the impression that the young man would be freed very soon because he was not known as an activist, and therefore had no business in prison. Gomes introduced himself with his real name. When the Brazilian officers arrived, though, everything changed. They looked at him and declared that nothing would be overlooked or forgiven. Gomes, after all, had left Brazil under a fake name, using the documents of a deceased young man. They soon noticed the discrepancy and took him to the Chilean officers. Brockes confirmed that Gomes was tortured, put in the pau-de-arara, and subjected to electric shocks by the Brazilian police in the National Stadium. He described Gomes as a very good and sweet person transfigured by the beatings. "When he left the lockup he couldn't hold up his neck. He suffered from fecal incontinence. His penis was all sore because they introduced a metal band and applied shocks. He left the pau-de-arara almost dead. Little by little, he recovered, but I don't know if he was ever able to live a normal life again. He was terribly shaken after that."[80]

Nielsen Pires also witnessed torture sessions perpetrated by three Brazilian men. According to him, besides the discretion and attempt to pass as civilians, the Brazilian agents had another particularity: they always carried files full of documents and pictures.[81] On Pires's first day at the stadium, the Chilean officers called all Brazilian prisoners to the center of the soccer field. They were roughly fifty men and ten women. The Brazilians officials approached them, opened their files, and kept comparing the faces of the prisoners to the images with disturbing patience and organization. They knew precisely who each one was. Still, the performance showed who was in control.

On Pires's second day at the stadium, the Chilean military and their Brazilian tutors divided the group of prisoners into three smaller groups. He was in the first one. Inside a room with four desks, he understood the interrogation was about to begin. "At each desk there was one officer seated wearing military attire. Right beside him there was a man wearing civilian clothes. We knew this would be the one to torture us. One of the exiles was barbarically tortured. I saw him later and he had burns all over his body."[82]

The Brazilian Ministry of Foreign Affairs ignored the calls to help the prisoners or even have them deported. There was only one request for safe-conducts for three prisoners in the stadium: Antônio Paulo Ferraz, Solange Bastos, and Ricardo de Azevedo. Ferraz was the son of a powerful Brazilian businessman, Paulo Ferraz, the owner of the oldest private shipyard of the country, Estaleiro Mauá.

Solange Bastos had arrived in Santiago only five months before the coup. On October 11, she received a letter from her mother at the National Stadium. Later she found out that her father had used his military rank to try to contact her. Her mother flew to Santiago and distributed letters to everyone who could contact her until she succeeded. Bastos states that Brazilian deputy-consul Luiz Loureiro Dias Costa "pretended to worry about the Brazilian citizens, roughly eighty, who were rotting for more than a month, arrested. We learned later that he went to the stadium on the insistence of the military attaché, who had received the request from CENIMAR, the Navy Intelligence Center, which demanded the freeing of the son of a renowned ship owner, who had been arrested with us." The three Brazilians who received the safe-conducts had one thing in common: their parents had flown to Santiago and went to the Brazilian embassy, pressuring the authorities for news of their children.[83]

The presence of Otto Brockes's family, along with his own ingenuity, also helped him escape the National Stadium. His sister and niece were in Santiago and managed to contact diplomats and other leaders. Meanwhile, he inserted documents describing torture and general treatment of prisoners in the stadium inside a sausage and sent it with a German prisoner who was being released. The Red Cross was informed and started working on his removal, worried that if the Chilean officers found out, he would be killed.

Being a foreign prisoner inside the stadium had several peculiarities. Inside that transnational authoritarian space, where the promise of socialism and democracy suddenly became a torture chamber, nationality mattered, even in practical terms. The Chilean military treated them as a separate group. In the first days, the foreign prisoners slept in shifts. While some lay down and slept, others would stand. However, having to coordinate dozens, sometimes hundreds, of people in each cell was impossible. Keeping track of who had slept and who had not was challenging, so Otto Brockes suggested they divide themselves into groups according to nationality. "There were people from all over the world, so we organized it like that. Brazilians, Argentineans, Uruguayans, they would all go together. It worked very well, and we managed to sleep well in that period."[84]

The role of the Brazilian government inside this space was not limited to torture. The country sent a plane full of products to help maintain the soccer stadium turned into an improvised prison. Journalist Pascale Bonnefoy Miralles suggests that the "generous" support of the Brazilian government started early enough to map where the most wanted political prisoners were. "It was not a coincidence that, in the first days of the Pinochet coup, more than a hundred Brazilians who were refugees in Chile under the protection of the United Nations were arrested and taken to the National Stadium."[85] The monitoring of exiles by the Brazilian Foreign Office's Intelligence Center

(CIEX) and other intelligence agencies during the Allende government made it easy for the Brazilian authorities to quickly find their enemies. The information had already been there for years. All they needed was the okay from the Chilean authorities.

"For breakfast, we had a mug of milk donated by the Americans. And after torture, if we needed medicine, they gave us samples distributed by the Brazilian Navy. We could read on the packaging 'Donated by the Brazilian Navy,'" remembers Nielsen Pires.[86] "After living in Chile, we got to know that those weapons, and even the orange neckband used by Chilean soldiers, came from Brazil," says Wilson Barbosa. "The two Hercules airplanes that arrived on September 10 brought not only Brazilian torturers to the National Stadium but also many supplies. We all knew that the United States was the father of all the supporters of the Chilean coup. But they would not get their hands dirty and that is why Brazil was important. To do the dirty work."[87]

CONCLUSION

One of the bravest and brightest men I have ever met was afraid to talk to me. I spent months sending messages, waiting for answers, but received only questions in return. Finally, he agreed to speak on one condition: I would have to be accompanied. Intrigued by the unusual request, my husband-turned-research-assistant joined me, and there we were on a foggy afternoon in São Paulo, inside a small building, speaking in hushed tones. Only over the course of our more than five-hour interview did I realize the reason: a request from a scholar with an Anglo-American surname, based in New York, was suspicious.

For those who have never gone through the trauma of torture and the loss of comrades at the hands of a repressive state, such caution can seem like an overreaction. However, this was someone who experienced two coups d'état and their full consequences, including his expulsion from two countries that he had once called home: first, during the 1964 military takeover in Brazil, and later as an enemy of the Chilean dictatorship installed in 1973. Both violent regimes had the support of the most powerful country in the world.

His trauma, however, was not collective or intergenerational. Both Chile and Brazil are still grappling with the full extent of the dictatorships' impact. Without constructing a shared memory of that period, its legacy lingers—like a ghost, unseen but ever-present. In all democratic elections in the two countries, the alignment with the dictatorship was crucial to defining the candidates. On December 19, 2021, Chileans went to the polls in record numbers to elect Gabriel Boric president. The turnout reflected a rejection of Augusto Pinochet's policies. Boric's adversary was José Antonio Kast, a far-right former lawmaker who sought to portray Boric as a radical communist and channeled the dictator's policies throughout the campaign.

Three years earlier, in Brazil, far-right former member of Congress Jair Bolsonaro had defeated Workers' Party candidate Fernando Haddad with a platform chillingly close to the one advocated at the Marches of the Family with God for Freedom, including anticommunism. A few years later, both countries faced shifts in these events. In 2022, Chileans massively rejected a new constitution, which would have replaced the one designed during Pinochet's rule.[1] In May 2023, Kast's far-right Republican Party secured twenty-two seats in the Chilean fifty-one-member assembly. Other right-wing parties won another eleven seats, making it virtually impossible for the Chilean Left to have a say in the writing of Chile's new constitution.[2]

In Brazil, meanwhile, Luís Inácio Lula da Silva put an end to Bolsonaro's reelection dreams but faced an irate mob of his supporters who attacked public buildings in the capital of Brasília, similar to what had happened in the United States on January 6, 2021.[3] All these campaigns had a similar questioning undertone: Did voters approve or not of the dictatorial regime and its policies? These tides show how fraught the relationship of the two countries with authoritarianism still is and how the memory of violence faded generation after generation.

Less than a month after the coup d'état in Chile, in 1973, when Gabriel García Márquez was still celebrating the popularity gained with his receipt of the Neustadt International Prize for Literature, the Colombian writer accused Brazil of being dangerous to all South American countries and charged it with orchestrating the overthrow of Salvador Allende in Chile, Juan José Torres in Bolivia, and the dissolution of Congress by Juan María Bordaberry in Uruguay. García Márquez warned that Argentina would be the next victim of the Brazilian dictatorship, united with other imperialist forces.[4]

He was right. The Brazilian dictatorial model went beyond its frontiers, arriving at other countries of the Southern Cone. The now public telegrams and reports from CIEX and from embassies attest to the fact that the proximity between Brazilian and Chilean right-wing groups, the military, and the US government was much closer than scholars have demonstrated so far. They also evidence that Brazil acted as an independent power that sought to interfere in the neighborhood by planting spies, sending weapons and torturers, and exporting its tactics to influence public opinion. Finally, they underline that the Brazilian dictatorship was a civilian-military one, in which diplomats played a central role.

The Brazilian Ministry of Foreign Affairs operated inside Chile with intelligence agents infiltrated among exiles. Brazilian ambassador Antônio Cândido da Câmara Canto was a close friend of most of the Chilean military personnel who became leaders during the dictatorship. The Brazilian regime not only inspired the Chilean but also fomented its existence with a constant interchange of information, strategies, ideas, military supplies, and even workers. Despite denunciations by exiles and scholars, the Brazilian government denied its participation in the Chilean coup and the Pinochet regime for years. In September 2023, in light of the fiftieth anniversary of the coup in Chile, then–Brazilian minister of justice Flávio Dino acknowledged the Brazilian government's responsibility for the Chilean coup and offered apologies for its support of Pinochet. A plaque with the names of the six Brazilians killed in Chile was unveiled in the Brazilian embassy in Santiago.[5]

Four years after the Chilean coup, Brazilian officers announced to their superiors the end of the resistance of the leftist groups in Chile. Now, they stated, the armed forces needed to implement the training of its personnel for the "upcoming antisubversive struggle. Such orientation would require an enormous effort, since the Chilean military needed an entirely new system of intelligence and specific training to confront urban guerrillas."[6] They acknowledged the presence in the government of the Chicago Boys, a group "proposing conservative economic guidelines." After the coup, Brazilian agents also kept track of Chilean exiles and their supposed attempts to remove Augusto Pinochet.[7]

The interventions of the United States and Brazil to create an unsustainable situation in Chile and destabilize the country's leftist movements were a proto–Operation Condor interaction that set the stage for transnational violence.[8] Before the election of Salvador Allende as president of Chile, Brazil, the United States, the Chilean military, and right-wing groups began to shape a structure that the South American dictatorships of Argentina, Bolivia, Brazil, Chile, Paraguay, and Uruguay would establish later, during the "Condor years."[9] They used political repression, propaganda, and intelligence operations to intimidate the opposition and weaken the connections among leftist organizations all over the Southern Cone.[10]

On September 12, 1973, the Brazilian Ministry of Foreign Affairs received the first telegram from Câmara Canto announcing the establishment of the military junta. It also described Allende's suicide, and the imposed curfew to "protect the population from suicidal extremist groups that are not yet disarmed."[11] He went on to write a series of memorandums, updating the situation according to what he had gathered from TV shows and newspapers. He wryly celebrated the fire in the office of "extreme leftist" newspaper *Puro Chile*, set "by a group of carabineros," stating that he was "watching from a box seat, since the mentioned paper, which has insulted the Brazilian government for so long, is based in front of our embassy."[12]

The embassy's lines of communication with Brasília were impaired in the coup's immediate aftermath. To let the government know they were safe, staff and diplomats looked for help from the US embassy, which first informed the US Department of State via radio. Later, the State Department sent the dispatch to the Brazilian embassy in Washington.[13] On September 14, when communications were still problematic in the country, the diplomat did a personal favor for Jorge Fontaine, vice president of the Federation of Chilean Industry (SOFOFA) and president of the Chilean Confederation of Production and Commerce. Canto asked the staff at the Ministry of Foreign Affairs in Brasília to send a telegram to Fontaine's daughter, who lived in the United States, attesting that the entire family was "happy and very well." In the message, the Brazilian ambassador justified the urgency of the favor, stating that Fontaine was his "personal friend, besides being anticommunist."[14]

Câmara Canto also asked the ministry to inform the families of a small number of Brazilians living in Santiago that they were protected from harm. All of them were students, friends, or staff members of the embassy. No political exile was mentioned. While most of the other embassies in Chile were working to protect their own citizens, the Brazilian ambassador left his compatriots helpless. Journalist Dorrit Harazim arrived in Santiago forty-eight hours before the coup to participate in an international seminar of the Economic Commission for Latin America and the Caribbean (ECLAC). She called the ambassador a few hours after the bombing of La Moneda asking him to inform the magazine for which she worked, *Veja*, that she was out of harm's way. "Câmara Canto heard everything, proclaimed that he would send *Veja* a message, asked me what the scene looked like (at La Moneda) from the perspective of the guests at Hotel Carrera, and hung up in a jovial tone, saying, 'We won, it's all in order.'"[15]

While the US government decided to maintain a public facade of noninvolvement with the Chilean coup d'état—only recognizing the military government on September 24—Brazil was the first country to officially support the new regime. It was a fast but thorough negotiation. First, the Chilean authorities demonstrated the need for the endorsement. A day after the coup, Augusto Pinochet sent a car to pick up military attaché Walter Mesquita de Siqueira and told him that he would appreciate it if Brazil became the first country to officially support his government. Ambassador Câmara Canto reinforced this proposal in a series of telegrams. The first, from September 12, stated that an endorsement was in Brazil's "maximum interest." A second telegram sent the same day suggested that it would be "very well perceived by the military junta and by the people." Finally, the minister of foreign affairs, Mário Gibson Barbosa, said the Brazilian government was willing to give the junta a green light as long as it followed some "minimal formalities."[16] The requirements were that the Chilean authorities make a public statement affirming that they controlled the entire territory, listing the names of members of the cabinet—even if they were temporary employees—and guaranteeing that they would respect international commitments. That night, in a televised pronouncement, these demands were fulfilled.

On the morning of September 13, Raúl Rettig, the Chilean ambassador to Brazil under Salvador Allende, resigned. That night, when the Brazilian Ministry of Foreign Affairs was already closed to its general staff and visitors, a group of Chilean diplomats went to Itamaraty.[17] From São Paulo, President Emílio Garrastazu Médici made a call ordering that Brazil become the first country to officially support the junta, and that it send "twenty tons of medicine" to Santiago.[18]

The United States followed the actions of its partner with relief. On that same September 13, William J. Jorden of the National Security Council staff told Henry Kissinger that Washington and Brasília could coordinate multiple forms of support for the newly installed dictatorship. After talking to Marcos Cortes, special assistant to Foreign Minister Barbosa, he concluded that it was clear that Brazil was acting to support Chile, as if it already anticipated requests for assistance, including "help in restoring essential services and in providing a better food supply for the Chilean people." They expected similar requests to be addressed to the United States. And he concluded, "The Brazilians are disposed to honor such a request one way or another."[19]

Most of the documents about the days following the coup available at the Central Archives of the Brazilian Ministry of Foreign Affairs, the Itamaraty, have been redacted and are now almost entirely illegible. But phrases such as "wipe communism out" can still be read.[20] In one telegram, from September 13, it is possible to grasp the influence of Câmara Canto in its first and only readable phrase: "I received from the Commander-in-chief of the Air Force and member of the military junta." Later, that same morning, in a less redacted document, Câmara Canto transcribed a letter from the new Chilean minister of foreign affairs, Ismael Huerta, informing the Brazilian government of the structure of the military junta that, according to him, "exercises absolute control over the national territory" and desires to keep "the best relation of friendship" with the Brazilian government.[21]

The Brazilian ambassador's access to privileged information is also clear in another telegram in which he communicates to the Division of Southern America in the Ministry of Foreign Affairs that "at this very moment I was informed that, possibly this afternoon, ambassador [Mario García] Inchaust-egui and his collaborators will board back to Cuba."[22] A day later, he contin-ued, "The chief of staff of the minister of foreign affairs confirmed that the Cuban ambassador, his staff, and a group of undesirable Cubans, have left the country yesterday in an airplane of the 'Cubana de Aviación.' . . . Out of respect for Sweden, which oversees the Cuban interests in this country, the embassy was not yet searched. It is a matter of days."[23]

The Swedish embassy became a shelter for hundreds of refugees. Ambas-sador Harald Edelstam was nicknamed "the Raoul Wallenberg of the 1970s" after helping the Cuban delegation, dozens of Uruguayan and Bolivians, and over 1,000 Chileans escape the Pinochet dictatorship.[24] His actions, however, went beyond simply offering shelter.[25] He influenced other European lead-ers to do the same and to be flexible in their interpretations of the Treaty of Caracas, which determines the rules for asylum and safe-conduct passes for victims of political upheaval.[26] In December 1973, he was declared persona non grata and expelled from Chile.

Nielsen Pires is still grateful for Edelstam's intervention. With the support of the French, Swiss, and Italian embassies, the Swedish ambassador created an improvised refuge inside a cloister for Belgian nuns. Pires describes the place as interminable rows of mattresses. They covered the floor of every room, the eatery, and even the hallways. The nuns were still there, living in a specific and greatly reduced area, while foreigners occupied most of the space. "There was a big room that was probably the eatery where we slept on the floor with thin mattresses and blankets, one beside the other." Despite the new challenges, the cloister was not comparable to the National Stadium. "In the stadium, there were machine guns in front of you, held by kids who were seventeen, eighteen years old, who could shoot if they got scared."[27] So-lange Bastos had a similar impression. She stated that in comparison to the treatment she received in prison in Brazil, the Chileans looked like amateurs. The soldiers had just arrived from smaller cities to work in the stadium. In the first days after the coup, some seemed to be as scared as the prisoners.[28] "The soldiers were young men, mostly of rural origin, serving in the army. They didn't know anything; they weren't part of the repressive forces."[29]

Four South American dictators reunite in Brasília during the inauguration of Ernesto Geisel on March 15, 1974. *Left to right:* Hugo Banzer (Bolivia), Juan María Bordaberry (Uruguay), Geisel (Brazil), and Augusto Pinochet (Chile). *Source: Centro de Pesquisa e Documentação de História Contemporânea do Brasil / Fundação Getulio Vargas.*

Chilean soldiers and authorities, however, quickly learned the lessons in brutality. The National Stadium became the most infamous of the dictatorship's torture centers. And in March 1974, a grateful Pinochet chose the inauguration of President Ernesto Geisel for his first international trip. There, he met with other Southern Cone dictators, Hugo Banzer of Bolivia and Juan María Bordaberry of Uruguay. As his government gained strength, Brazilian exiles looked for shelter in other countries and the activities of CIEX became less and less necessary. The monitoring of political enemies moved on to other countries and practically disappeared from Chile.

Still, the years of being constantly watched caused psychological traumas that continue today. Otto Brockes began to tell me the story of Osni Geraldo Gomes without mentioning his name. When I asked whom he was talking about, he said he did not remember the name of the person. Only when I directly asked if he was talking about Osni did he confirm and began to tell the full story. The same impulse and habit of protecting his peers that he felt in the 1970s, he demonstrated again. Osni Gomes states that the torture

Brazilian agents perpetrated against him at the National Stadium is still part of his life. "My capacity for physical and psychological adaptation was profoundly affected. And I have been dealing for more than forty years with periods of psychic and emotional instability. This situation prevented me from having stable professional development and stained my entire life. Only today, after all this time, has it been possible for me to rethink my story with enough balance to withhold my indignation, anger, and hate without being completely overtaken by these feelings."[30]

Differently from most of the exiles who tried to start new lives in other countries, Brockes did not settle down after the Chilean coup. First, he moved to Germany, with the intention of spending only a few months while planning his clandestine return to Brazil. However, when he read the news about the Carnation Revolution in April 1974, he traveled to Portugal to join the movement against the dictator António Salazar and the Estado Novo. He then enlisted to finally fulfill his dream to work as a volunteer doctor. In Angola, where he helped the proindependence forces, he said, "I worked nonstop. I was alone in charge of an entire hospital in the northern area. My ears were swollen by the repetition of the movement of putting the stethoscope in and out." He worked from early in the morning until late at night, treating all kinds of diseases, from tuberculosis to leprosy. When the Cuban army arrived to support Angola's independence, he joined them as a doctor and provided logistical support. "At that point I was just a doctor, trying to help."[31] Brockes was only able to return to Brazil after the Amnesty Law of 1979, which exempted exiles as well as torturers from any crimes committed during the dictatorship.

For René-Louis de Carvalho, exile in Chile shifted his focus from ending the Brazilian dictatorship to a Latin American project. Following the steps of his father, Apolônio de Carvalho, who fought against fascism in Brazil, Spain, and France, he viewed the fight as universal. "In Algeria, I had a lot of contact with the leadership of the African Liberation Movement, particularly the Portuguese-speaking ones. I met Agostinho Neto, Angola's first president. So, it was like I was finally an internationalist, you know? When I returned to France, after the coup in Chile, solidarity was internationalist, although it was very focused on Latin America. I know there was an internationalist idea, but the main focus was Latin America."[32]

Most of the foreigners who survived the National Stadium were transferred to UN camps or embassies in Chile. A delegation from Amnesty International visited the stadium on November 7, 1973, and confirmed that only twenty foreigners were still imprisoned there. However, there were groups detained in other parts of the country. The embassies of Argentina, Mexico, Venezuela, Ecuador, Peru, Panama, and many European countries continued to give shelter to exiles and Chileans.

Meanwhile, the Brazilian embassy closed its doors to political enemies of the Chilean regime, including Brazilian citizens. Câmara Canto nevertheless continued tracking the actions of other ambassadors. On September 14, he wrote to the Ministry of Foreign Affairs about the Mexican embassy's offering shelter to sixty people, including the widow and grandsons of Salvador Allende.[33] Reinaldo Guarany, Maria Auxiliadora Barcelos, Wilson Barbosa, and other Brazilian exiles took the same route. Barbosa recalls that a Mexican government plane took them to Mexico City, but upon their arrival, an agent told him and his wife that they needed to find another country. For Barbosa, it was a disappointment and a confirmation that Mexican president Luis Echeverría "was a CIA agent who only declared that he had a commitment with Allende as a façade, so he would give asylum to his family and guarantee transit to those whom Allende had accepted in Chile."[34] But the Mexican police and government made it clear that they could not stay there.[35] They spent a month in Mexico and were ordered to leave. "I was simply social garbage. That was when I formed an understanding of the nature of Latin America. This category so many talk about. I understood what the problem was." Barbosa and his wife boarded a plane to Sweden. While they waited, a Mexican police officer who conducted them to the airplane kept telling Barbosa what a coward he was for flying to Europe instead of going back to Brazil and fighting the dictatorship. "The humiliation of an exile has no limits—oh, the things you have to hear and how much you have to be degraded to remain alive!"[36]

Nancy Mangabeira Unger, a Brazilian and US citizen, experienced the lack of support from both nations. In July 1970, Unger was sleeping in her house in Brazil when around twenty soldiers invaded it, shooting. She was shot in the lungs, liver, ribs, and hand, losing her right thumb.[37] Her mother contacted the US embassy, sent letters to Senator Edward Kennedy, and asked Brazilian politicians for help.[38] But Nancy was arrested and only released as one of the seventy prisoners exchanged by the Swiss ambassador to Brazil. After the 1973 coup, she did not find help in either the Brazilian or the US embassy in Santiago.

Several of the foreigners residing in Santiago started looking for political asylum in embassies a few hours after the first bombs. For the enemies of the new regime, getting a safe-conduct and leaving the country was the best hope for survival. However, although the Chilean government had signed the American Convention of Human Rights in 1969, which states that "every person has the right to seek and be granted asylum in a foreign territory, in accordance with the legislation of the state and international conventions, in the event that he is being pursued for political offenses or related crimes," the junta refused safe-conducts for approximately 500 politicians. It claimed that they had committed common crimes or participated in Plan Zeta, a supposed scheme by the Allende administration to impose a Marxist government.[39] Plan Zeta was, according to the junta, the main reason why the coup was an emergency.[40] Many ambassadors, including Mexico's, were able to negotiate safe-conducts in return for resuming commercial and diplomatic ties with Chile. Neither the United States nor Brazil was willing to negotiate on those terms.

After the coup, Maria do Carmo Brito tried to no avail to contact her Chilean friends and offer help in the fight against the military. She discovered that the lack of responses was because she had become a burden as soon as Chilean radio stations announced that all foreigners should voluntarily present themselves to the authorities. More than a week after the coup, she decided to ask for asylum, but at this point the Mexican and Argentine embassies were packed. She finally found shelter at the Embassy of Panama, located in a small apartment in a four-story building.[41]

Many Brazilians went to the same location, where there were already several Uruguayans and Chileans. The embassy consisted of a living room, three small bedrooms, two bathrooms, a kitchen, and an external area visible from all the other apartments. Every day, increasing numbers of people arrived. Brito estimates that over 200 people shared that same space. It was so crowded that when her son became ill with diarrhea and vomiting, the solution was to grab him, naked and dirty, and place him in the care of one of the neighbors. The ambassador's office became an improvised infirmary, and he did not like the changes. "As the days passed, he started making more and more aggressive speeches, menacing to remove the Panamanian flag and leave the entire group with no diplomatic protection."[42] The exiles slept, ate, smoked, and went to the restrooms in shifts.

When the situation became unsustainable, one of the Brazilian exiles suggested transferring the embassy to his house, which was much more spacious than the apartment. Theotônio dos Santos and his then wife, renowned political scientist and sociologist Vânia Bambirra, had been in Chile since 1965 with their two children. They lived in an old house that suddenly had a Panamanian flag planted in the front yard. According to Brito, "271 people left the apartment and 273 arrived at the new address. Don't ask me how.

I have no idea. But that is what happened." At night, Brazilians and Uruguayans got together to play the guitar, sing, and tell jokes. In the background, they could hear bombs. According to Brito, in these homely moments she felt all the weight of cultural differences and of having seen a similar scenario before. For the Chileans, the singing seemed like disrespect, as if Brazilians did not care for their tragedy. "For us, it was another defeat. Starting all over again. Horrible. But the songs were like an exorcism. They helped."[43] In August 1974, the house was taken over by the National Intelligence Directorate and turned into a detention and torture center.

Vera Vital Brasil remembers hearing stories about the days in that house. She also heard about the terrors of the coup in Chile. Nevertheless, she decided to stay. With a steady job and many Chilean friends, she moved to a house in Macul, in Greater Santiago, and remained there until 1976, having witnessed the brutality of the Pinochet regime and experienced a constant "feeling of fear in the air."[44] However, as soon as she found out that she was found not guilty in a Brazilian court, she returned home.

Eliete Ferrer learned to call Sweden home after the trauma in Chile. She learned the language, taught it for years, made friends, and decided to make the most of her life in the new country. "In Sweden, I found everything I could ask from a country. If I am breathing today, it was due to Harald Edelstam and Olof Palme's intervention. I promised to never go back to Chile and I never did. But as much as I told everyone I hated Brazil, I always thought of coming back. As soon as the Amnesty Law started and I could return, I did."[45]

So did most exiles. Their transnational experience was essential for the subsequent fight for democratization in Brazil. They brought ideas of equality that flourished in the late 1960s and early 1970s in the countries they had to call home after being expelled from Brazil. In France, England, Italy, Sweden, and other places, they joined movements in defense of human rights. In Brazil, they organized and conducted demonstrations against the dictatorship and in defense of civil rights, including the movement Diretas Já, which demanded universal suffrage. Many of the exiles became politicians, including former president Fernando Henrique Cardoso, former presidential candidate and São Paulo governor José Serra, and federal representative Fernando Gabeira. Others, such as Chico Buarque, Caetano Veloso, and Gilberto Gil, became symbols of the democratization and are among the greatest stars of Brazilian music.

Over half a century after the 1973 coup in Chile, it is still hard to determine the number of victims of the imposed government. The Rettig Commission stated in its report of 1991 that 2,296 people were killed, including almost 1,000 cases of disappearances.[46] Between 2003 and 2005, the Valech Commission concluded that 28,459 people were arrested and that most of them had also been victims of torture.[47] Five years later the commission was reopened, and this time settled the number of people killed between 1973 and 1990. Survivors stand at 38,254.[48] Beyond colluding to support authoritarianism, Brazil and Chile have similarities in how they punished (or did not punish) perpetrators of crimes during their civilian-military dictatorships. In 1979, Brazilians approved the Amnesty Law, which guaranteed impunity for torturers and murderers. In Chile, the Amnesty Decree Law, passed in 1978, absolved human rights violators between September 11, 1973, and March 10, 1978, from any criminal responsibility.

Sometimes investigating South America's history feels like reading a book for the second time. Many things appear to be mere repetitions; others seem like brand new passages. One can easily identify political trends in the region, but it is difficult to demonstrate to what extent they are due to mutual influence. In the case of the dictatorships from the 1960s to the 1990s, the "coincidence" of having all the countries experiencing similar regimes resulted from external influence as well as a broad and long regional collaboration to fight against common enemies. The cooperation was not only military but also relied on diplomats and civilians.

This book is an attempt to listen to what exiles have been saying for decades and to contribute to broadening the memory of human rights violations in the region. May greater knowledge of the scope of the atrocities committed by the Brazilian regime, beyond the national sphere, add to the consolidation of democracy in the region.

NOTES

ABBREVIATIONS

ACI-SERE Arquivo Central do Itamaraty, Secretaria de Estado das
          Relações Exteriores, Brasília
AGH-MRE   Archivo General Histórico del Ministerio de Relaciones
          Exteriores de Chile
ANB-B   Arquivo Nacional do Brasil, Brasília
ANB-RJ   Arquivo Nacional do Brasil, Rio de Janeiro
CIEX   Brazilian Foreign Office's Intelligence Center
          (Centro de Informações do Exterior)
CNV   Comissão Nacional da Verdade
CPDOC   Centro de Pesquisa e Documentação, Fundação Getúlio Vargas
EMFA   General Staff of the Armed Forces
GWU   National Security Archives, George Washington University

INTRODUCTION

1. Some of the Brazilian exiles published these accusations in their memoirs. See Sirkis, *Roleta*; and Gabeira, *O que é isso*.

2. One of the first works on the US support was Armando Uribe's *The Black Book*. The poet and writer, who served as Chile's ambassador to China during the Allende government, focused on the US role and mentioned the propaganda against the Popular Unity government as inspired by what the United States had done against João Goulart in Brazil in the early 1960s (148). In 1982, the national security adviser at the time of the Chilean coup, Henry Kissinger, dedicated an entire chapter of his book to the fall of Salvador Allende, attesting that "contrary to anti-American propaganda around the world and revisionist history in the United States, our government had nothing to do with planning his overthrow

and no involvement with the plotters." See Kissinger, *Years of Upheaval*, 374. Propelled by the Church Committee, investigations of the terrors of the Pinochet regime emerged in the late 1970s and early 1980s, including Herman, *Real Terror*; Valenzuela, *Political Brokers*; and Muñoz, Tulchin, and Becker, *Latin American Nations*, among many others. The 2000s saw a broader wave of scholarship on the US role, including Crandall, *United States and Latin America*; Sikkink, *Mixed Signals*; Bandeira, *Fórmula para o caos*; Klein, *Shock Doctrine*; McSherry, *Predatory States*; Haslam, *Nixon Administration*; Guardiola-Rivera, *Story of a Death*; Qureshi, *Nixon, Kissinger, and Allende*; and Stern, *Remembering Pinochet's Chile*.

3. A series of eight cables known as Korrygrams reveals how the United States reacted to Allende's election and worked to prevent his inauguration. Then–US ambassador to Chile Edward Korry wrote the documents, which are available at the George Washington University National Security Archive, Electronic Briefing Book 8, https://nsarchive2.gwu .edu/NSAEBB/NSAEBB8/docs/doc18.pdf.

4. Salvador Allende's last speech has been printed and reproduced in multiple sources. His emotional farewell to the Chilean people was broadcast in its entirety from La Moneda Palace by Radio Magallanes. Allende states that the moment can serve as a lesson: "Foreign capital, imperialism, together with reaction, created the climate in which the armed forces broke with their tradition, the tradition taught by General Schneider and reaffirmed by Commander Araya, victims of the same social sector who today are hoping, with foreign assistance, to reconquer power to continue defending their profits and their privileges [El capital foráneo, el imperialismo, unido a la reacción, creó el clima para que las Fuerzas Armadas rompieran su tradición, la que les enseñara Schneider y que reafirmara el comandante Araya, víctimas del mismo sector social que hoy estará en sus casas, esperando con mano ajena reconquistar el poder para seguir defendiendo sus granjerías y sus privilegios]." All translations in this book are by me unless otherwise indicated.

5. Among the most recent works that look at the leftist movements' criticisms of Allende and the internal fragilization of the Left are Fermandois, *La revolución inconclusa*; Núñez M., *El gran desencuentro*; and Gaudichaud, *Chile*.

6. Rollemberg, *Exílio*. Some place France as the top country to receive exiles from Brazil. Because of the lack of reliable numbers, it is impossible to make objective comparisons between countries, but it is clear that the wave of exiles to Chile increased after Institutional Act no. 5, in 1968. For an example that identifies France as the top destination of exiles, see Vitor Amorim de Angelo, "Exílio: Intelectuais saíram do Brasil durante a ditadura," *UOL*, March 7, 2014, https://educacao.uol.com.br/disciplinas/historia-brasil /exilio-intelectuais-sairam-do-brasil-durante-a-ditadura.htm.

7. "Militares e policiais brasileiros torturaram presos no Estádio Nacional do Chile," April 15, 2014, CNV, http://cnv.memoriasreveladas.gov.br/outros-destaques/470-militares -e-policiais-brasileiros-torturaram-presos-no-estadio-nacional-do-chile.html.

8. Bambirra's *El capitalismo dependiente latinoamericano* was published after she left Chile and went into exile in Mexico.

9. Carvalho, "Paulo Freire"; Freire, *Pedagogy of the Oppressed*.

10. Cardoso and Faletto, *Dependência e desenvolvimento*.

11. Rollemberg, *Exílio*, 97–98.

12. Document ACM pm 1964.04.09, 09/04/1964–04/1975, microfilm 1, fot. 619–29, CPDOC; Comissão Especial sobre Mortos e Desaparecidos Políticos, *Direito à memória*, 89.

13. Kushnir, *Cães de guarda*.

14. Brasil, "Presidência da República, Casa Civil, Subchefia para Assuntos Jurídicos, Ato Institucional no. 5, de 13 de dezembro de 1968," www.planalto.gov.br//CCIVIL_03 /AIT/ait-05-68.htm.

15. Comissão Especial sobre Mortos e Desaparecidos Políticos, *Direito à memória*, 89.

16. Rollemberg, *Exílio*, 49–50.

17. Salvador Allende introduced his Chilean Path to Socialism in a speech to Congress on May 21, 1971. See Allende, *La vía chilena*.

18. Interview with Otto Brockes by the author, video recording, Goiás, Brazil, July 15, 2014.

19. Telegram, September 11, 1973, ACI-SERE.

20. Telegram, DMP/600 (B39) (571), September 13, 1973, ACI-SERE.

21. CIEX, report no. 487/73, BRAN, BSB, IE 11.3, p. 28/121, October 5, 1973, ANB-B.

22. CIEX, report no. 522/73, II, no. 671-90/91, October 15, 1973, ANB-B.

23. "Observações da realidade chilena feitas na visita do Comandante do Estado-Maior da Marinha, 1972 a 1980," report no. 600 (B39), ANB-B. The information was confirmed by Chilean businessman Orlando Sáenz Rojas. Interview with Orlando Sáenz Rojas by the author, audio recording, Santiago, December 2, 2021.

24. Amnesty International, *Chile*, 64. Exile Nielsen Pires remembers seeing the name of the Brazilian government on the label of the medicine he received at the National Stadium. Interview with Nielsen Pires by the author, video recording, São Paulo, July 11, 2014.

25. Júnia Gama, "Ditadura forneceu armas para a repressão no Chile," *O Globo*, June 30, 2012, https://oglobo.globo.com/politica/ditadura-forneceu-armas-para-repressao -no-chile-5361897.

26. Some works that encompass relations between Brazil and Chile during the dictatorial period focus on the study of exiles. Historian Denise Rollemberg devoted her seminal book to such research. Historian Teresa Cristina Schneider Marques leaned into the same subject. There are also many publications whose authors are themselves exiles. Their scope is limited to individual life stories and to the political situation in each country, without necessarily investigating its transnational or diplomatic nature. See Rollemberg, *Exílio*; Marques, "Lembranças do exílio"; Costa et al., *Memórias das mulheres*; and Cavalcanti, Celso, and Ramos, *Memórias do exílio*.

27. Davis, *Last Two Years*, 331, 333.

28. The clandestine nature of Operation Condor makes it impossible to ascertain the precise number of its victims. Slack, "Operation Condor"; Bevins, *Jakarta Method*, 266–67.

29. The periodization of Operation Condor is still a source of discussion among scholars. John Dinges considers 1973–80 to be the "Condor Years." Edward S. Herman refers to 1976, when "Argentina, Bolivia, Brazil, Chile, Paraguay and Uruguay entered into a system for the joint monitoring and assassinating of dissident refugees in member countries." Greg Grandin mentions the CIA support for Condor "throughout the 1980s." However, taking into consideration J. Patrice McSherry's explanation of the three levels of the operation, one can notice that a similar project started much earlier, with the connections between Brazil, the United States, and the Chilean military, right after the election of Salvador Allende. The first consisted of the "cooperation among military intelligence services, to coordinate political surveillance of targeted dissidents and exchange of intelligence

information." The second was covert action, and the third, known as "Phase III," was the murdering of enemies of the dictatorial governments, especially political leaders. See Dinges, *Condor Years*, 1; Herman, *Real Terror*, 70; Grandin, *Last Colonial Massacre*, 75; and McSherry, *Predatory States*, 4–5.

30. According to the Church Committee, "The Central Intelligence Agency spent three million dollars in an effort to influence the outcome of the 1964 Chilean presidential elections. Eight million dollars was spent, covertly, in the three years between 1970 and the military coup in September 1973, with over three million dollars expended in fiscal year 1972 alone." See US Senate, *Covert Action in Chile*, 1.

31. A decade ago, scholars opened an avenue to a less North-South reading of the Cold War in South America, notably Harmer, *Allende's Chile*. See also Grandin, *Last Colonial Massacre*; and Brands, *Latin America's Cold War*. More recent works with a similar perspective are Field, Krepp, and Pettinà, *Latin America*; Keller, *Mexico's Cold War*; and Marchesi, *Latin America's Radical Left*. Historians Olivier Compagnon and Caroline Moine advocated for a global history of the Chilean September 11, pointing to the urgency of moving beyond Chile's borders to investigate the coup and the subsequent Augusto Pinochet regime. See Compagnon and Moine, "Pour une histoire globale."

32. After years of work to declassify documents attesting to the role of the United States in the Chilean coup, new scholarship on the topic emerged. See Kornbluh, "Declassifying U.S. Intervention," 36–42; and Kornbluh, *Pinochet File*. See also Herman, *Real Terror*; Muñoz, Tulchin, and Becker, *Latin American Nations*; Cockcroft, *Neighbors in Turmoil*; Tulchin and Varas, *From Dictatorship to Democracy*; and Verdugo, *Interferencia secreta*.

33. Journalist Roberto Simon starts his investigation at the time of the election of Salvador Allende, in 1970. Alessandra Beber Castilho's MA thesis begins earlier, in 1968. See Simon, *O Brasil*; and Castilho, "Diplomacia."

34. "Ata da trigésima nona sessão do Conselho de Segurança Nacional," October 24, 1966, no. 85, Conselho de Segurança Nacional, ANB-B.

35. Oliveira, "Os primórdios."

36. Gonzalo Monsálvez Araneda, "Discurso y legitimidad."

37. "Comemoração do sete de setembro," September 8, 1973, telegram 641.7 (148), ACI-SERE.

38. For more on this debate, see Reis, "Ditadura, anistia e reconciliação"; Melo, "Ditadura civil-militar'?"; and Pagliarini, "De Onde?"

39. Penna Filho, "O Itamaraty nos anos."

40. Magalhães, "A lógica da suspeição."

41. Marques, "Militância política," 112.

42. Pio Corrêa, *O mundo*.

43. Aldo Marchesi states that "it is clear that several different aspects of US bilateral relations with Mexico, Peru, and, in particular, Brazil were strongly influenced by the policies implemented by Washington for Allende's Chile." Furthermore, "the Inter-American system shaped the transnational development of political culture." Marchesi, *Latin America's Radical Left*, 11.

44. Between the late 1960s and mid-1970s, the dictatorship destroyed at least thirty-nine secret reports produced by the Brazilian Army and the General Staff of the Armed Forces. In addition, nearly 19,400 documents from the SNI were reduced to ashes. It is impossible to determine exactly what was lost, but there are a few clues. According to the

"terms of destruction," the punishment of the poet Vinícius de Moraes by the Ministry of Foreign Affairs and the medical record of the Catholic archbishop Dom Hélder Câmara are among the papers burned in 1981, during the government of João Baptista Figueiredo (1979–85). See Rubens Valente, "Ditadura destruiu mais de 19 mil documentos secretos," *Folha de S. Paulo*, July 2, 2012, https://www1.folha.uol.com.br/fsp/poder/52189-ditadura-destruiu-mais-de-19-mil-documentos-secretos.shtml.

45. For more on the characteristics of the Brazilian military, see Castro, *O espírito militar*.

46. "Meeting with President Emílio Garrastazu Médici of Brazil on Thursday, December 9, 1971, at 10:00 a.m., in the President's Office, the White House," White House memorandum, GWU, https://nsarchive.gwu.edu/document/2075-04.

47. Soares, dal Maso Jardim, and Hermont, "Lei de Acesso."

48. The commission has made documents, pictures, and interviews available at http://cnv.memoriasreveladas.gov.br/ (accessed October 5, 2021).

49. Argentina established its Comisión Nacional sobre la Desaparición de Personas (National Commission on the Disappearance of Persons) in 1983; in Chile, President Patricio Aylwin signed Decree 355 on April 24, 1990, creating the Comisión Nacional de Verdad y Reconciliación (National Truth and Reconciliation Commission). Ecuador, Uruguay, Peru, and Panama followed suit. See Cuya, "Las comisiones."

50. Instituto Nacional de Derechos Humanos, *Informe de la Comisión Nacional de Verdad y Reconciliación (Informe Rettig)*, https://bibliotecadigital.indh.cl/items/edb83a4d-9121-48ee-8e66-09fe31e926fe.

51. The Aviation Information Service (Serviço de Informações da Aeronáutica) was later renamed the Aviation Security Information Center (Centro de Informações de Segurança da Aeronáutica), the Aviation Security Information Service (Serviço de Informações de Segurança da Aeronáutica), and finally the Aviation Information Center (Centro de Informações da Aeronáutica). Journalist Lucas Figueiredo unearthed some of these documents. See Figueiredo, *Lugar nenhum*. An earlier contribution to the declassification of these documents is Santos, *Desarquivando a ditadura*.

52. Few books have focused on the relations between Chile and Brazil with other regimes. Tanya Harmer argues that the Chilean coup was part of an inter-American Cold War shaped by disputes between Cuba, Chile, the United States, and Brazil. Harmer's deep archival research offered a plethora of new hypotheses to explain the extent of US support for the Chilean coup. A decade later, journalist Roberto Simon argued that the Brazilian support had been fundamental to the fall of Allende, focusing on the Allende administration and the Operation Condor years. See Harmer, *Allende's Chile*; and Simon, *O Brasil*.

53. Many scholars have described the influence of the United States in the Brazilian coup. See Parker, *1964*; Bandeira, *Brasil—Estados Unidos*; and Fico, *O grande irmão*.

54. Black, *United States Penetration of Brazil*, xiii.

55. Gillmore, "Bolivia."

56. Hermann, "Reformas," 82.

57. Spektor, *Kissinger*, 45.

58. Fermandois, *La revolución inconclusa*, 448.

59. Richard Nixon, "Toasts of the President and President Medici of Brazil, December 7, 1971," "Spoken Remarks and Addresses," American Presidency Project, University of California, Santa Barbara, www.presidency.ucsb.edu/ws/?pid=3247.

60. "Meeting with President Emílio Garrastazu Médici."

61. "Meeting with President Emílio Garrastazu Médici."

62. Kornbluh, *Pinochet File*.

63. Brazilian historian Carlos Fico dedicated several books to the 1964 coup d'état and its consequences. The influence of the United States is at the core of his research. See esp. Fico, *Como eles agiam* and *O grande irmão*.

64. Herman, *Real Terror*, 70.

65. The most frequent estimate is of "60,000 to 80,000 deaths." Víctor Flores Olea, "Editoriales: Operación Cóndor," *El Universal*, April 10, 2006.

66. "Morte de João Goulart: Laudo pericial inconclusivo não afasta outros meios de prova," Ministério Público Federal, www.jusbrasil.com.br/noticias/morte-de-joao-goulart -laudo-pericial-inconclusivo-nao-afasta-outros-meios-de-prova/154797529 (accessed February 20, 2024).

67. Simone Iglesias, "Fleury deu a ordem final, diz ex-agente," *Folha de S. Paulo*, January 27, 2008. In 2009, another publication reinforced the theory of a "B Agent" who had poisoned Goulart. See Gilberto Nascimento, "Documentos inéditos produzidos por agente infiltrado no Uruguai reforçam a tese do 'envenenamento' do ex-presidente," *CartaCapital*, March 3, 2009.

68. Nascimento, "Documentos inéditos." See also William, *Uma mulher*.

69. "Ata da trigésima nona sessão do Conselho de Segurança Nacional."

70. "Resolutions Adopted at the Eighth Meeting of Consultation of Ministers of Foreign Affairs, Punta del Este, Uruguay, January 22–31, 1962," Yale Law School, Avalon Project, http://avalon.law.yale.edu/20th_century/intam17.asp.

71. Spektor, *Kissinger*.

72. Hermann, "Reformas," 71.

73. To define "organic elites," Dreifuss uses the Gramscian concept of "organic intellectual," a group connected to a class project, responsible for emanating the "organic ideology," a unified, "hegemonic," ideological system, a "hegemonic principle." For Dreifuss, "organic elites" are a group of agents specialized in strategic planning and in the implementation of political class action. The organic elite establishes "the organizational and political unity in the diversity internal class ideology, incorporated and internalized in its program of action and in its State project." Dreifuss, *A Internacional Capitalista*, 26. See also Dreifuss, *1964*. For an insightful analysis of the concept of organic elites, see Hoeveler, "René Dreifuss."

74. Hoeveler, "(Neo)liberalismo," 51.

75. Crummett, "El Poder Feminino."

76. Spektor, "Origens."

77. Davis, *Last Two Years*.

78. "Chile: 'Dictatorship' Stays in Books," *New York Times*, January 7, 2012, A6.

79. Odette Magnet, "Chile Begins 'Beautiful Challenge' of Drafting New Constitution," *Al Jazeera*, July 4, 2021, www.aljazeera.com/news/2021/7/4/chile-beautiful-challenge -of-drafting-new-constitution; Rafael Romo, Maija Ehlinger, Marlon Sorto, and Simone McCarthy, "Chilean Voters Overwhelmingly Reject Proposed Leftist Constitution," *CNN*, September 5, 2022, www.cnn.com/2022/09/04/americas/chile-constitution -vote-intl/index.html.

80. Güell, "El Estallido Social"; Jiménez-Yañez, "#Chiledespertó"; Waissbluth, "Orígenes."

81. "Quién es Javier Iturriaga, el general encargado del estado de emergencia en Chile?," *El Comercio*, October 21, 2019, https://elcomercio.pe/mundo/latinoamerica /protestas-en-chile-quien-es-javier-iturriaga-el-general-del-ejercito-encargado -del-estado-de-emergencia-en-chile-perfil-noticia/; Alejandra Valderrama, "Javier Iturriaga: El hombre duro del ejercito familiar de violadores de DDHH," *La Izquierda Diario*, October 19, 2019, www.laizquierdadiario.cl/Javier-Iturriaga-El-hombre-duro-del-ejercito -familiar-de-violadores-de-DDHH.

82. "Andrés Pío Bernardino Chadwick Piñera: Reseñas biográficas parlamentarias." Biblioteca del Congreso Nacional de Chile, www.bcn.cl/historiapolitica/resenas_parlam entarias/wiki/Andrés_P6o_Bernardino_Chadwick_Piñera (accessed December 7, 2021).

83. José Piñera was a candidate for the Chilean presidency in 1993. At the time, he defended his neoliberal agenda in Piñera, *Camino nuevo*.

84. "Jair Bolsonaro: Biografia," Câmara dos Deputados do Brasil, www.camara.leg.br /deputados/74847/biografia (accessed December 7, 2021).

85. Mariana della Barba and Marina Wentzel, "Discurso de Bolsonaro deixa ativistas 'estarrecidos' e leva OAB a pedir sua cassação," *BBC*, April 19, 2016, www.bbc.com /portuguese/noticias/2016/04/160415_bolsonaro_ongs_oab_mdb.

CHAPTER ONE

1. The CSN was one of the three agencies focused on homeland security that directly advised the president, along with the Brazilian National Intelligence Service (SNI) and the General Staff of the Armed Forces. It produced more than 3,000 pages of classified documents between 1964 and 1980, including the thirty-nine-page minutes of the meeting in question. Institutional Act no. 2, published on October 27, 1965, gave ample powers to the CSN, stipulating that complementing acts (*atos complementares*) could be established at any time as long as the council approved of it. The CSN also gained the capacity to fire, remove, and force the retirement of anyone it deemed "incompatible with the objectives of the Revolution" (*que demonstrem incompatibilidade com os objetivos da Revolução*). With the support of the CSN, the president could now cancel the political rights of any citizen for up to ten years. Brasil, "Presidência da República, Casa Civil, Subchefia para Assuntos Jurídicos, Ato Institucional no. 2, de 27 de outubro de 1965," www.planalto.gov.br /ccivil_03/ait/ait-02-65.htm.

2. "Ata da trigésima nona sessão do Conselho de Segurança Nacional," October 24, 1966, no. 85, Conselho de Segurança Nacional, ANB-B.

3. "Juracy Magalhães," CPDOC, www.fgv.br/cpdoc/acervo/dicionarios/verbete-biografico /juraci-montenegro-magalhaes.

4. "Ata da trigésima nona sessão do Conselho de Segurança Nacional," 1–2.

5. The minister was referring to a small gathering of nations in Bogotá in August 1966. At the end of the summit, countries published the "Declaration of Bogotá." The leaders of the "democratic nations" of Colombia, Chile, Ecuador, Peru, and Venezuela reiterated the need for economic cooperation in the region and condemned Argentina's military coup d'état. "Declaration of Bogota," *New York Times*, August 27, 1966, 22.

6. "Ata da trigésima nona sessão do Conselho de Segurança Nacional," 3.

7. Besides Chile, Magalhães also visited Bolivia, Argentina, and Uruguay. He began praising the tour by saying that the promotion of Brazil on the continent was the means through which to achieve global recognition. Although Magalhães was not a professional diplomat and had had a long and successful military career, the phrase clarified his involvement with the policy of multilateralization of Brazilian foreign relations during the dictatorship. The idea was to expand the country's international influence, going beyond its alignment with the United States. The South American expedition, therefore, was made to measure. Paulo Fagundes Vizentini defines the multilateralization of foreign relations as "the search for new spaces, regional and institutional ones, in addition to traditional relationships (which are not interrupted), of political and economic performance of Brazilian diplomacy." Vizentini, *A política externa*, 10.

8. Vizentini, *A política externa*, 50.

9. The Tricontinental was an anticapitalist movement comprised of eighty-two countries at the height of the Cold War. With debates on race, inequality, and social justice, it had the revolutions in Cuba and Vietnam at the center of its agenda. See Mahler, *From the Tricontinental*; and Young, "Disseminating the Tricontinental."

10. "Ata da trigésima nona sessão do Conselho de Segurança Nacional," 7. For more on the history of the Chilean Communist Party, see Angell, *Partidos políticos*; Labarca Goddard, *Corvalán*; and Ulianova, Loyola, and Álvarez, *1912–2012*.

11. "Ata da trigésima nona sessão do Conselho de Segurança Nacional," 7.

12. "Ata da trigésima nona sessão do Conselho de Segurança Nacional," 7. For more on Argentina, see Eidelman, "El desarrollo."

13. Gabriel Valdés Subercaseaux served as Chile's minister of foreign affairs from 1964 to 1970 and would later become one of the most vocal critics of the Augusto Pinochet regime. In the 2000s, his son, Juan Gabriel Valdés Soublette, served as Chile's ambassador to the United Nations.

14. Brazilian minister of planning Roberto Campos asserted that Magalhães's achievements were fundamental for the country's economic leadership in the region. He affirmed that Brazil was now in better financial shape than in the first years of the civilian-military regime and could negotiate better terms with the International Monetary Fund, adding that it was a very different situation from 1963, when he had presided over the Committee of the Alliance for Progress that analyzed Chile. At the time, under civilian president João Goulart, Brazil had followed a less austere and prodevelopment approach, raising taxes and using that income for governmental spending. For Campos, the most important differences between the two nations were that Chile had a "lower inflation rate—only 38 percent—and a financial administration in order," besides having received more international support than Brazil. At the time, Campos was facing criticism of his Government Economic Action Program (PAEG), which prescribed tax reform and reduced spending to combat inflation. Campos would leave the ministry a few months after the meeting, in March 1967. See Hermann, "Reformas." See also "Ata da trigésima nona sessão do Conselho de Segurança Nacional," 18.

15. The belief in a connection between elites and foreign capital that perpetuated the hegemony of powerful nations was widely debated among left-wing intellectuals in 1960s Brazil. Its critics came not only from the political realm. Businessmen, Church authorities, politicians, and intellectuals were among the conservative leaders who condemned Marxist thinkers such as Manoel Bonfim, Octávio Brandão, and Caio Prado Júnior, who contended

that Brazil's backwardness could only be explained by colonialism and US imperialism. See Almeida, "Do alinhamento."

16. Burns, *History of Brazil*, 398–99.

17. Vargas served as president from 1930 to 1945. First, as interim president, then as a constitutional president, and finally, as a dictator from 1937 to 1945. After resigning in 1945, he returned to power in 1951. He served until his suicide in 1954. See Neto, *Getúlio 3*; and Vizentini, *Relações internacionais*.

18. Moura, *O alinhamento*.

19. During the 1950s, however, the Brazilian government did little to address this disapproval, embracing a foreign policy that continued to prioritize US interests. The Cuban Revolution of 1959 brought to light the conflicting anti-US domestic demands and the continuation of the US-oriented foreign policy. See Hershberg, "United States."

20. Rogério de Souza Farias analyzes the Brazilian role in the creation of a system of rules for international trade established after World War II, arguing that the country's participation was instrumental in the negotiations with industrialists, economists, and diplomats. See Farias, "Industriais."

21. Vizentini, "Da barganha nacionalista."

22. Public opinion about the expansion of communism in Latin America changed during the 1950s. In an analysis of several polls, Rodrigo Patto Sá Motta demonstrates the shifts. In March 1955, 58 percent of the population in the cities of Rio de Janeiro and São Paulo stated that communism was bad for the people, while 2 percent considered it to be good. In the same survey, 23 percent declared that communists in Latin America were a very serious danger, 8 percent saw them as not very serious, and 3 percent considered them not to be dangerous at all. In March 1959, research about an eventual trade with the Soviet Union showed that, although most Brazilians were sympathetic to the United States, the majority was pragmatic about the Soviet Union, defending ties if they benefited the country economically. Motta, "O anticomunismo."

23. Between 1955 and 1958, South America entered a period of redemocratization, with elections in multiple countries. The fall of authoritarian regimes that Eisenhower had supported—Gustavo Rojas Pinilla (Colombia), Marcos Pérez Jiménez (Venezuela), and Manuel Odría (Peru)—increasingly weakened the image of the North American president in the region. See Rabe, *Eisenhower*; and Silva, *A política externa de JK*, 5.

24. "Memorandum of a Telephone Conversation Among the Minister-Counselor of the Embassy in Venezuela (Burrows), the Assistant Secretary of State for Inter-American Affairs (Rubottom) in Caracas, and the Deputy Director of the Office of South American Affairs (Sanders)," Washington, May 13, 1958, in Glennon, *Foreign Relations, 1958–1960*, doc. 46, https://history.state.gov/historicaldocuments/frus1958-60v05/d46.

25. Farias, "Industriais."

26. "Marxists Are Organizing Peasants in Brazil; Leftist League Aims at a Political Army 40 Million Strong," *New York Times*, November 1, 1960, 3.

27. Leacock, *Requiem for Revolution*, 14.

28. Gordon only arrived in Brazil in October 1961, after Jânio Quadros's resignation and the inauguration of João Goulart. The Alliance for Progress was developed through the Agency for International Development, also established in 1961. The plan was to loan more than $20 billion to nations in the region. It was the largest aid program in US

history at the time. For more on the Alliance for Progress, see Taffet, *Foreign Aid*; Latham, "Ideology"; and DeWitt, "Alliance for Progress."

29. Markun and Hamilton, *1961*; Gualazzi and Quadros Neto, *Jânio Quadros*.

30. Memorial da Democracia, a virtual museum developed by Instituto Lula, recovered documents, videos, and newspaper stories about this moment. See "Brasil reata com União Soviética," November 23, 1961, Memorial da Democracia, http://memorialdademocracia.com.br/card/brasil-reata-com-uniao-sovietica. See also Dantas, *Política externa*; "Discurso pronunciado na Câmara dos Deputados, em 23 de novembro de 1961," in Dantas, *Política externa independente*, 47–99. For an analysis of Goulart's foreign policy and the US reaction, see Domingos, "A política externa independente," 266.

31. Vizentini, *A política externa*, 23.

32. The most popular interpretation of Quadros's move is that he expected Congress to reject his resignation because Vice President João Goulart had even less political capital then Quadros. Goulart was a *getulista*, a Getúlio Vargas supporter and mentee. However, Congress did accept Quadros's resignation. Arnt, *Jânio Quadros*; Valente, *Jânio Quadros*; Castello Branco, *A renúncia*.

33. Ferreira and Castro Gomes, *Jango*.

34. Caio Navarro de Toledo argues that the 1964 coup was a reaction to reform and democracy. See Toledo, "1964."

35. Agee, *Inside the Company*, 216.

36. Leacock, *Requiem for Revolution*, 72–73.

37. US Senate, *Covert Action in Chile*, 1. This number differs greatly from source to source. Historian Luiz Alberto Moniz Bandeira, for instance, claims the figure was from $12 million to $20 million. See Bandeira, *Fórmula para o caos*, 85–86.

38. Dreifuss, *1964*, 102; Green and Jones, "Reinventing History."

39. Military ministers in the cabinet tried to stop João Goulart's inauguration. Goulart was in his second term as vice president. At the time, Brazilians voted for the president and vice president separately. In 1956, Goulart became vice president and Juscelino Kubitschek president. In 1960, he was reelected, but the president elect, Jânio Quadros, was a member of a different party. After Quadros's decision to resign, Goulart's brother-in-law and renowned politician Leonel Brizola created a pool of radio stations branded the Cadeia da Legalidade (Chain of Legality), calling on the population to take to the streets to ensure the vice president's right to take office. Goulart was only proclaimed president after he agreed to a constitutional amendment abolishing the presidential executive and after creating a parliamentary government, which would be rejected only a year later, in a plebiscite. See d'Avila, *Um olhar*.

40. Pontes, *Julio de Mesquita Filho*, 64.

41. Weis, *Cold Warriors*; Black, *United States Penetration of Brazil*.

42. Goulart's opposition worked to contain the Peasant League's movements and to keep a close relationship with the Brazilian military. The manipulation of the media and "penetration" of Brazilian elites, focusing on key businessmen, were parts of this strategy. See Black, *United States*, 95–110.

43. Tollerson, "Developing Democracy," 2.

44. Black, *United States Penetration of Brazil*, 85.

45. Kennedy's Alliance for Progress was the most important economic aid program of the 1960s. Research on the multibillion-dollar program is abundant. Among the works

that focus on Brazil and Chile is Taffet, *Foreign Aid*. For a more general perspective, see Rabe, *Most Dangerous Area*. See also Field, *From Development to Dictatorship*.

46. John F. Kennedy, "Latin American Diplomatic Corps Reception Speech," March 13, 1961, East Room, White House, American Rhetoric Online Speech Bank, www.americanrhetoric .com/speeches/jfklatinamericadiplomaticcore.htm.

47. The Eduardo Frei administration is an example of the changes in the agenda of the Alliance for Progress. In its first years, the program was dedicated to tax and land reforms. With the difficulties of the Frei government, the project shifted to focus on military rule, especially in Brazil. See Sigmund, *Overthrow*.

48. Chilean scholars have questioned the myth of Chilean long-lasting democracy in recent years. See Avendaño, *Los partidos*; and Fermandois, *La revolución inconclusa*. Thomas Tunstall Allcock demonstrated that the shift in the US policy toward Latin America—with the abandonment of noninterference and the embrace of actions against leftist governments, culminating in the Alliance of Progress—started before protests against Richard Nixon's May 1958 goodwill tour and the Cuban Revolution. See Allcock, "First Alliance for Progress."

49. US Senate, *Covert Action in Chile*, 1.

50. San Francisco, Millar Carvacho, and Soto, *Camino a La Moneda*.

51. Bandeira, *Fórmula para o caos*, 99.

52. Castro, "Castro Announces the Revolution."

53. "Resolutions Adopted at the Eighth Meeting of Consultation of Ministers of Foreign Affairs, Punta del Este, Uruguay, January 22–31, 1962," Yale Law School, Avalon Project, http://avalon.law.yale.edu/20th_century/intam17.asp.

54. "Eighth Meeting of Consultation of Ministers of Foreign Affairs," Punta del Este, Uruguay, January 22–31, 1962, Final Act, www.oas.org/consejo/MEETINGS%20OF%20 CONSULTATION/Actas/Acta%208.pdf.

55. "Eighth Meeting of Consultation."

56. "A política externa independente durante o governo João Goulart," CPDOC, www .fgv.br/cpdoc/acervo/dicionarios/verbete-tematico/politica-externa-independente.

57. In her study of ECLAC, historian Margarita Fajardo demonstrates that the Cepalinos' agenda—which included more trade and aid—became dominant in Latin America, successfully establishing the commission as more influential than the United States and the International Monetary Fund. See Fajardo, *World That Latin America Created*.

58. In 1964, Furtado worked on the implementation of the UN Conference on Trade and Development (UNCTAD) and became an internationally renowned economist, despite his "Marxist tendencies." See Vieira, "Celso Furtado"; and Furtado, *Teoria e política*.

59. Santos and de Mulder Fuentes, "Celso Furtado."

60. "A política externa independente."

61. "Actitud que observará Brasil en Punta del Este, oficio confidencial no. 77/9 enviado por el Embajador Marcelo Ruiz Solar al Ministerio de Asuntos Exteriores," Rio de Janeiro, January 15, 1962, Embajada de Chile en Brasil, año 1962, AGH-MRE.

62. Soto Ángel and Garay, *Las relaciones chileno-brasileñas*, 167. Although criticized, Goulart's neutral stance allowed him to act as a secret mediator between John Kennedy and Fidel Castro. See André Duchiade, "Documentos indicam que João Goulart atuou como mediador secreto entre Kennedy e Fidel Castro," *O Globo*, April 29, 2021, https://oglobo .globo.com/mundo/documentos-indicam-que-joao-goulart-atuou-como-mediador-secreto -entre-kennedy-fidel-castro-1-24994882.

63. Weis, *Cold Warriors.*

64. Under the agreement, the two countries committed $276 million to investments in the region. See John F. Kennedy, "Letter to President Goulart of Brazil on the Signing of an Alliance for Progress Agreement with Brazil," "Letters," American Presidency Project, University of California, Santa Barbara, www.presidency.ucsb.edu/node/236413.

65. Hershberg, "Soviet-Brazilian Relations."

66. Bandeira, *O governo João Goulart,* 79. See also Keller, "Latin American Missile Crisis."

67. Hershberg, "Soviet-Brazilian Relations."

68. Bustos Díaz, *Diplomacia chilena,* 398.

69. *Memoria del Ministerio de Relaciones Exteriores de Chile, 1962,* AGH-MRE, 70.

70. The length of the presidential term in Chile has varied in the twentieth century. The 1925 Constitution established a period of six years. That was the rule when Alessandri was elected. The original text of the 1980 Constitution defined a term of eight years with no possibility of reelection. In March 1994, a reform defined six years again as the length of the term. Finally, in 2005, it was reduced to four years with no possibility of reelection.

71. *Memoria del Ministerio de Relaciones Exteriores de Chile, 1962,* 98.

72. "Instrucciones al Embajador de Chile, D. Marcelo Ruiz Solar, Estrictamente Confidencial no. 3," Santiago de Chile, May 15, 1962, Oficios Archivo MRREE Departamento Político, año 1962, AGH-MRE.

73. "La política exterior de Brasil," *El Mercurio,* April 23, 1963.

74. Soto Ángel and Garay, *Las relaciones chileno-brasileñas,* 169.

75. "Vibrante recibimiento al Presidente João Goulart," *El Siglo,* April 21, 1963; "Aclamado Goulart," *El Siglo,* April 23, 1963.

76. Ferreira and Castro Gomes, *Jango.*

77. Ferreira, *João Goulart.* For more on the "Reformas de Base," see Moreira, "O projeto de nação."

78. "A Eletrobrás e a história do setor de energia elétrica no Brasil: Ciclo de palestras," Centro da Memória da Eletricidade no Brasil, 1995, Rio de Janeiro. See also "Eletrobras (Centrais Elétricas Brasileiras S.A.)," CPDOC, www.fgv.br/cpdoc/acervo/dicionarios /verbete-tematico/eletrobras-centrais-eletricas-brasileiras-s-a.

79. Dreifuss, *1964.*

80. Soto-Ángel and Garay, *Las relaciones chileno-brasileñas,* 177.

81. Fermandois, "Chile y la 'cuestión cubana,'" 143–44.

82. In the 1960s, the country ranked second in per capita economic aid, behind only Vietnam. See Michaels, "Alliance for Progress," 77.

83. "Para conseguir ayuda financiera de EE.UU. Brasil seguiría confiando más que en la Alianza para el Progreso en el argumento político que le da su importancia territorial, demográfica y geográfica: Oficio confidencial no. 38/4 enviado por el Embajador Marcelo Ruiz Solar al Ministerio de Asuntos Exteriores," Rio de Janeiro, August 1, 1962, Embajada de Chile en Brasil, año 1962, AGH-MRE.

84. Vizentini, *A política externa,* 24.

85. "Telegram from the Department of State to the Embassy in Brazil," March 31, 1964, in Keefer, *Foreign Relations, 1964–1968,* vol. 31, doc. 198, https://history.state.gov /historicaldocuments/frus1964-68v31/d198. See also Parker, *1964.* Although Operation Brother Sam is occasionally called Contingency Plan 2-61, these two actions were in fact

different. Plan 2-61 was a larger project that encompassed the operation and was organized in advance. It included logistical support and the provision of arms and ammunition. See Fico, *O grande irmão*, 87–88; Bandeira, *Brasil—Estados Unidos*; and Joffily, "A política externa."

86. The thesis that Brazil and the United States conspired even before Allende's inauguration was noted by journalist Mónica González, who worked closely with the Brazilian Truth Commission. Emílio Ariel Crenzel also mentions the Brazilian influence on other South American regimes as a possibility but does not dedicate his work to this question. See González, *Chile*; and Crenzel, *Memory of Argentina*.

87. US Senate, *Covert Action in Chile*.

88. Hurtado-Torres, *Gathering Storm*. The investment intensified after Allende was elected president in 1970. Between then and the coup of 1973, the government agency spent, covertly, over $8 million, according to US Senate, *Covert Action in Chile*.

89. US Senate, *Covert Action in Chile*. The report stresses that the amount was much more significant due to the price of the dollar on the Chilean black market, "where the unofficial exchange rate into Chilean *escudos* often reached five times the official rate" (1).

90. "The Country That Saved Itself," *Reader's Digest*, November 1964, BR AN, RIO. QL.O.CDI.22, ANB-RJ.

91. The US ambassador to Brazil at the time of Goulart's overthrow, Lincoln Gordon, is a central figure in the articulation between Brazilian and North American diplomats in the coup of 1964. Skidmore, *Politics of Military Rule*; Skidmore, *Politics in Brazil*; and Spektor, *Kissinger*.

92. "Remessa de filmes," May 25, 1970, telegram no. 6073, DDC/540.612(32), ACI-SERE.

93. "XXV Assembleia Geral da ONU, 1970: Candidatura do Brasil," April 10, 1970, telegram no. 2 349, DNU/DBP/604(04)5, ACI-SERE.

94. "Andamento administrativo do Chile: Mensagem do Presidente Frei," May 22, 1970, telegram no. 5 892, DBP/601.4(32) 600(32) 900.1(32), ACI-SERE.

95. Pio Corrêa, *O mundo*.

96. "Organização Latino-Americana de Solidariedade: Comitês nacionais," July 24, 1967, no. 415, BR AN, BSB, IE 027, 64–72, ANB-B.

97. "Organização Latino-Americana," 65–72.

98. Valle, *1968*.

99. "New Ambassador to Brazil Predicts No Big Shift in U.S. Latin America Policy," *Baltimore Sun*, August 31, 1969, 6.

100. Green, "Clérigos," 20.

101. "Controls Stiffened in Brazil," *Washington Post*, December 15, 1968, A1.

102. Green, *We Cannot Remain Silent*. See also Sales, "*The Economist*," for a compelling look into the *Economist*'s coverage of the Brazilian dictatorship in this period in comparison to fellow British publications the *Times* and the *Guardian*.

103. "Hopes Rise in Washington," *New York Times*, December 18, 1968, 3.

104. Fico, *O grande irmão*, 80.

105. Spektor, *Kissinger*, 40–41.

106. Vizentini, *A política externa*.

107. CIA Memorandum, "Chile: A Status Report," September 21, 1970, US State Department, Freedom of Information Act (FOIA), Virtual Reading Room. The nickname was coined in Silveira, *Frei, el Kerensky chileno*. See also Hurtado-Torres, *Gathering Storm*.

108. Santos, *Poder e dominação*.

109. The Brazilian government followed a similar strategy with its intelligence agencies, modeled after the CIA. See Cepik, "Sistemas nacionais"; and Andrade, "A Escola Nacional."

110. In 1970, when Brazil had been a dictatorship for six years and Chile was still under Salvador Allende's socialist presidency, Ambassador Willard L. Beaulac, who served in US diplomatic institutions in five Latin American countries, released a book about the multibillion-dollar US aid program to the continent. A supporter of such initiatives, Beaulac gives clues about how US officials acknowledged the instrumentality of keeping the continent under control during the Cold War. Beaulac, *Diplomat Looks at Aid*.

111. Benjamin A. Cowan discusses sexuality at the Escola Superior de Guerra and demonstrates how discourses of masculinity spread among the youth. See Cowan, *Securing Sex*. A similar approach regarding homosexuality in Cuba is developed in Guerra, *Visions of Power*.

112. "Aviso no 05/ FA-2 204," July 20, 1973, EMFA, ANB-B.

113. "Aviso no 008/ FA-10 238," September 5, 1973, EMFA, ANB-B.

114. "Da embaixada em Santiago," September 22, 1970, telegram no. 17534, DBP /600(32)35, ACI-SERE.

115. Hurtado-Torres, *Gathering Storm*.

116. "Intercâmbio cultural Brasil-Chile: Incidentes com estudantes brasileiros," June 27, 1970, telegram no. 9125, DCInt/DBP/542.6(32) and 542.64(32)14, ACI-SERE.

117. "Comentários políticos desfavoráveis ao Brasil em emissora chilena," June 16–18, 1970, telegram no. 8 251, AIG/DBP/DSI/500, ACI-SERE.

118. "Informes sôbre o Chile," May 18, 1970, Parte S/No. EMFA, ANB-B.

119. The document only became public in August 2012, as a result of the work of the Brazilian Truth Commission, which had been implemented three months earlier to investigate human rights violations in Brazil from September 18, 1946, to October 5, 1988, a period when the country was under different dictatorial regimes.

120. "Informes sôbre o Chile."

121. "Informes sôbre o Chile."

122. "Informes sôbre o Chile."

123. "Informação para o Senhor Presidente da República: Eleição presidencial no Chile," September 22, 1970, 00183, ACI-SERE.

124. "Informação para o Senhor Presidente."

125. "Informação para o Senhor Presidente."

126. "Allende já diz que seu governo não será marxista," *Folha de S. Paulo*, September 6, 1970, 1.

CHAPTER TWO

1. Interview with Otto Brockes by the author, video recording, Goiás, Brazil, July 15, 2014.

2. The debate on the geographical border (or lack thereof) among groups of resistance, activism, and guerrillas against authoritarianism in South America is a central topic in Aldo Marchesi's book about the radical Left in the region. Although Brazilian guerrillas

are not the focus of this work, several of the exiles I have interviewed refer to the regional character of the revolution. See Marchesi, *Latin America's Radical Left*.

3. "O médico Otto Brockes aborda aspectos de sua experiência durante o golpe que depôs presidente chileno," April 14, 2014, video recording of testimony to the CDHMVJ, YouTube video, 38:12, posted by TV Senado on July 11, 2014, 07:48–7:54, www.youtube .com/watch?v=Mdo3SxFSnJY.

4. Blanc, *Searching for Memory*.

5. Interview with Aluízio Palmar by the author, audio recording, Foz do Iguaçu, Brazil, August 10, 2020.

6. Rollemberg, *Exílio*, 49–50; Marchesi, *Latin America's Radical Left*.

7. Scelza, "Entre o controle."

8. Gaspari, *A ditadura escancarada*, 263.

9. Palmar, *Onde foi*.

10. Reis and Pereira, *Imagens da revolução*.

11. Codarin, *O MR-8*; Herler, "Formação e trajetória."

12. Juan de Onis, "Kidnapping Diplomats Is Becoming a Latin Custom," *New York Times*, March 15, 1970, 176.

13. Silva, "Vanguarda Popular Revolucionária"; Guttmann, *Origins of International Counterterrorism*. For more information about Ambassador Giovanni Enrico Bucher, see Swiss Academy of Humanities and Social Sciences, Dodis Research Centre, dodis.ch/ P10060 (accessed September 9, 2022).

14. Interview with Brockes.

15. Eisenber, Husid, and Luco, "Preliminary Report."

16. Mario Alves, Jacob Gorender, and Apolônio de Carvalho, all dissident members of the Communist Party, founded the PCBR in 1968. The group questioned the need for an alliance with the Brazilian bourgeoisie and maintained that only a rural guerrilla group combined with urban activism could deliver the promise of a popular revolutionary government. Della Vechia, "Origem e evolução."

17. Silveira, "Dissidência comunista," 292. See also Sales, *Entre a revolução*.

18. In his book about executions inside guerrilla groups during the years of the dictatorship, journalist Lucas Ferraz describes the importance of "cachorros," guerrillas turned spies who received financial compensation to provide information to the military. See Ferraz, *Injustiçados*.

19. Several documents describing Maria Tereza Ribeiro da Silva's activities are now available at the online archive Documentos Revelados. "Espiões: Agente do CENIMAR Maria Thereza [sic] Ribeiro da Silva infiltrada no PCBR," November 26, 2018, https:// documentosrevelados.com.br/espioes-agente-do-cenimar-maria-thereza-ribeiro-da-silva -infiltrada-no-pcbr/. The Federal University of Minas Gerais (UFMG) compiled documents about the civilian-military dictatorship in the Projeto República initiative. The ones about CENIMAR moles, including Ribeiro da Silva, are available at Brasil Doc, "3.1. CENI-MAR," www.ufmg.br/brasildoc/temas/3-informantes-infiltrados-agentes-e-centros-de -repressao/3-1-cenimar/ (accessed August 31, 2022).

20. "Espiões."

21. In three pages, Maria Tereza asks for money, describing her precarious life at length. The letter is from February 26, 1973, and she signs with her code name, Renata. The document is available at Brasil Doc, "3.1. CENIMAR."

22. Rollemberg, *Exílio*.

23. Amnesty International, *Chile*, 64. The Amnesty International report, written a year after the coup, states several times that there is a "problem of statistics" under the Chilean dictatorship. The numbers are not precise and estimates from international organizations differ greatly from the official figures of the Chilean government. However, the report states that "many thousands of Latin American refugees had been granted asylum in Chile during the government of the Unidad Popular [Popular Unity]. Although the exact number is unknown and was almost certainly unknown even to the Allende government, the figure is estimated as being between 13,000 and 15,000. The French newspaper *Le Monde*, on September 24, 1973, estimated that there were '4,000 Bolivians, 3,000 Uruguayans, 2,000 Argentinians, 1,200 Brazilians, and a small number from other Latin American countries.' Other newspaper sources gave far higher figures."

24. "Exílio é a saída para milhares de brasileiros," Memorial da Democracia, https://memorialdademocracia.com.br/card/exilio-e-a-saida-para-milhares-de-brasileiros (accessed September 12, 2024).

25. For the multiple definitions of exile, see Ferreira, "Anthropology of Exile."

26. The problem of conceptualizing exile can be considered the result of a still present challenge to the exclusionary nation-states of the region. James N. Green, Luis Roniger, and Pablo Yankelevich contend that "the study of exile highlights an ongoing tension between the principle of national membership and the principle of citizenship. Once pushed into exile, people may lose the entitlements attached to citizenship but at the same time may become even more attached than before to what is perceived as the 'national soul.'" Green, Roniger, and Yenkelevich, *Exile*, 4.

27. Considering that displacement is a central characteristic of diasporic communities, it is possible to conclude that exiles develop a sense of self that is the result not of the state but of its absence and its impossibility. In the case of Brazilian exiles in Chile, this sentiment is complicated by the fact that, after some years, the new place also became oppressive. This sense of self, furthermore, is inspired by notions of nationhood and citizenship that the Brazilian dictatorship had been imposing for almost a decade, resorting to torture and violence.

28. When defining cosmopolitism and transnationalism in his discussion of the future of the nation-state, Jürgen Habermas dealt with a global order in which democratic states predominated. To a considerable extent, respect for individualism, freedom of speech, and human rights are inherent in cosmopolitism. Habermas would later revise his definition, noticing that transnational movements could happen between nondemocratic institutions. See Habermas, "Kant's Idea."

29. The debate on the construction of exile, refugees, and displacement as anthropological fields of study has been a fruitful one among anthropologists. See Malkki, "Refugees and Exile"; Lumsden, "Broken Lives?"; Ballinger, *History in Exile*; Bender and Winer, *Contested Landscapes*; and Roniger, "Reflexões."

30. Amnesty International, *Chile*, 64.

31. Interview with Jean Marc von der Weid by the author, video recording, Rio de Janeiro, September 1, 2020.

32. Apolônio de Carvalho is a mythical figure in Brazilian activism. He fought in multiple political conflicts in Brazil and Europe. See Pereira, "Apolônio de Carvalho."

Notes to Chapter Two

33. Costa et al., *Memórias das mulheres*.

34. Interview with Solange Bastos by the author, video recording, Rio de Janeiro, February 23, 2024.

35. Rollemberg, "Cultura política brasileira."

36. The process of expelling professors who were seen as menaces to the regime, known as *expurgo*, is central to the understanding of how the policies instated during the regime of exception shaped ideas of nationhood in the transition to democracy. Rodrigo Patto Sá Motta discusses the topic at length when looking at Brazilian universities under the military regime. Motta, *As universidades*.

37. Serbin, *From Revolution to Power*; Silva, "Resistência no exterior"; Marques, "O exílio"; Rojas Aravena, "Chile"; Pericás, *Caio Prado Júnior*; Rabêlo and Rabêlo, *Diáspora*.

38. Serra, *Cinquenta anos*, 163.

39. Frank, *Autobiographical Essays*.

40. Some of their most influential works published in the late 1960s and early 1970s include Bambirra, *El capitalismo dependiente latinoamericano*; Marini, *Subdesarrollo* and *Dialéctica*; and Santos, *Dependencia y cambio social*.

41. Wasserman, "Transição ao socialismo," 88. See also Johnson, "Dependency Theory."

42. Cerda, "Aspectos internacionales," 60–61. Aldo Marchesi states that Marini's view was connected to that of the Junta de Coordinación Revolucionária, which also argued that Argentina was a critical place for the success of the revolution. See Marchesi, *Latin America's Radical Left*.

43. Telegram no. 062195, BBP/600(32), November 3, 1971, ACI-SERE.

44. Aggio, "A esquerda brasileira," 3.

45. Marques, "O exílio"; Araújo, "Paixões políticas."

46. González Errázuriz, *Partido Demócrata Cristiano*, 189–91.

47. Azevedo, *Por um triz*, 110.

48. Interview with von der Weid.

49. Interview with Reinaldo Guarany by the author, video recording, Rio de Janeiro, August 28, 2020.

50. Interview with Guarany.

51. Interview with Guarany.

52. Interview with René de Carvalho by the author, audio recording, Rio de Janeiro, August 17, 2020.

53. Interview with Wilson Barbosa by the author, video recording, São Paulo, July 11, 2014.

54. Interview with Barbosa.

55. "Brazil Releases 40 Prisoners to Ransom Bonn Ambassador," *New York Times*, June 16, 1970, 1.

56. A full list of the exiles freed on January 13, 1971, is available at Geni Public Access, www.geni.com/projects/Exilados-brasileiros-os-70-do-Chile/26365 (accessed December 13, 2021).

57. Interview with Barbosa.

58. Interview with Bruno Dauster, in Silveira, *Setenta*.

59. Interview with Marco Maranhão, in Silveira, *Setenta*.

60. Interview with Jaime Cardoso, in Silveira, *Setenta*.

61. Interview with Cardoso.

62. Apolônio de Carvalho's biography reads like a movie. He served in the Brazilian Army, volunteered in the International Brigades of the Spanish Civil War, was a colonel in the French Resistance in the fight against Nazism in World War II, and was one of the founders of the Brazilian Revolutionary Communist Party. See Carvalho, *Renée France de Carvalho*; and Carvalho, *Vale a pena sonhar*.

63. Interview with Carvalho.

64. Stuart Angel was the son of fashion designer Zuzu Angel, who started a crusade to punish the murderers. In 1971, she launched a fashion show in protest. See Simili, "Tecidos."

65. The airbase is one of the seven official settings of the military where torture and murders were confirmed in the first preliminary report of the Brazilian Truth Commission. CNV, *Relatório final da Comissão Nacional da Verdade*, http://cnv.memoriasreveladas .gov.br/images/pdf/relatorio_versao_final18-02.pdf (accessed September 17, 2024). In 1970, after the outrage over the killing of Stuart Angel, Burnier was discharged and forced into retirement with enlisted pay. See Memorial da Resistência de São Paulo, https:// memorialdaresistenciasp.org.br/vocabulario-controlado_referencias/joao-paulo-moreira -burnier (accessed September 17, 2024).

66. Interview with von der Weid.

67. One of Frei Tito's interviews in Chile can be found at "Frei Tito: Depoimento no Chile 1971," YouTube video, 3:07, posted by Juventude Dominicana on November 16, 2011, 3:07, www.youtube.com/watch?v=q3TEIv_Q4p0.

68. Interview with Maranhão.

69. Interview with Barbosa.

70. Interview with Barbosa.

71. Gabeira, *O que é isso*, 11. Gabeira's book inspired the movie *Four Days in September*. Barreto et al., *Four Days in September*.

72. Amnesty International, *Chile*, 67.

73. Gabeira, *O que é isso*, 13.

74. Swyngedouw, "Globalisation."

75. James Clifford's articulation of anti-Zionist Judaism's diaspora in relation to Paul Gilroy's *Black Atlantic* results in a deconstruction of nationalism that can be useful in the case of the Brazilian exiles' transnational experience. See Clifford, *Routes*; and Gilroy, *Black Atlantic*.

76. Clifford, *Routes*, 263.

77. Laguerre, "Homeland Political Crisis."

78. In *Imagined Communities*, Benedict Anderson defines the idea of nation as an object of transnational exchange. The formation of communities is the result not of state imposition but of a socially constructed process of identity perception. Violence is an instrumental part of the national character in moments of authoritarian leadership, not only when it comes to torture and physical abuses, which were daily practices of the Brazilian dictatorship, but also when the state determines that a citizen born and raised in a country can no longer remain in the national space. See Anderson, *Imagined Communities*; and Anderson, *Spectre of Comparisons*, 3–4.

79. Rollemberg, "As trincheiras da memoria," 103. Rollemberg argues that "the memory of the *abertura*, according to which the society was the big actor that generated the transformation of a dictatorship into a democratic regime, transcends the period of 1974–1985." See also Rollemberg, "Brazilian Exile."

80. Marchesi, *Latin America's Radical Left*.

81. Rollemberg, *Exílio*, 33.

82. Interview with Nielsen Pires by the author, video recording, São Paulo, July 11, 2014.

83. Sá, "Ação Popular do Brasil."

84. Dom Hélder Câmara was also known as the Red Bishop due to his connections with communism. He once stated, "When I give food to the poor, they call me a saint. When I ask why the poor have no food, they call me a communist." See Rocha, *Helder*, 53. For more on the actions of progressive bishops during the Brazilian dictatorship, see Gomes, *Os bispos*; Serbin, *Diálogos na sombra*; and Bandeira, *A Igreja Católica*.

85. Interview with Pires.

86. Interview with Pires.

87. Denise Rollemberg uses the term "generation" due to the number of different experiences and events that characterized the groups who were forced to leave the country prior to Institutional Act no. 5 or between the act and the process of "opening," the *abertura*, in 1979. Rollemberg, *Exílio*, 49–50. For a parallel between 1968 in Brazil and the rest of the world, see Ventura, *1968*; and Kurlansky, *1968*.

88. Langland, *Speaking of Flowers*.

89. Interview with Vera Vital Brasil by the author, video recording, Rio de Janeiro, March 4, 2024.

90. Interview with Vital Brasil.

91. Serra, *Cinquenta anos*, 171.

92. Serra, *Cinquenta anos*, 179.

93. Rabêlo and Rabêlo, *Diáspora*, 83–84.

94. Rabêlo and Rabêlo, *Diáspora*.

95. Interview with Armênio Guedes, *Roda Viva*, August 11, 2008, transcript, Marxists Internet Archive, www.marxists.org/portugues/guedes/2008/08/11.htm.

96. Amnesty International, *Chile*, 23.

97. Cruz, "Frente Brasileiro de Informacões."

98. Interview with Barbosa.

99. At the time of his death in 2013, journalist Fernando Rabelo, the son of an exile family in Chile, wrote about Fonseca as the person who made him believe in Santa, for he would bring presents for the kids at Christmas. Images and Visions, https://imagesvisions.blogspot.com/2013/05/morre-edmur-fonseca.html (accessed December 14, 2021).

100. "Jaques de Sousa Coimbra," DPN PES 323, p. 57–127 Arquivo Nacional, Brasília, Divisão de Segurança e Informações do Ministério das Relações Exteriores, Documentos Revelados, https://documentosrevelados.com.br/wp-content/uploads/2021/01/dedoduro-informante-resumido-paginas-57–66.pdf (accessed September 14, 2024).

101. "Jaques de Sousa Coimbra."

102. Interview with Guedes.

103. Interview with Guedes.

104. Rollemberg, "Brazilian Exile," 95.

105. Interview with Barbosa.

106. Interview with Ubiramar Peixoto by the author, video recording, Brasília, July 14, 2014.

107. Interview with Peixoto.

108. Interview with Peixoto.

109. The escudo was the Chilean currency until 1975, when the Decree 1123 replaced it with the peso as part of an anti-inflation economic plan, at a rate of one peso for 1,000 escudos.

110. Interview with Pires.

111. Interview with Pires.

112. Interview with Guarany.

113. Interview with Guarany.

114. Interview with Guarany.

115. Palmar, *Onde foi*.

116. Palmar, *Onde foi*.

117. Frei Tito was a Brazilian Dominican friar and the director of the Association of Youth Catholic Students. He was arrested and tortured several times by the civilian-military regime and died in 1974. He became a symbol of resistance to the dictatorship, and of the support of a sector of the Church. Duarte-Plon and Duarte, *Um homem torturado*.

118. Cavalcanti, Celso, and Ramos, *Memórias do exílio*.

119. Cavalcanti, Celso, and Ramos, *Memórias do exílio*, 9.

120. Cavalcanti, Celso, and Ramos, *Memórias do exílio*, 10.

121. Angela Neves-Xavier de Brito separates the waves of female exiles in two: the 1964 group, which moved right after the coup d'état, mainly to other Latin American countries, and the 1968 group, who looked for destinations in Europe and Africa. The first faced a return to the status they had before they had engaged in political activism. According to the author, this was due to the structure of Latin American leftist political organizations, which held women in an inferior position with no possibility of incorporating a new feminine identity. In Europe, in contrast, the process for Brazilian women of building a new consciousness began to emerge. "The process of reflection on the conditions of oppression of women could only be done in exile and especially in societies whose social conditions favored its appearance. It never could have been done in societies such as Brazil or Chile, imbued in patriarchal values." Brito, "Brazilian Women."

122. Costa et al., *Memórias das mulheres*.

123. Costa et al., *Memórias das mulheres*, 17.

124. Angela Neves-Xavier de Brito broadened the question by looking at identity among exiles in several countries. She called attention to a large gap in the historiography of the Brazilian dictatorship and urged scholars to move away from first-person narratives and memoirs, especially because most of them were authored by men. For her, it was urgent to shift from personal accounts to understanding the political and social impact of exiles in Brazil. Brito uses as her main sources the interviews in Costa et al., *Memórias das mulheres*. Brito, "Brazilian Women."

125. Ana Vazquez's work also focuses on female exiles' perceptions of identity. In a series of articles published in 1982, she looked at narratives of Brazilian exiles in France.

See Vazquez, "Des troubles d'identité." For more on the emergence of debates on gender equality in the last years of the Brazilian dictatorship, see Burns, *Dona Ivone Lara's "Sorriso Negro."*

126. The shift was also present in other disciplines, including anthropology, that embraced the "anthropology of exile." See, e.g., Ferreira, "Anthropology of Exile."

127. One major moment was the publication, in 2007, of a volume dedicated to the topic in *Latin American Perspectives,* edited by James N. Green, Luis Roniger, and Pablo Yankelevich. This collection of articles remains an influential work on the subject. See Green, Roniger, and Yankelevich, *Exile.*

128. "Amnesty Law" is the popular name for Law Number 6.683, signed by then-president João Batista Figueiredo on August 28, 1979. The legislation absolved civilians and military personnel of any political crimes committed in the context of the dictatorship, from September 2, 1961, to August 16, 1979.

129. Leonelli and Oliveira, *Diretas Já*; Nery, *Diretas Já.*

130. Carvalho, *Cidadania no Brasil.*

131. Fico, Araújo, and Grin, *Violência na história.*

CHAPTER THREE

1. Almeida, "Do alinhamento."

2. Pio Corrêa, *O mundo*, 2:657–58, 854. In the original, Pio Corrêa's prose can be difficult to read because of the often-pretentious language, very different from the structure of modern Portuguese.

3. Pio Corrêa, *O mundo*, 2:655–56.

4. Report no. 154/77, April 14, 1977, BR AN, BSB, IE 16.4, 1/52, CIEX, ANB-B.

5. Penna Filho, "O Itamaraty e a repressão," 163–69.

6. Marques, "Militância política," 112.

7. Penna Filho, "O Itamaraty nos anos de chumbo." See also Pio Corrêa, *O mundo.*

8. Claudio Dantas Sequeira, "O pai do serviço secreto do Itamaraty," *Correio Braziliense*, July 23, 2007.

9. Carvalho e Souza was the first woman to serve as ambassador in the history of Brazil. Von der Weid and Uziel, "Odette de Carvalho e Souza."

10. Pio Corrêa, *O mundo*, 580, 814.

11. Claudio Dantas Sequeira, "O serviço secreto do Itamaraty," *Correio Braziliense*, July 22, 2007.

12. "Octubre 1975—Primera reunión de trabajo de Inteligencia Nacional," Fotograma 00022F 0155–0165, GWU, Archivo del Terror Digital, https://nsarchive2.gwu.edu /NSAEBB/NSAEBB239b/PDF/19751000%20Primera%20reunion%20de%20Trabajo %20de%20Inteligencia%20Nacional.pdf (accessed September 14, 2024).

13. Multiple documents describing Operation Condor refer to the fact that Brazil had been working independently and with individual countries, spying on political enemies. See, e.g., "Julio 10, 1980—Ingreso de terroristas argentinos a su país a través del nuestro," Fotograma 00019F 0876, GWU, Archivo del Terror Digital, https://nsarchive2.gwu.edu /NSAEBB/NSAEBB239d/index.htm. It mentions close alliances with Paraguay and Argentina to locate and imprison members of the guerrilla group Montoneros.

14. There were periods in certain countries of the Southern Cone when the Brazilian ambassadors were military men. General Fernando Belford Bethlem, for example, ambassador to Paraguay, was replaced in 1984 by another military man, General Mario de Melo Matos. See Abreu et al., *Dicionário*, 1:650 and 4:3640.

15. Abreu et al., *Dicionário*, 1:650 and 4:3640.

16. Guena, *Arquivo do horror*.

17. "Consbras Montevideu para Secretaria Estado: Atividades subversivas na Argentina, Chile, Paraguai, Bolivia e Uruguai," April 7, 1976, EMFA, ANB-B.

18. Interview with Wilson Barbosa by the author, video recording, São Paulo, July 11, 2014.

19. Interview with Nielsen Pires by the author, video recording, São Paulo, July 11, 2014.

20. See, e.g., "Chile: Asilados brasileiros, plano subversivo da 'VPR' para o Brasil—Amarílio Vasconcelos," June 1, 1971, BR AN BSB IE 06.6, p. 5/80, CIEX, ANB-B.

21. "Chile: Reunião de refugiados brasileiros com o Presidente Allende," June 1, 1971, BR AN BSB IE 06.6, no. 176, 6/80, CIEX, ANB-B.

22. "Chile: Nomeação de asilados brasileiros—Cândido da Costa Aragão, Amarílio Vasconcelos, governo da 'UP,'" June 28, 1971, BR AN BSB IE 06.6, no. 212, 78/80, CIEX, ANB-B.

23. Report no. 217, May 13, 1972, BR AN, BSB, IE 08.5, 16/97, CIEX, ANB-B.

24. Rodrigues, *Vozes do mar*. José Anselmo dos Santos was widely known as Cabo Anselmo. In August 1973, he began using the fake name Alexandre da Silva Montenegro, registered in São Paulo. He fought in the courts to recover his baptismal name but when he died, in March 2022, he was buried as Alexandre da Silva Montenegro. In this book, I will refer to him mostly as Cabo Anselmo, which translates as Corporal Anselmo, a military rank that became his nickname. In 2015, he published an autobiography under the name José Anselmo dos Santos. See Santos, *Cabo Anselmo*.

25. Rodrigues, *Vozes do mar*, 174. See also Silva, "Os não-anistiados."

26. "Cândido Aragão," *Dicionário histórico biográfico brasileiro pós 1930*, CPDOC, https://cpdoc.fgv.br/acervo/dicionarios/dhbb (accessed September 30, 2024).

27. The actual date of the coup is still debated in Brazil, with most considering March 31 to be the official date and some implying that the removal of the president only happened on April 1. To avoid being remembered as a regime that started on April Fools' Day, the government made official the celebration on March 31. See more at Mario Magalhães, "Por que a data do golpe é 1 de abril de 1964, e não 31 de março," *UOL*, March 30, 2014, https://blogdomariomagalhaes.blogosfera.uol.com.br/2014/03/30/por-que-a-data-do-golpe-e-1o-de-abril-de-1964-e-nao-31-de-marco-2.

28. Danilo Thomaz, "Cabo Anselmo, famoso agente duplo da ditadura, agora é palestrante de direita," *Época*, July 16, 2018, https://oglobo.globo.com/epoca/cabo-anselmo-famoso-agente-duplo-da-ditadura-agora-palestrante-de-direita-22891376.

29. Cabo Anselmo asked for compensation in the amount of R$100,000. The Amnesty Commission of the Ministry of Justice denied the request.

30. Lucas Ferraz, "União terá de devolver documento a Cabo Anselmo," *Folha de S. Paulo*, December 19, 2008, A17.

31. Institutional Act no. 1 considered it "essential to establish the concept of the civil and military movement that has just opened a new perspective on Brazil for its future.

What happened and will continue to happen at this moment, not only in the spirit and behavior of the armed officials, but also in national public opinion, is a real revolution." Brasil, Presidência da República, Casa Civil, Subchefia para Assuntos Jurídicos, Ato Institucional no. 1, de 9 de abril de 1964, www.planalto.gov.br/ccivil_03/AIT/ait-01-64.htm (accessed November 30, 2023).

32. Renata Keller explores the role of Mexico as a haven for leftist exiles from Latin American countries under dictatorships during the Cold War. See Keller, *Mexico's Cold War*.

33. Marchesi, "Revolution."

34. Thomaz, "Cabo Anselmo."

35. Interview with Cabo Anselmo by the author, São Paulo, October 25, 2021.

36. Interview with Aluízio Palmar by the author, audio recording, Foz do Iguaçu, Brazil, August 10, 2020.

37. Inês Etienne Romeu was held in an extrajudicial detention center called the Casa da Morte (House of Death), a place where state officers tortured political prisoners to convince them to serve as double agents. Romeu was the only captive to survive the camp. The Brazilian Truth Commission published a video with testimonies from Romeu's friends and family. See "Depoimentos dos familiares e amigos de Inês Etienne Romeu," YouTube video, 50:26, posted by Comissão Nacional de Verdade on March 27, 2014, www.youtube .com/watch?v=MCxW3WoQu9w.

38. Pinpointing the exact moment when Cabo Anselmo turned from a VPR guerrilla to a DOPS informant is still a challenge. Elio Gaspari traces his steps since his arrival from Cuba, in September 1970, when he was still using the nickname Jadiel, to when he replaced someone known only as Joel as director of the VPR in São Paulo. He then became Jônatas. See Gaspari, *A ditadura escancarada*, 344–48. However, documents from the Brazilian Truth Commission suggest that he had been an informant since the early years of the dictatorship, in 1964. See Lucas Ferraz, "Cabo Anselmo já era agente duplo em 64, dizem documentos," *Folha de S. Paulo*, October 17, 2011.

39. Souza, *Eu, Cabo Anselmo*, 52–53. In an interview for Brazilian TV Cultura's show *Roda Viva*, reporter Monica Bergamo asks Cabo Anselmo about a 1984 interview with *Istoé* magazine, in which Cabo Anselmo stated that he became an informant voluntarily. He contends that it was not true. "I lied in 1984. Who was the Brazilian government in 1984? What could I have done as a person who had been arrested, tortured, who had known part of all that terror, and who had contributed, as a police dog? Because you cannot believe that they thought I was really a voluntary collaborator! What could I do?" See interview with Cabo Anselmo, *Roda Viva*, October 17, 2011, YouTube video, 1:20:04, posted by Roda Viva on March 19, 2015, www.youtube.com/watch?v=s1MbYiJz9LE.

40. Campos, *O massacre*.

41. Maria do Carmo Brito and her husband, Juarez Guimarães de Brito, were part of the POLOP until 1968, when they founded the Comando da Libertação Nacional (COLINA), which would later merge with the Popular Revolutionary Vanguard (VAR), originating the Palmares Armed Revolutionary Vanguard (VAR-Palmares). VAR-Palmares divided again and became a new version of the VPR, now commanded by Brito, after the successful political burglary known as "Adhemar's Safe." The guerrilla members stole over $2.5 million from a safe connected to former São Paulo governor Adhemar de Barros. Juarez

Guimarães de Brito died after military officers ambushed him in Rio de Janeiro in 1970. Maria do Carmo Brito was arrested on the same occasion. See Vianna, *Uma tempestade*.

42. "Relatório de 'Paquera,' elaborado por Cabo Anselmo e enviado ao DOPS/SP." Documento no. 09/143 DOPS/SP, Documentos Revelados, https://documentosrevelados .com.br/wp-content/uploads/2017/04/relatorio-de-paquera-1.pdf (accessed September 14, 2024).

43. Palmar, *Onde foi*.

44. Interview with Palmar.

45. Interview with Palmar.

46. Interview with René de Carvalho by the author, audio recording, Rio de Janeiro, August 17, 2020.

47. "Soledad Barrett Viedna: Dados," February 2, 1973, BR.AN.BSB.IE.10–2, CIEX (originally CENIMAR), ANB-B.

48. "Soledad Barrett Viedna." Another famous double agent of the military was known as Alberi Vieira dos Santos. The military sent him to Chile to dissipate what was left of the VPR. However, due to the military coup in Chile, he ended up in Mexico, where he was issued a passport. Alberi then went to Argentina following other groups of exiles. Aluízio Palmar dedicated his life to uncovering what happened to these exiles, eventually finding out that they were victims of an armed ambush in a national park. See Palmar, *Onde foi*.

49. "Hace 43 años asesinaron en Brasil a la paraguaya Soledad Barrett," *Última Hora*, January 8, 2016.

50. Mota, *Soledad no Recife*.

51. Borba, *Cabo Anselmo*.

52. "Relatório de 'Paquera.'"

53. Claudio Dantas Sequeira, "O pai do serviço secreto do Itamaraty," *Correio Braziliense*, July 23, 2007.

54. Report no. 209, May 13, 1972, BR AN, BSB, IE 08.5, 7/97, CIEX, ANB-B.

55. Report no. 213, May 13, 1972, BR AN, BSB, IE 08.5, 12/97, CIEX, ANB-B.

56. CNV, *Relatório final da Comissão Nacional da Verdade*, https://www.gov.br /memoriasreveladas/pt-br/assuntos/comissoes-da-verdade/volume_1_digital.pdf (accessed May 8, 2025), 232. CIEX reported on the arrival of Tupamaros in Chile on June 1, 1971. See "Chile: Chegada de 'Tupamaros' uruguaios," June 1, 1971, BR AN BSB IE 06.6, 1/80, CIEX, ANB-B.

57. Calirman, *Brazilian Art*. The exhibition's full catalog can be found at ISUU Inc., https://issuu.com/bienal/docs/name9839c4/82 (accessed September 17, 2024).

58. "Chile: Asilados e refugiados brasileiros—'Jornada de Solidariedade com o Povo Brasileiro,' Takao Amano, Amadeo Thiago de Mello, Amarilio Vasconcellos, Edmur Camargo," June 1, 1971, BR AN BSB IE 06.6, 2/80, CIEX, ANB-B.

59. "Mortos e desaparecidos políticos, Edmur Péricles Camargo," CNV, www.cnv.gov .br/images/pdf/publicacoes/claudio/publicacoes_edmur_pericles.pdf (accessed September 17, 2024).

60. Vizentini, *A política externa*.

61. "Statement by H. E. Mr. João Augusto de Araújo Castro, Minister of State for External Relations of the United States of Brazil, Head of the Delegation at the Fourth Plenary Meeting, Held on 24 March 1964," in United Nations, *Proceedings*, 117.

62. "Statement by the Representative of Brazil, Closing Statements, June 16, 1964," in United Nations, *Proceedings*, 473.

63. "Discurso de posse, Ministro das Relações Exteriores Juracy Magalhães, 17 de janeiro de 1966," Fundação Alexandre de Gusmão, Centro de História e Documentação Diplomática (CHDD), www.gov.br/funag/pt-br/chdd/historia-diplomatica/ministros-de-estado-das-relacoes-exteriores/juracy-montenegro-magalhaes-discurso-de-posse.

64. "Discurso de posse."

65. Vizentini, *A política externa*, 31.

66. Bandeira, *Brasil—Estados Unidos*, 114.

67. Rodrigues, *Aspirações nacionais*, 17.

68. Edward M. Korry, "Confronting Our Past in Chile," *Los Angeles Times*, March 8, 1981, sec. 6, 5.

69. Davis, *Last Two Years*, 331–33.

70. In 2012, the Brazilian Truth Commission announced that it would investigate the role of Brazilian businessmen in the Chilean coup d'état. For more information, see João Paulo Charleaux, "Comissão da Verdade deve investigar participação de brasileiros no golpe do Chile," *OperaMundi*, May 5, 2012.

71. Marlise Simons, "The Brazilian Connection," *Washington Post*, January 6, 1974, B3.

72. Davis, *Last Two Years*, 332.

73. "Ex-embaixador dos EUA conta a 'conexão brasileira' no Chile," *Jornal do Brasil*, November 8, 1985.

74. "Diplomatas refutam livro de Davis," *Jornal do Brasil*, November 6, 1985, 15. The line of credit for buses is registered in the documents of the Brazilian Ministry of Foreign Affairs, such as Telegram, February 4, 1972, DPR/DPB/DALALC/845.15(32) (254), ACI-SERE.

75. Telegram no. 067561," November 20, 1971, DPB/DPF/DPr/DBP/845.72(32)(42) (202), ACI; and Telegram no. 073101," December 8, 1971, DPR/DTU/DBP/845.15(32)(42) (223), ACI-SERE.

76. William Montalbano, "Allende Finding New Credit Sources," *Miami Herald*, October 20, 1972.

77. Sigmund, "'Invisible Blockade,'" 336.

78. Telegram no. 079039, December 30, 1971, DALALC/DPF/DPC/DPR/800(20) (234), ACI-SERE.

79. Telegram no. 065983, November 16, 1971, DFE/DPr/DBP/(190), ACI-SERE.

80. Telegram no. 003543, January 14, 1972, DFE/DBP/DPC/(243), ACI-SERE.

81. Telegram no. 011923, February 2, 1973, DBP/600(B39)602.2(B39) (385), ACI-SERE.

82. Telegram, June 11, 1973, DAM-I/600(B39)611.5(B39) (455), ACI-SERE.

83. Telegram, August 4, 1973, DAM-I/600(B39) (518), ACI-SERE.

84. "Câmara Canto, um diplomata valente," *Jornal do Brasil*, November 8, 1985. In the original, "Fostes punido porque eres (impublicável, designando homossexual)."

85. "Itamaraty usou AI-5 para investigar vida privada e expulsar diplomatas," *O Globo*, June 28, 2009.

86. Adam Bernstein, "Sergio Arellano Stark, Driver of the 'Caravan of Death' under Pinochet, Dies at 94," *Washington Post*, March 10, 2016.

87. "Brasil: A conexão secreta," *La Tercera*, September 8, 2013.

88. " Informes sôbre o Chile," May 18, 1970, Parte S/No. EMFA, ANB-B.

CHAPTER FOUR

1. Assis, *Propaganda e cinema*, 21.

2. Loureiro, *A Aliança para o Progresso*.

3. John F. Kennedy, "Latin American Diplomatic Corps Reception Speech," March 13, 1961, East Room, White House, American Rhetoric Online Speech Bank, www.american rhetoric.com/speeches/jfklatinamericadiplomaticcore.htm.

4. *Mater et magistra*, Encyclical of Pope John XXIII on Christianity and Social Progress, May 15, 1961, www.vatican.va/content/john-xxiii/en/encyclicals/documents/hf_j -xxiii_enc_15051961_mater.html.

5. The Frente Nacionalista Patria y Libertad, also known as Patria y Libertad, was an ultranationalist group formed in April 1971 to oppose the socialist government of Salvador Allende. In June 1973, the group attempted a coup against the Allende government, now known as the Tancazo. With the support of the Chilean Navy, it was behind acts of violence and sabotage of Chile's infrastructure, including power cuts while Allende was broadcast on television. See Gomés, "Héroes y demonios"; Boisard, "La matriz antiliberal"; and Vera and Díaz Nieva, "Frente Nacionalista."

6. Dreifuss, *1964*, 102.

7. "The Country That Saved Itself," *Reader's Digest*, November 1964, BR AN, RIO. QL.O.CDI.22, ANB-RJ.

8. Crummett, "El Poder Feminino"; Cordeiro, *Direitas em movimento*; Power, "Who but a Woman?"

9. The connection started right after Allende's inauguration, when Chilean business-people decided to invest in São Paulo and other large cities in Brazil. Luis Fuenzalida was one of them. He connected with Brazilian American entrepreneur Gilberto Huber, who commanded the company Listas Telefônicas Brasileiras, a manufacturer of telephone directories. Huber diversified the business, investing in metallurgy, paper, and insurance companies. See Bandeira, *Fórmula para o caos*, 286–87.

10. Hoeveler, "(Neo)liberalismo," 51.

11. Poggi, "A política."

12. Valdés, *Pinochet's Economists*.

13. Cysne, "A economia brasileira"; Resende, "A política brasileira"; Assunção, "PAEG"; Malloy, *Authoritarianism and Corporatism*.

14. Barbosa, Pessoa Brandão, and Faro, "Fiscal Reform."

15. Beired, *Sob o signo*.

16. Black, *United States Penetration of Brazil*, 78.

17. Bortone, "O Instituto de Pesquisas."

18. "Fundo Instituto de Pesquisas e Estudos Sociais—IPES (QL), Coordenação Geral de Processamento e Preservação do Acervo Coordenação de Documentos Audiovisuais e Cartográficos Equipe de Documentos Iconográficos, Arquivo Nacional, Brasília," 6, www .gov.br/arquivonacional/pt-br/servicos/copy_of_instrumentos-de-pesquisa/ipes_final _iconografico.pdf (accessed September 14, 2024).

19. "Silva, Golberi do Couto," CPDOC, www.fgv.br/cpdoc/acervo/dicionarios/verbete -biografico/silva-golberi-do-couto-e (accessed September 17, 2024).

20. Historian Thomas E. Skidmore referred to Golbery as "an important minister in the Geisel administration who became notable for his efforts to democratize the military regime." "General Golbery do Couto e Silva (1911–1987)," Thomas E. Skidmore Collection, Brown University Library Collections, https://library.brown.edu/collections/skidmore /portraits/generalGolberyCoutoESilva.html (accessed January 10, 2023).

21. "Golbery do Couto e Silva, Leader in Brazil Coup," *New York Times*, September 20, 1987.

22. Bortone, "O Instituto de Pesquisas."

23. The focus on the Brazilian youth has been discussed in Cowan, *Securing Sex*. Many of these videos can be found online. "Assista à propaganda anticomunista do Ipes," excerpt of documentary movie, YouTube video, 10:52, posted by Estado de S. Paulo on April 2, 2014, 0:19, www.youtube.com/watch?v=zN6tIZEHXr8.

24. The ESG was another common thread among Brazilian, Chilean, and other South American dictatorships. In his address celebrating the third anniversary of the coup, on September 11, 1976, Pinochet declared that the National Security Doctrine was the official ideology of Chile.

At the height of the Cold War narrative, the Brazilian and the Chilean DSN contended that the only way to achieve safety at home was by guaranteeing a safe state. The notion of national security connected to international affairs, however, was replaced by a focus on domestic enemies. The war on communism should not only focus on the fear of another Cuba—the prevention of which was the responsibility of the United States—but also on prioritizing local supporters of communism, who could be individuals, companies, or any entity perceived as an enemy of the government. All basic instruments for the functioning of the society, including education, internal affairs, foreign relations, and the economy, represented fronts of a "total war," which justified the state of exception. The rule of law, therefore, could be ignored if the government understood it was menacing the public good. For more on the US approach to national security, which addresses Latin America's role in US national security, see Schoultz, *National Security*; and Arriagada Herrera, "National Security Doctrine."

25. "Fundo Instituto de Pesquisas e Estudos Sociais."

26. Sonia Seganfreddo, "UNE instrumento de subversão; Série de quatorze reportagens, publicada sob o título UNE—menina dos olhos do PC," *O Jornal*, September 1962, www.ebooksbrasil.org/eLibris/une.html (accessed December 3, 2021). See also Barbosa, "Fazendo-os obedecer."

27. Seganfreddo, "UNE instrumento de subversão."

28. "Fundo Instituto de Pesquisas e Estudos Sociais."

29. Moreira, "O partido do empresariado."

30. Stepan, *Military in Politics*, 154.

31. "Silva, Golberi do Couto."

32. Starling, "Golpe militar."

33. Interview with Orlando Sáenz Rojas by the author, audio recording, Santiago, December 2, 2021.

34. Interview with Sáenz Rojas.

35. Dreifuss, *1964*, 61–62.

36. Bandeira, *O governo João Goulart*, 65.

37. Simons, "Brazilian Connection."

38. Simons, "Brazilian Connection." Simons also suggests that institutions from other countries contributed to anti-Allende groups, including those from Argentina, Venezuela, and Bolivia.

39. Paiva, *BNDES*, 26, 35.

40. Paiva, *BNDES*, 19.

41. Simons, "Brazilian Connection."

42. Interview with Aristóteles Drummond by the author, Rio de Janeiro, February 3, 2017.

43. Simons, "Brazilian Connection."

44. Drummond, *Memórias.*

45. Interview with Drummond.

46. There are two versions of the history of the creation of IBAD; one places it in the late 1950s, as a result of the strengthening of commercial groups in Rio de Janeiro. The other connects it to conservatives from the state as a reaction to Goulart's presidency. See Dreifuss, *1964,* 102.

47. Black, *United States Penetration of Brazil,* 72.

48. Bandeira, *O governo João Goulart,* 67.

49. Dreifuss, *1964,* 103.

50. Integralismo was a Brazilian fascist movement. See Gonçalves and Caldeira Neto, *O fascismo.*

51. Although IBAD was dissolved along with ADEP on December 20, 1963, accused of "carrying out illicit activity and contrary to the security of the state and the community," the model of creating "caixinhas," or collective funding to support political candidates, survived. In 1985, Congressman Maurício Ferreira Lima denounced an attempt to resurrect IBAD. "Deputado denuncia 'caixinha' de empresários para a Constituinte," *Jornal do Brasil,* June 12, 1985, Senado Federal, https://www2.senado.leg.br/bdsf/bitstream/handle/id/110570/Jun_1985%20-%200119.pdf?sequence=3&isAllowed=y (accessed September 17, 2024).

52. "1963: É constituída CPI para apurar candidatos que teriam recebido financiamento do Ibad e Ipes," *Rádio Câmara,* May 14, 2006, www.camara.leg.br/radio/programas/270928-1963-e-constituida-cpi-para-apurar-candidatos-que-teriam-recebido-financiamento-do-ibad-e-ipes-07—00/. The Arquivo Público Estadual Jordão Emerenciano, a public archive in Pernambuco, has preserved all the volumes of documents and interviews from the 1963 CPI. They are available at Comissão da Verdade do Estado de Pernambuco, www.comissaodaverdade.pe.gov.br/index.php/vol01-pdf (accessed November 23, 2021).

53. Moreira, "O partido do empresariado."

54. Interview with Drummond.

55. "Intercâmbio Comercial Brasileiro—Chile," Ministério do Desenvolvimento, Indústria e Comércio Exterior (MDIC), Secretaria de Comércio Exterior (SECEX), and Departamento de Planejamento e Desenvolvimento do Comércio Exterior (DEPLA), www.gov.br/produtividade-e-comercio-exterior/pt-br/assuntos/comercio-exterior/estatisticas/outras-estatisticas-de-comercio-exterior (accessed December 2, 2021). According to the same source, trade between the two countries increased dramatically after the 1973 coup. Even then, however, Chile's participation in Brazil's total trade volume never surpassed 2 percent of exports or imports from 1966 to 1975.

Table 1. Chile's participation in Brazil's total trade volume

FREE ON BOARD (FOB) (IN US$1,000)

Year	Exports	Imports
1967	21,737.80	14,462.40
1968	23,184.90	18,819.70
1969	24,096.40	26,299.80
1970	23,714.60	32,669.50
1971	31,645.30	28,573.00
1972	54,941.00	20,726.00
1973	34,542.10	32,975.00
1974	91,778.10	137,422.90
1975	99,849.00	103,105.70
1976	81,844.20	266,772.70

It is important to clarify that the data in the table were compiled using methodologies very different from the current ones, at a time when the UN international compatibility manual did not exist. See United Nations Department of Economic and Social Affairs, *International Merchandise Trade Statistics*. That said, for aggregate and historical comparison purposes, they are valid.

56. Arquivo Nacional, Rio de Janeiro, Coordenação de Documentos Escritos, Equipe de Documentos Privados, *Campanha da Mulher pela Democracia: Inventário das Coleções* (Rio de Janeiro, 2005), 1:199–218, digital, AN/SCO/SDP 064.

57. "Histórico," Fundo CAMDE, ANB-RJ, 1967, 2. See also Moreira, "Em defesa da Igreja."

58. Pollanah, "D. Amélia Molina Bastos," 161.

59. The so-called Lei do Divórcio (Law 6515/1977) finally allowed matrimonial ties to be legally broken. Until then, the only possibility for couples who wanted a divorce was "desquite," similar to what some US states call "divorce from bed and board," in which the couple is separated in terms of "bodies and goods" but still legally married. See Tatiana Beltrão, "Divórcio demorou a chegar no Brasil," *Agência Senado*, December 4, 2017, https://www12.senado.leg.br/noticias/especiais/arquivo-s/divorcio-demorou-a-chegar-no-brasil.

60. "San Tiago Dantas," *Dicionário histórico biográfico brasileiro pós 1930*, CPDOC, https://cpdoc.fgv.br/producao/dossies/Jango/biografias/san_tiago_dantas (accessed September 17, 2024).

61. Cordeiro, *Direitas em movimento*.

62. Power, *Right-Wing Women*.

63. "Marcha de las cacerolas vacías, contra el gobierno de Salvador Allende," *El Mercurio*, December 2, 1971, 1.

64. Feminist communications theorist Michèle Mattelart recorded a fascinating studio program rich in images of female participation in the protests against Allende. "Michelle Mattelart Reads the Chilean Press avant Coup: Every Day It Gets Harder to Be a Good Housewife," Vimeo, https://vimeo.com/212132375 (accessed September 17, 2024).

65. Cordeiro, *Direitas em movimento*.

66. Simons, "Brazilian Connection."

67. White, *Chile's Days of Terror*, 24.

68. Camilla Townsend presents a new perspective on the role of working-class women, arguing that dissatisfaction with the leftist administration was latent. See Townsend, "Refusing to Travel."

69. Andreas, *Nothing*, 8–9. Nathaniel Davis suspected that "the loyal or gentrified maids from the better suburbs made up more of the 'working-class' contingent than women of the shantytowns and poorer districts." See Davis, *Last Two Years*, 47–48.

70. Betilde V. Muñoz contends that a similarly varied demography could be observed in protests against Augusto Pinochet. See Muñoz, "Where Are the Women?"

71. Crummett, "El Poder Feminino," 105.

72. Power, "Engendering of Anticommunism."

73. Apiolaza and Salgado Ferrufino, "Gremios empresariales."

74. Campero, *Los gremios empresariales*.

75. Gaudichaud, *Chile*.

76. Vilarín was consulted by the military and the CIA constantly. Closer to the September 11 coup, "Admiral Patricio Carvajal, Chief of the National Defense staff, tried to persuade" him to "postpone his strike" until the counterinsurgency planning by the military was finished. "Central Intelligence Agency Information Report," July 25, 1973, in Howard, *Foreign Relations, 1969–1976*, vol. 21, doc. 338, https://history.state.gov/historicaldocuments/frus1969-76v21/d338.

77. "El sórdido mundo del fascismo," *Punto Final*, October 24, 1972. See also Díaz Nieva, "Patria y Libertad."

78. Poggi, "A política."

79. Dreifuss, *1964*; Dreifuss, *A Internacional Capitalista*.

80. Dreifuss, *1964*, 161.

81. Dreifuss, *1964*; Hoeveler, "René Dreifuss."

82. Interview with Sáenz Rojas.

83. Pompeu would also have his turn presiding over AILA. His tenure coincided with the early years of the Pinochet regime, from May 29, 1974, to May 7, 1975.

84. Interview with Sáenz Rojas.

85. Interview with Sáenz Rojas.

86. Marta Sánchez Leiva, "Orlando Sáenz: 'Estábamos atentos y contentos,'" *La Tercera*, September 8, 2018.

87. Sánchez Leiva, "Orlando Sáenz."

88. Gaudichaud, *Chile*, 145.

89. Jonathan Kandell, "Foreign Companies Aided Anti-Allende Strikers, Chileans Say," *New York Times*, October 16, 1974, 8. The companies cited in the article denied the accusations. Kandell's interviewees stated that the funds amounted to $200,000 and also came from Mexican, Venezuelan, and Peruvian companies. The dollar-escudo rate on the black market was cited as evidence of CIA support for strikers. The influence of other countries, however, could also be part of the explanation.

90. "El sórdido mundo del fascismo," *Punto Final*, October 24, 1972. See also Díaz Nieva, "Patria y Libertad."

91. Bandeira, *Conflito e integração*, 414. Ibañez's role is also mentioned in Simons, "Brazilian Connection."

92. Gaspari, *O sacerdote*, 348.

93. Seymour M. Hersh, "The Price of Power: Kissinger, Nixon, and Chile," *Atlantic*, December 1982, www.theatlantic.com/magazine/archive/1982/12/the-price-of-power/376309/.

94. Hersh, "Price of Power."

95. This is how the "About" section of COA's website defines its objectives. Americas Society / Council of the Americas, www.as-coa.org/about/about-ascoa (accessed September 17, 2024).

96. Hoeveler, "(Neo)liberalismo."

97. Frei's suggestion would eventually result in the creation of the Latin American Integration Association via the 1980 Montevideo Treaty.

98. "Memorandum from Richard T. Kennedy and Arnold Nachmanoff of the National Security Council Staff to the President's Assistant for National Security Affairs (Kissinger)," November 17, 1970, in Howard, *Foreign Relations, 1969–1976*, vol. 21, doc. 182, https://history.state.gov/historicaldocuments/frus1969-76v21/d182.

99. Hoeveler, "(Neo)liberalismo," 244.

100. Interview with Sáenz Rojas.

101. Ramírez, "Trayectoria intelectual."

102. Fajardo, *World That Latin America Created*.

103. Campos, *A lanterna na popa*, 164, 268, 165.

104. Campos was one of the most frequent lecturers at the Brazilian Escola de Guerra. See Simons, "Brazilian Connection."

105. Campos, *A lanterna na popa*, 164–65.

106. Campos, *A lanterna na popa*, 749.

107. Campos was appointed ambassador in August 1961 by Jânio Quadros. After the president's resignation, the appointment was delayed and he was only confirmed after Goulart took office, agreeing with a parliamentary system, which reduced his powers. He decided to maintain Campos as an ambassador-at-large (*embaixador extraordinário*). However, influenced by his business partner, Jorge Flores, Campos supported the 1964 coup d'état in Brazil and became a powerful adviser during the entire period of the dictatorship. See Simon Romero, "Jorge Flores, 88; Influenced a Coup in Brazil," *New York Times*, August 3, 2000. Criticizing João Goulart, Campos classified his administration as a "bitter experience of the radicalization of political attitudes that were leading us to administrative inertia, galloping inflation, economic backwardness and the loss of substance of democratic institutions." See Campos, *Política econômica*, 36.

108. Campos, *A lanterna na popa*, 556.

109. Fico, *O grande irmão*, 78–80.

110. Campos, *A lanterna na popa*, 559.

111. Campos, *A lanterna na popa*, 640. Campos nominally cited projects by Mario Simonsen for tax reform, Paulo Assis Ribeiro for agrarian reform, Dénio Nogueira for bank reform, and Jorge Flores for housing. He added, "Fortunately, the IPES texts were quite readable, as the writer Rubem Fonseca was in charge of the editorial revision."

112. Blume, "Pressure Groups," 213, 218.

113. "Programa de Ação Econômica do Governo (PAEG)," CPDOC, www.fgv.br/cpdoc /acervo/dicionarios/verbete-tematico/programa-de-acao-economica-do-governo-paeg (accessed September 3, 2024).

114. "Ingreso silenciosamente al país teórico de la dictadura brasileña toma contactos con la derecha," *Última Hora*, November 26, 1971, 3.

115. Telegram 069743, AIG/DSI/DBP/591.71, November 26, 1971, ACI-SERE.

116. Valdés, *Pinochet's Economists*.

117. Friedman and Friedman, *Two Lucky People*, 398. Milton Friedman's point of view is criticized by economists such as Paul Krugman, who states that "Chile had a huge economic crisis in the early 70s, which was, yes, partly due to Allende and the accompanying turmoil. Then the country experienced a recovery driven in large part by massive capital inflows, which mostly consisted of making up the lost ground. Then there was a huge crisis again in the early 1980s—part of the broader Latin debt crisis, but Chile was hit much worse than other major players. It wasn't until the late 1980s, by which time the hardline free-market policies had been considerably softened, that Chile finally moved definitively ahead of where it had been in the early 70s." See Paul Krugman, "Fantasies of the Chicago Boys," *New York Times*, March 3, 2010.

118. Foxley, *Latin American Experiments*, 103–5.

119. Gárate Chateau, *La revolución capitalista*; Silva, "La política económica."

120. Campos, *A lanterna na popa*, 560.

121. Becker, "What Latin America Owes."

122. Veloso, "Determinantes do 'milagre,'" 222–24.

123. Valenzuela, "Six Years," 8.

124. Campos, *A moeda*, 41.

125. For a concise account of the critique of the statist politics of the Brazilian military government, see Cysne, "A economia brasileira."

126. In his memoirs, Campos asserts that "in the early 1970s statism was still the dominant ideology in Latin America. Brezhnevian socialism continued to grow, and only the intelligence agencies of some countries perceived the great operational failures of Marxism-Leninism, which had the promise of rapid industrialization with social justice. False but seductive to the Third World." Campos, *A lanterna na popa*, 910.

127. Campos, *O século esquisito*, 19–21.

128. Campos, *O século esquisito*, 105.

129. Gramsci, *Prison Notebooks*.

130. Campos, *A lanterna na popa*, 640.

131. Campos, *A lanterna na popa*, 248.

CHAPTER FIVE

1. Embajada de Chile, "Dirección General Departamento de Coordinación y análisis, ref.: Estudios que estaría realizando el Ejército brasileño sobre el establecimiento de guerrillas en Chile, 0912, estrictamente confidencial DG no. 18," Brasília, March 23, 1971, AGH-MRE.

2. Embajada de Chile, "Dirección General," 1.

3. Embajada de Chile, "Dirección General," 2.

4. In 1972, the Navy Intelligence Center (CENIMAR) dramatically increased the geographical research and mapping of the area, as demonstrated in its annual report. Divisão de Registro do CENIMAR, *Relatório anual e estatístico da Divisão de Registro do CENIMAR em 1972, assinado pelo capitão Ronaldo Velloso Netto dos Reys, s.d. Sem grau de sigilo*, PR/UFMG/Cenimar/LR., Projeto República, Universidade Federal de Minas Gerais, www.ufmg.br/brasildoc/mdocs-posts/documento-cenimar-operação-registro-relatorio -anual-de-1972, cited in Figueiredo, *Lugar nenhum*, 26.

5. Navarro, "*Fiducia,*" 24–25.

6. Necochea, "El fascismo," 145.

7. Embajada de Chile, "Dirección de Relaciones Internacionales: Departamento Asun- tos Americanos, ref.: Visita del Canciller de Panamá, Planes y comentarios, no. 501/130, 18679," Brasília, June 2, 1971, AGH-MRE.

8. Embajada de Chile, "Informativo económico no. 3," Brasília, May 15, 1971, AGH-MRE.

9. "Declaração de Eduardo Frei: Atuação do PCCh," no. 441, BR AN, BSB, IE 07.2, p. 66/85, October 21, 1971, CIEX, ANB-B.

10. Spektor, "Origens."

11. The partnership to remove Allende came as the result of a solid relationship of trust with the United States, which began when Brazil helped General Hugo Banzer come to power in Bolivia. Two weeks before Médici's visit, the countries had worked together to prevent the leftist "Frente Amplio" from winning the Uruguayan presiden- tial elections of 1971. See Rabe, *Kissinger*, 95–96. See also "Secret Department of State Telegram to U.S. Embassies in Brazil and Argentina," August 20, 1971, Department of State Subject Numeric Files 1970–73, GWU, https://nsarchive2.gwu.edu/NSAEBB /NSAEBB71/#docs.

12. US Department of State, "The New Course in Brazil," A/ISS/IPS, Department of State NIE 93–72, January 13, 1972, GWU, http://nsarchive.gwu.edu/NSAEBB/NSAEBB282 /Document%20146%201.13.72.pdf.

13. Gaspari, *A ditadura escancarada*, 298–99; Grael, *Aventura*, 19.

14. Cockcroft, *Neighbors in Turmoil*; Bandeira, *Fórmula para o caos*; Haslam, *Nixon Administration*; Guardiola-Rivera, *Story of a Death*; Qureshi, *Nixon, Kissinger, and Allende*; Stern, *Remembering Pinochet's Chile*; Uribe, *Black Book*.

15. Kornbluh, *Pinochet File*, 83.

16. US Senate, *Covert Action in Chile*, 3.

17. "Chile: Encontro dos Presidentes Lanusse e Allende—Intervenção do Brasil no Uruguai," no. 470, BR AN, BSB, IE 07.3, p. 17/86, November 1, 1971, CIEX, ANB-B.

18. Gerald R. Ford, "Press Conference on Questions Related to Nixon," September 16, 1974, video recording of press conference, 11:44–13:59, Gerald R. Ford Foundation, https://geraldrfordfoundation.org/press-conference-on-questions-related-to-nixon/.

19. US Senate, *Covert Action in Chile*.

20. Uribe, *Black Book*.

21. Salvador Allende, "Speech to the United Nations," December 4, 1972, excerpts, Marxists Internet Archive, www.marxists.org/archive/allende/1972/december/04.htm.

22. Paul E. Sigmund discusses at length the participation of US private institutions, including banks and International Telephone and Telegraph (ITT), owner of 70 percent of the Chilean Telephone Company. See Sigmund, "'Invisible Blockade,'" 323. ITT was also a major actor in the years that preceded the 1964 coup in Brazil. Robert Kennedy traveled

to the country in 1963, at the request of his president brother, to demand support for the company; otherwise, Brazil could have suffered a decrease in economic cooperation. See Dreifuss, *1964*, 100.

23. Track Two was also the nickname of Project FUBELT, a secret CIA operation to prevent Salvador Allende from taking power in 1970. For more on the definition and instances in which the United States has applied Track Two diplomacy, see Jones, *Track Two*.

24. "Developments in Brazil: Significance of Institutional Act no. 5," telegram no. 292127. December 25, 1968, Brown University Digital Repository, https://repository .library.brown.edu/studio/item/bdr:336519/.

25. "South American Portion of Secretary Connally's Trip," memorandum 5001, June 23, 1972, Department of State EO 12958.

26. A brief biography of Emílio Garrastazu Médici can be found at Biblioteca Presidência da República, www.biblioteca.presidencia.gov.br/presidencia/presidencia/ex -presidentes/emilio-medici (accessed September 18, 2024).

27. "Brasil hablará en Washington como potencia mundial," *Qué pasa*, no. 8, December 1971.

28. Gabeira, *O que é isso*.

29. "Seqüestrado cônsul japonês," *O Estado de S. Paulo*, March 12, 1970, 16.

30. "Embaixador alemão é seqüestrado," *Jornal do Brasil*, June 19, 1970, 1.

31. Telegram no. 19187," DFE/DPR/660.7(32), June 18, 1971, ACI-SERE.

32. Veloso, "Determinantes do 'milagre,'" 222, 224.

33. Spektor, *Kissinger*, 45.

34. Green, *We Cannot Remain Silent*, 194.

35. "Student Disrupts a Meeting of O.A.S. during Medici Talk," *New York Times*, December 8, 1971.

36. "The Torture of a Brazilian," *Washington Post*, September 19, 1971, 83.

37. Sattamini, *Mother's Cry*, 21, 37.

38. Interview with Marcos Arruda by the author, via Skype, March 8, 2012.

39. Richard Nixon, "Toasts of the President and President Medici of Brazil, December 7, 1971," "Spoken Remarks and Addresses," American Presidency Project, University of California, Santa Barbara, www.presidency.ucsb.edu/ws/?pid=3247.

40. "Meeting with President Emílio Garrastazu Médici of Brazil on Thursday, December 9, 1971, at 10:00 a.m., in the President's Office, the White House," White House memorandum, GWU, https://nsarchive.gwu.edu/document/20757-04.

41. "Meeting with President Emílio Garrastazu Médici."

42. "Meeting with President Emílio Garrastazu Médici."

43. Henry A. Kissinger, "The President's Private Meeting with British Prime Minister Edward Heath on Monday, December 20, 1971, 1:30–5:00 p.m., in the Sitting Room of Government House, Bermuda," memorandum for the President's File, GWU, http://nsarchive.gwu.edu/NSAEBB/NSAEBB71/doc15.pdf.

44. Burns, *History of Brazil*, 449.

45. Telegram 2162 from Rio de Janeiro, RG 59, Central Files 1964–66, POL 23–9 BRAZ, April 2, 1964, National Archives and Records Administration, https://catalog .archives.gov/id/331238367.

46. The maneuver to give a positive tone to a military coup worked so well that for decades Brazilians, including victims of the dictatorship, referred to it as a "revolution." Even

Brazilian leftist president Luís Inácio Lula da Silva did that in his third term, in June 2023, during a political event. See "Lula comete gafe ao chamar golpe military de revolução," *UOL*, June 29, 2023, https://noticias.uol.com.br/politica/ultimas-noticias/2023/06/29/lula-comete-gafe-ao-chamar-golpe-militar-de-revolucao.htm.

47. Burns, *History of Brazil*, 78–80.

48. Galeano, *As veias abertas*, 235–38.

49. Almeida, "Do alinhamento," 10.

50. The comparison of small Latin American countries to Cuba and geographically larger ones, such as Brazil, to China was frequent in the media and in official documents. See Vizentini, *A política externa*, 42.

51. Santos, "Brazilian Foreign Policy," 62.

52. Burns, "Tradition and Variation," 208.

53. Stallings, *Class Conflict*, 65.

54. Dattwyler, "La vivienda social"; Tinsman, *Partners in Conflict*.

55. Boorstein, *Allende's Chile*, 39.

56. Stallings, *Class Conflict*, 126.

57. US Senate, *Covert Action in Chile*, 19–20. This amount refers to the sum spent before Allende's election. In a top-secret hearing at the US Congress, CIA director William E. Colby testified that the agency had spent over $8 million on covert actions during the Allende administration. See Seymour M. Hersh, "C.I.A. Chief Tells House of $8-Million Campaign against Allende in '70–73," *New York Times*, September 8, 1974, 26.

58. See Georgetown University Political Database of the Americas, https://pdba.georgetown.edu/Elecdata/Chile/pres_totals.html (accessed August 7, 2024). Other sources, however, give slightly different numbers.

59. "Texto refundido de la Ley General de Elecciones de Chile," law no. 12.891, established in Santiago, July 10, 1958, Biblioteca del Congreso Nacional de Chile, www.leychile.cl/Navegar?idNorma=253140.

60. García, *El Caso Schneider*; Varas, *Conversaciones con Viaux*.

61. Sigmund, "CIA in Chile," 11–17; Gustafson, "CIA Machinations."

62. Boorstein, *Allende's Chile*, 67.

63. Beaulac, *Diplomat Looks at Aid*.

64. The CIA estimated that Cuba had provided Allende's campaign with $350,000. See US Senate, *Covert Action in Chile*, 21. For an analysis of US operations in Chile during the 1960s and 1970s, see Gustafson, *Hostile Intent*.

65. "EM no 01," FA-2–25, January 21, 1971, Estado Maior das Forças Armadas, ANB-B.

66. Castro, *Cuba-Chile*, 13.

67. José Rodríguez Elizondo, "El invierno del Mesías," *Caretas*, November 8, 2001, 9.

68. Telegram no. 21612, AIG/DBP/601.4(32)47, October 30, 1970, ACI-SERE.

69. Telegram no. 469, BR AN, BSB, IE 07.3, p. 16/86, November 1, 1971, CIEX, ANB- B.

70. Telegram no. 064043, DBP/DAC/430(24h) (32)169, November 9, 1971, ACI-SERE.

71. Telegram no. 064860, DBP/DAC/430(24h) (32)174, November 11, 1971, ACI-SERE.

72. Telegram no. 065394, DBP/DEOc/920(85)(32)178, November 12, 1971, ACI-SERE.

73. Telegram no. 065769, DBP/DAC/920(24h) (32)179, November 14, 1971, ACI-SERE.

74. Telegram no. 066067, DBP/DAC/430(52) (32)186, November 16, 1971, ACI-SER.

75. Fermandois, *Chile y el mundo*, 240; Aggio, *Democracia e socialismo*, 184.

76. Aggio, "Uma insólita visita."

77. Rojas, *Salvador Allende*, 100.

78. "Visita de Fidel Castro ao Chile," telegram no. 067211, DBP/DAC/DCInt/AIG430(24h)(32), November 19, 1971, ACI-SERE.

79. Bandeira, *Fórmula para o caos*.

80. Castro, *Cuba-Chile*, 265.

81. Telegram no. 066067, DBP/DAC/430(52)(32)186, November 16, 1971, ACI-SERE.

82. Castro, *Cuba-Chile*, 265.

83. Qureshi, *Nixon, Kissinger, and Allende*, 112.

84. Pedemonte, "Castro's Position."

85. Harmer, *Allende's Chile*, 94–95.

86. For a rich source of images and testimonials of this day, see Guzmán, *Battle of Chile*.

87. Stern, *Remembering Pinochet's Chile*.

88. Allende, *Compañero Presidente*, 155, 157.

CHAPTER SIX

1. "O médico Otto Brockes aborda aspectos de sua experiência durante o golpe que depôs presidente chileno," April 14, 2014, video recording of testimony to the CDHMVJ, YouTube video, 38:12, posted by TV Senado on July 11, 2014, 07:48–7:54, www.youtube.com/watch?v=Mdo3SxFSnJY.

2. Interview with Otto Brockes by the author, video recording, Goiás, Brazil, July 15, 2014.

3. Interview with Brockes.

4. Report no. 173/73, BR AN, BSB, IE 10.4, p. 13/157, April 5, 1973, CIEX, ANB-B.

5. Report no. 225/73, BR AN, BSB, IE 10.5, p. 13/375, May 4, 1973, CIEX, ANB-B.

6. When writing about the Tancazo, also known as Tanquetazo, Franck Gaudichaud argues that it served more as a demonstration of popular resistance than as a rehearsal for the September 11 coup. See Gaudichaud, *Chile*, 258.

7. Interview with Jean Marc von der Weid by the author, video recording, Rio de Janeiro, September 1, 2020.

8. Report no. 314/73, BR AN, BSB, IE 10.6, p. 51/93, June 20, 1973, CIEX, ANB-B.

9. Report no. 402/73, BR AN, BSB, IE 11.1, p. 55/61, August 20, 1973, CIEX, ANB-B.

10. Report no. 389/73, BRAN, BSB, IE 11.1, p. 25/61, August 8, 1973, CIEX, ANB-B.

11. Report no. 389/73.

12. Harmer, *Allende's Chile*, 233.

13. Telegram 641.7 (148), "Comemoração do sete de setembro," September 8, 1973, ACI-SERE.

14. Padrós and Simões, "A ditadura brasileira," 241.

15. Telegram 641.7 (148).

16. McPherson, *Ghosts of Sheridan Circle*.

17. Desabastecimento: Pão—Agudização do problema," September 11, 1973, ACI-SERE.

18. "Situação econômica: Greve dos trabalhadores—Apoio de outros gremios," September 11, 1973, ACI-SERE.

19. Silveira, *Setenta*.

20. Interview with Wilson Barbosa by the author, video recording, São Paulo, July 11, 2014.

21. Interview with Ubiramar Peixoto by the author, video recording, Brasília, July 14, 2014.

22. Gabeira, *O que é isso*, 11.

23. A short description of Gabeira's political career is available on his website, http://gabeira.com.br/biografia/ (accessed September 26, 2024).

24. Amnesty International, *Chile*, 6.

25. Amnesty International, *Chile*, 64.

26. Interview with René de Carvalho by the author, audio recording, Rio de Janeiro, August 17, 2020.

27. The radio was also an important instrument for contesting the dictatorial regime since its inception. Salvador Allende's iconic farewell speech arrived in Chilean households via Radio Magallanes. For more on the role of opposition radio, see Herrera and Reyes, "El rol de las radios"; and Solari Orellana, "Una voz."

28. Interview with Aluízio Palmar by the author, audio recording, Foz do Iguaçu, Brazil, August 10, 2020.

29. Interview with Eliete Ferrer by the author, video recording, Rio de Janeiro, August 15, 2024.

30. Interview with Nielsen Pires by the author, video recording, São Paulo, July 11, 2014.

31. Interview with Pires.

32. Interview with Carvalho.

33. Interview with Carvalho.

34. "Nilton Rosa da Silva," in Comissão Nacional da Verdade, *Relatório*, 1248.

35. Brum, "Um jacarandá."

36. Eduardo Santa Cruz, "El fascismo mató a combatiente brasileño," *Punto Final*, July 3, 1973.

37. Amnesty International, *Chile*.

38. CNV, *Relatório final da Comissão Nacional da Verdade*, http://cnv.memoriasreveladas.gov.br/images/pdf/relatorio_versao_final18-02.pdf (accessed September 17, 2024).

39. Estadio Nacional Memoria Nacional ex Prisioneros/as Políticos/as is a nonprofit created by former prisoners of the Chilean dictatorship. Its work has been catalogued at Memoria Estadio Nacional, www.memoriaestadionacional.cl/ (accessed July 17, 2023).

40. Comisión Nacional de Verdad y Reconciliación, *Informe*, 115.

41. Comisión Nacional sobre Prisión Política y Tortura, *Informe*, 524.

42. Comissão da Verdade do Estado de São Paulo, "Wânio José de Mattos," http://comissaodaverdade.al.sp.gov.br/mortos-desaparecidos/wanio-jose-de-mattos (accessed September 16, 2024).

43. Interview with Brockes.

44. Interview with Brockes.

45. Bonnefoy Miralles, *Terrorismo de estadio*.

46. Comissão da Verdade do Estado de São Paulo, "Wânio José de Mattos."

47. "Patriota brasileiro vítima do fascismo no Chile," Vaz 3, 110, 4/4, report no. 389/73, ANB-B.

48. Memórias da Ditadura, "Jane Vanini," Secretaria de Direitos Humanos da Presidência da República, https://memoriasdaditadura.org.br/biografias-da-resistencia/jane-vanini/ (accessed July 17, 2023).

49. Sales, "A Ação Libertadora Nacional."

50. Merlino and Ojeda, *Direito à memória*, 163–66.

51. Merlino and Ojeda, *Direito à memória*, 163–66. The note read, "Perdóname mi amor, fue un último intento por salvarte."

52. Mario Magalhães, "Ditadura chilena matou e sumiu com cinco brasileiros," *UOL*, September 11, 2013, https://blogdomariomagalhaes.blogosfera.uol.com.br/2013/09/11/ditadura-chilena-matou-e-sumiu-com-cinco-brasileiros/ (accessed September 26, 2024).

53. The play *Jane Vanini: Uma vida em favor da liberdade*, by Grupo Cena Onze, was performed at the theater of the Instituto Federal Professor Olegário Baldo, in Cáceres, Mato Grosso. The documentary titled *Missivas: As cartas de Jane Vanini* was directed by Carolina Araújo and Maurício Pinto. More information can be found at https://missivas.com/ (accessed July 18, 2023). See also Araújo, "Um mundo feminino."

54. "VANINI CAPOZI, Jane—Dossier 33 Pág.—23 artículos." Centro de Estudios Miguel Enríquez (CEME), Archivo Chile, www.archivochile.com/Memorial/caidos_mir/V/vanini_capozi_jane.pdf (accessed July 18, 2024). Carlos Marighella (1911–69) was a Brazilian guerrilla leader and founder of ALN.

55. CHILE—Comisión Nacional de Verdad y Reconciliación.

56. CHILE—Comisión Nacional de Verdad y Reconciliación.

57. The criminal trial no. 368/2012 opened on December 12, 2012. Some of its documents, including Carmen Fischer's testimony, were unearthed by the Brazilian Truth Commission. "Depoimento de Carmen Fischer, 27 de maio de 1993," CNV, http://cnv.memoriasreveladas.gov.br/images/pdf/docs/pg_51.pdf.

58. "Mortos e desaparecidos, Luiz Carlos Almeida," Comissão da Verdade do Estado de São Paulo, http://comissaodaverdade.al.sp.gov.br/mortos-desaparecidos/luiz-carlos-almeida (accessed September 16, 2024).

59. "Depoimento de Elaine Beraldo, de 26 de julho de 1993, que relata as circunstâncias do sequestro e desaparecimento de Nelson de Souza Kohl," CNV, www.cnv.gov.br/images/pdf/docs/pg_360_a_366.pdf.

60. "Cópia do Ofício no 175, de 29 de dezembro de 2011, do Cemitério Geral Recoleta, que certifica que Nelson de Souza Kohl teria sido cremado naquele cemitério em 4 de janeiro de 1974," CNV, www.cnv.gov.br/images/pdf/docs/pg_140.pdf.

61. Silveira, *Setenta*.

62. "Maria Auxiliadora Lara Barcelos," Memórias da Ditadura, Secretaria de Direitos Humanos da Presidência da República, http://memoriasdaditadura.org.br/biografias-da-resistencia/maria-auxiliadora-lara-barcelos/ (accessed July 17, 2024).

63. Wexler, *Brazil*.

64. Interview with Reinaldo Guarany by the author, video recording, Rio de Janeiro, August 28, 2020.

65. Silveira, *Setenta*.

66. Interview with Solange Bastos by the author, video recording, Rio de Janeiro, February 23, 2024.

67. Interview with Bastos.

68. Hopenhayn, *Así se torturó*.

69. Interview with Ferrer.

70. Amnesty International, *Chile*, 19.

71. Guimarães, "45 dias prisioneiro," 569.

72. Guimarães, "45 dias prisioneiro," 571.

73. "Capitão Mike" and "Alemão" were the nicknames of Alfredo Magalhães (1913–96), who served at the Centro de Informações da Marinha (CENIMAR). There are accounts of his participation in multiple infamous torture sessions of the Brazilian dictatorship, including at the Navy branch of Ilha das Flores, in Niterói, and at the killing of Stuart Angel. See more at Caldas, *Tirando o capuz*; and "Veja a lista dos 377 apontados como responsáveis por crimes na ditadura," *G1*, December 10, 2014, http://g1.globo.com/politica/noticia/2014/12/veja-lista-dos-377-apontados-como-responsaveis-por-crimes-na-ditadura.html.

74. Amnesty International, *Chile*, 7.

75. Guimarães, "45 dias prisioneiro," 571.

76. Amnesty International, *Chile*, 65.

77. "Osni Gomes depõe sobre tortura no Chile," video testimony of Osni Geraldo Gomes to the Brazilian Truth Commission, YouTube video, 12:52, posted by Mauro Gomes on April 13, 2014, www.youtube.com/watch?v=-OM1eh3rb1U.

78. "Osni Gomes."

79. Interview with Brockes.

80. Interview with Brockes.

81. Interview with Pires.

82. Interview with Pires.

83. Bastos, "Eu estive presa," 573–76.

84. Interview with Brockes.

85. Bonnefoy Miralles, *Terrorismo de estadio*, 119.

86. Interview with Pires.

87. Interview with Barbosa.

CONCLUSION

1. See Vanessa Buschschlüter, "Chile Constitution: Voters Overwhelmingly Reject Radical Change," *BBC News*, September 5, 2022, www.bbc.com/news/world-latin-america-62792025.

2. See Vanessa Buschschlüter, "Chile Constitution: Far-Right Party Biggest in New Assembly," *BBC News*, May 8, 2023, www.bbc.com/news/world-latin-america-65524068.

3. Chris Cameron, "The Attack on Brazil's Seat of Government Resembles the Storming of the U.S. Capitol on Jan. 6, 2021," *New York Times*, January 8, 2023, www.nytimes.com/2023/01/08/world/americas/brazil-jan-6-riots.html.

4. Report no. 543/73, BRAN, BSB, IE 11.3, p. 114/121, October 30, 1973, CIEX, ANB-B.

5. "No Chile, ministros participam da inauguração de placas em homenagem a brasileiros exilados no país latino-americano," *Agência Estado*, December 9, 2023, https://agenciagov.ebc.com.br/noticias/202309/no-chile-silvio-almeida-participa-da-inauguracao-de-placas-em-homenagem-a-brasileiros-exilados-no-pais-latino-americano.

6. Report no. 566/73, BRAN, BSB, IE 16.4, 1/52, April 14, 1977, CIEX, ANB-B.

7. Report no. 154/77, BRAN, BSB, IE 11.4, 45/109, November 13, 1973, CIEX, ANB-B.

8. New research points to the continuing influence of Chilean foreign policy for years after the coup. See Avery, "Promoting a 'Pinochetazo.'"

9. The Brazilian influence in other countries has yet to be investigated, and so do other aspects of the violence of the Brazilian dictatorship. The Brazilian government confirmed in 2019 that diplomat José Jobim was one of the victims of the dictatorship and altered his death certificate to confirm that he was murdered after menacing to denounce corruption in the construction of Itaipu Dam, a partnership between Brazil and Paraguay. See Hellen Guimarães, "Diplomata foi morto pela ditadura antes de denunciar corrupção no regime, confirma nova certidão," *O Globo*, September 21, 2018, https://oglobo.globo.com/epoca /diplomata-foi-morto-pela-ditadura-antes-de-denunciar-corrupcao-no-regime-confirma -nova-certidao-23089585/. See also Dinges, *Condor Years*, 1.

10. McSherry, *Predatory States*, 4–5.

11. "Constituição de Junta Militar de Governo," 601.3(B39), September 12, 1973, ACI-SERE.

12. "Incêndio do *Puro Chile*," 600(B39), September 13, 1973, ACI-SERE.

13. Bandeira, *Fórmula para o caos*, 551.

14. "Pedido de retransmissão de telegrama," telegram no. 106282, 341.75, September 14, 1973, ACI-SERE.

15. Bandeira, *Fórmula para o caos*, 575.

16. Bandeira, *Fórmula para o caos*, 552, 595.

17. Roberto Simon, "Diplomata brasileiro tinha laços com oficiais," *O Estado de S. Paulo*, September 1, 2013; Roberto Simon, "O Brasil de Pinochet," *O Estado de S. Paulo*, August 31, 2013.

18. Simon, "Diplomata brasileiro"; Simon, "O Brasil de Pinochet."

19. "Memorandum from William J. Jorden of the National Security Council Staff to the President's Assistant for National Security Affairs (Kissinger)," September 13, 1973, in Howard, *Foreign Relations, 1969–1976*, vol. E-11, doc. 90, https://history.state.gov/historicaldocuments /frus1969-76ve11p2/d90.

20. "Revolta militar," 600(B39), September 12, 1973, ACI-SERE.

21. "Novo governo chileno," 600(B39), September 13, 1973, ACI-SERE.

22. "Ruptura de relações com Cuba: Partida de embaixador e colaboradores," 920(B39) (B36), September 12, 1973, ACI-SERE.

23. "Ruptura de relações com Cuba: Partida do embaixador e colaboradores—Suécia encarregada dos interesses cubanos," September 13, 1973, ACI-SERE.

24. Padilla, "Los asilados."

25. Harald Edelstam became the topic of a 2007 movie by director Asa Faringer, *The Black Pimpernel*. This was another of his nicknames, a reference to the title character of Baroness Orczy's first novel in a series of historical fictions, *Scarlet Pimpernel*. Pimpernel was an English aristocrat who risked his life to rescue French citizens from the guillotine at the time of the French Revolution. The nickname became synonymous with heroic people who risk themselves to save people from other countries. See also Perotti, *Harald Edelstam*.

26. Amnesty International, *Chile*, 67. See also "Chilean Troops Assault Swedish Envoy," *New York Times*, November 26, 1973, 4.

27. Interview with Pires.

28. Bastos, "Eu estive presa," 574.

29. Interview with Solange Bastos by the author, video recording, Rio de Janeiro, February 23, 2024.

30. "Osni Gomes depõe sobre tortura no Chile," video testimony of Osni Geraldo Gomes to the Brazilian Truth Commission, YouTube video, 12:52, posted by Mauro Gomes on April 13, 2014, www.youtube.com/watch?v=-OM1eh3rb1U.

31. Interview with Otto Brockes by the author, video recording, Goiás, Brazil, July 15, 2014.

32. Interview with René de Carvalho by the author, audio recording, Rio de Janeiro, August 17, 2020.

33. "Exilados na embaixada do México," telegram 904.924.31 (00) (B14), September 14, 1973, ACI-SERE.

34. Interview with Wilson Barbosa by the author, video recording, São Paulo, July 11, 2014.

35. For more on the dubious and complex Mexican diplomacy of the Cold War, see Keller, *Mexico's Cold War*. Former CIA secret operations officer Philip Agee also discusses the connections between Echeverría and the CIA in Agee, *Inside the Company*.

36. Interview with Barbosa.

37. Wexler, *Brazil*.

38. "Nancy Mangabeira Unger, American Citizen Arrested for Terrorist Activities in Recife," July 31, 1970, record group 84, Records of the Foreign Service Posts of the Department of State, 1788–ca. 1991, series: Classified Central Subject Files, 1964–1975, file unit: PS-7-1, National Archives and Records Administration, www.archives.gov/research/foreign-policy/brazil-human-rights.

39. On September 18, 1973, the Chilean newspaper *El Mercurio* published a story titled "Ex gobierno marxista preparaba autogolpe," stating that Plan Zeta was Allende's attempt to remain in power. Therefore, the September 11 coup was urgent. Historian Gonzalo Vial Correa also supported the theory in Correa, *Libro blanco*. For the CIA, however, it was clearly a strategy to promote psychological insecurity and support the Chilean military. For more, see "Plan Zeta," Memória Chilena, www.memoriachilena.gob.cl/602/w3-article-96802.html (accessed September 16, 2024); and "Plan Zeta," *El Mercurio*, February 7, 1999, p. D5.

40. Amnesty International, *Chile*, 67–68.

41. Brito, "Embaixada do Panamá," 592–93.

42. Brito, "Embaixada do Panamá," 594.

43. Brito, "Embaixada do Panamá," 594, 597.

44. Interview with Vera Vital Brasil by the author, video recording, Rio de Janeiro, March 4, 2024.

45. Interview with Eliete Ferrer by the author, video recording, Rio de Janeiro, August 15, 2024.

46. *Report of the Chilean National Commission on Truth and Reconciliation*, United States Institute of Peace, www.usip.org/sites/default/files/resources/collections/truth_commissions/Chile90-Report/Chile90-Report.pdf (accessed July 19, 2024).

47. United States Institute of Peace, "Commission of Inquiry: Chile 03," September 1, 2003, www.usip.org/publications/2003/09/commission-inquiry-chile-03.

48. Amnesty International, "Chile: 40 Years on from Pinochet's Coup, Impunity Must End," September 10, 2013, www.amnesty.org/en/latest/news/2013/09/chile-years-pinochet-s-coup-impunity-must-end/.

BIBLIOGRAPHY

ARCHIVES

Brazil

Arquivo Central do Itamaraty, Secretaria de Estado das Relações Exteriores, Brasília
Arquivo Nacional do Brasil, Brasília
Arquivo Nacional do Brasil, Rio de Janeiro
Brasil Doc, Universidade Federal de Minas Gerais, www.ufmg.br/brasildoc
Centro de Pesquisa e Documentação de História Contemporânea,
    Fundação Getúlio Vargas, Rio de Janeiro
Comissão Nacional da Verdade, https://cnv.memoriasreveladas.gov.br/
Documentos Revelados, Foz do Iguaçu, https://documentosrevelados.com.br
Memorial da Resistência de São Paulo, https://memorialdaresistenciasp.org.br
Projeto República, Brasil Doc, Universidade Federal de Minas
    Gerais, Belo Horizonte, www.ufmg.br/brasildoc/

Chile

Biblioteca del Congreso Nacional de Chile, Santiago
Cancillería de Chile, Santiago
Colección Museo Histórico Nacional de Chile, Santiago

Paraguay

Archivo del Terror, Asunción

United States

Brown University Digital Repository, https://repository.library.brown.edu/
Brown University Library Collections, https://library.brown.edu/collections/
Gerald Ford Presidential Library and Museum, Ann Arbor, Michigan
John F. Kennedy Presidential Library and Museum, Boston, Massachusetts
Lyndon B. Johnson Presidential Library, Austin, Texas
Marxists Internet Archive, www.marxists.org
National Archives and Records Administration, https://catalog.archives.gov/
National Security Archives, George Washington University
Richard Nixon Presidential Library and Museum, Yorba Linda, California

PERIODICALS AND WEBSITES

Agência Estado

Agência Senado

Al Jazeera

The Atlantic

Baltimore Sun

BBC News

CartaCapital

CNN

Correio Braziliense

Diários Associados

El Comercio

El Mercurio

El Siglo

El Universal

Época

Folha de S. Paulo

G1

Jornal do Brasil

La Izquierda Diario

La Tercera

Los Angeles Times

Miami Herald

New York Times

O Estado de S. Paulo

O Globo

O Jornal

OperaMundi

Punto Final

Qué pasa

Rádio Câmara

Reader's Digest

The Times

Última Hora

UOL

Washington Post

INTERVIEWS BY THE AUTHOR

Arruda, Marcos. Via Skype, March 8, 2012.

Barbosa, Wilson. Video recording. São Paulo, July 11, 2014.

Bastos, Solange. Video recording. Rio de Janeiro, February 23, 2024.

Brockes, Otto. Video recording. Goiás, July 15, 2014.

Cabo Anselmo. São Paulo, October 25, 2021.

Carvalho, René de. Audio recording. Rio de Janeiro, August 17, 2020.

Drummond, Aristóteles. Rio de Janeiro, February 3, 2017.

Ferrer, Eliete. Video recording. Rio de Janeiro, August 15, 2024.

Guarany, Reinaldo. Video recording. Rio de Janeiro, August 28, 2020.

Palmar, Aluízio. Audio recording. Foz do Iguaçu, Paraná, Brazil, August 10, 2020.

Peixoto, Ubiramar. Video recording. Brasília, July 14, 2014.

Pires, Nielsen. Video recording. São Paulo, July 11, 2014.

Sáenz Rojas, Orlando. Audio recording. Santiago, December 2, 2021.

Vital Brasil, Vera. Video recording. Rio de Janeiro, March 4, 2024.

von der Weid, Jean Marc. Video recording. Rio de Janeiro, September 1, 2020.

PUBLISHED SOURCES

Abreu, Alzira Alves de, Israel Beloch, Fernando Lattman-Weltman, and Sérgio Tadeu de Niemeyer. *Dicionário histórico-biográfico brasileiro pós-1930*. Rio de Janeiro: Editora da Fundação Getúlio Vargas, 2001.

Adair, Jennifer. *In Search of the Lost Decade: Everyday Rights in Post-Dictatorship Argentina*. Oakland: University of California Press, 2019.

Adams, Jefferson. *Strategic Intelligence in the Cold War and Beyond*. Making of the Contemporary World. New York: Routledge, 2015.

Agee, Philip. *Inside the Company: CIA Diary*. New York: Stonehill, 1975.

Aggio, Alberto. *Democracia e socialismo: A experiência chilena*. São Paulo: Annablume, 2002.

———. "A esquerda brasileira vai ao Chile." *História Viva*, no. 42 (2007): 3.

———. "Uma insólita visita: Fidel Castro no Chile de Allende." *História* 22, no. 2 (2003): 151–66.

Allcock, Thomas Tunstall. "The First Alliance for Progress? Reshaping the Eisenhower Administration's Policy toward Latin America." *Journal of Cold War Studies* 16, no. 1 (2014): 85–110.

Allende, Salvador. *Compañero Presidente: Ideario político de Salvador Allende*. Mexico City: Samoc, 1973.

———. *La vía chilena al socialismo*. Puebla, Mexico: Universidad Autónoma de Puebla, 1988.

Almeida, Paulo Roberto de. "Do alinhamento recalcitrante à colaboração relutante: O Itamaraty em tempos de AI-5." In *Tempo negro, temperatura sufocante: Estado e sociedade no Brasil do AI-5*, edited by Oswaldo Munteal Filho, Adriano de Freixo, and Jacqueline Ventapane Freitas, 65–89. Rio de Janeiro: Editora PUC-Rio, Contraponto, 2008.

Amaral, Ricardo Batista. *A vida quer é coragem: A trajetória de Dilma Rousseff, a primeira presidenta do Brasil*. Rio de Janeiro: Primeira Pessoa, 2012.

Amnesty International. *Chile: An Amnesty International Report*. London: Amnesty International Publications, 1974. www.amnesty.org/en/documents/amr22/001/1974/en/.

Anderson, Benedict. *Imagined Communities: Reflections on the Origin and Spread of Nationalism*. New York: Verso, 1983.

———. *The Spectre of Comparisons: Nationalism, Southeast Asia and the World*. New York: Verso, 1998.

Andrade, Fabiana de Oliveira. "A Escola Nacional de Informações: A formação dos agentes para a inteligência brasileira durante o regime militar." Master's thesis, Universidade Estadual Paulista, 2014.

Andreas, Carol. *Nothing Is as It Should Be: A North American Woman in Chile*. New York: Schenkman, 1976.

Angell, Alan. *Partidos políticos y movimiento obrero en Chile*. Mexico City: Era, 1974.

Apiolaza, Pablo Rubio, and Xaviera Salgado Ferrufino. "Gremios empresariales y derecha chilena: Redes de poder y propuestas programáticas de la Sociedad Nacional de Agricultura, 1952–1958." *Amérique Latine, Histoire et Mémoire: Les Cahiers ALHIM* 32 (2016). https://journals.openedition.org/alhim/5573.

Araújo, Maria Paula Nascimento. *A utopia fragmentada: As novas esquerdas no Brasil e no mundo na década de 1970*. Rio de Janeiro: Editora da Fundação Getúlio Vargas, 2000.

Araújo, Maria do Socorro de Sousa. "Paixões políticas em tempos revolucionários: No traço da militância, o percurso de Jane Vanini." Master's thesis, Universidade Federal de Mato Grosso, Cuiabá, 2002.

———. "Um mundo feminino entre a razão e as paixões." *Labrys, Études Féministes / Estudos Feministas*, January–December 2009. www.labrys.net.br/labrys15/ditadura/socorro.htm.

Arceneaux, Craig L. *Bounded Missions: Military Regimes and Democratization in the Southern Cone and Brazil*. University Park: Pennsylvania State University, 2001.

Archetti, Eduardo P. *Masculinities: Football, Polo and the Tango in Argentina*. New York: Berg, 1999.

Arnt, Ricardo. *Jânio Quadros: O prometeu de Vila Maria*. Rio de Janeiro: Ediouro, 2004.

Arriagada Herrera, Genaro. *De la vía chilena a la vía insurreccional*. Santiago: Del Pacífico, 1974.

———. "National Security Doctrine in Latin America." *Peace & Change* 6, no. 1–2 (January 1980): 49–60.

———. *Por la razón o la fuerza: Chile bajo Pinochet*. Buenos Aires: Sudamericana, 1998.

Arroyo, Gonzalo. *Coup d'État au Chili*. Paris: Cerf, 1974.

Assis, Denise. *Propaganda e cinema a serviço do golpe, 1962/1964*. Rio de Janeiro: Mauad/ Faperj, 2001.

Assunção, Matheus. "PAEG: O Programa de Ação Econômica do Governo e a economia brasileira nos anos 1960." Universidade de Brasília, December 2021.

Avendaño Pavez, Octavio. *Los partidos frente a la cuestión agraria en Chile, 1946–1973*. Santiago: LOM, 2017.

Avery, Molly. "Promoting a 'Pinochetazo': The Chilean Dictatorship's Foreign Policy in El Salvador during the Carter Years, 1977–81." *Journal of Latin American Studies* 52, no. 4 (2020): 759–84.

Azevedo, Ricardo. *Por um triz: Memórias de um militante da AP*. São Paulo: Plena, 2010.

Bailey, Norman A. *Latin America: Politics, Economics, and Hemispheric Security*. New York: Center for Strategic Studies, Georgetown University, 1965.

Ballinger, Pamela. *History in Exile*. Princeton, NJ: Princeton University Press, 2018.

Bambirra, Vânia. *El capitalismo dependiente latinoamericano*. Mexico City: Siglo XXI, 1974.

———. *Teoría de la dependencia: Una anticrítica*. Mexico City: Era, 1978.

Bandeira, Luiz Alberto Moniz. *Brasil—Estados Unidos: A rivalidade emergente (1950–1988)*. Rio de Janeiro: Civilização Brasileira, 1989.

———. *Conflito e integração na América do Sul: Brasil, Argentina e Estados Unidos: Da Tríplice Aliança ao Mercosul, 1870–2003*. Rio de Janeiro: Revan, 2003.

———. *Fórmula para o caos: A derrubada de Salvador Allende, 1970–1973*. Rio de Janeiro: Civilização Brasileira, 2008.

———. *O governo João Goulart: As lutas sociais no Brasil (1961–1964)*. Rio de Janeiro: Civilização Brasileira, 1978.

Bandeira, Marina. *A Igreja Católica na virada da questão social (1930–1964)*. Curitiba, Brazil: Vozes, 2000.

Barbosa, Caio Fernandes. "Fazendo-os obedecer: Moralidade, educação e trabalho nas políticas do IPES para a juventude brasileira durante a Guerra Fria (1961–1969)." PhD diss., Universidade Federal da Bahia, 2021.

Barbosa, Fernando de Holanda, Antônio Salazar Pessoa Brandão, and Clovis de Faro. "Fiscal Reform and Stabilization: The Brazilian Experience." *Ensaios Econômicos* (Fundação Getúlio Vargas), no. 147 (January 1989): 2–24.

Barreto, Lucy, Luiz Carlos Barreto, Mario Barrozo, Mary Ann Braubach, Adair Roberto Carneiro, Cristina Cirne, and Lucíola Vilella. *Four Days in September*. DVD. Directed by Bruno Barreto. Sunrise, FL: Alliance, 1997.

Barr-Melej, Patrick. *Psychedelic Chile: Youth, Counterculture, and Politics on the Road to Socialism and Dictatorship*. Chapel Hill: University of North Carolina Press, 2017.

Bastos, Solange. "Eu estive presa no Estádio Nacional do Chile." In *68, a geração que queria mudar o mundo: Relatos*, edited by Eliete Ferrer, 573–76. Brasília: Ministério da Justiça / Comissão da Anistia / Projeto Marcas da Memória, 2011.

Beaulac, Willard L. *A Diplomat Looks at Aid to Latin America*. Carbondale: Southern Illinois University Press, 1970.

Becker, Gary S. "What Latin America Owes to the Chicago Boys." *Hoover Digest* (Stanford University), no. 4 (1997): 11–14.

Beired, José Luis. *Sob o signo da nova ordem: Intelectuais autoritários no Brasil e na Argentina, 1914–1945*. São Paulo: Loyola, 1999.

Bender, Barbara, and Margot Winer, eds. *Contested Landscapes: Movement, Exile and Place*. New York: Routledge, 2020.

Berger, Mark T. *Under Northern Eyes: Latin American Studies and U.S. Hegemony in the Americas, 1898–1990*. Bloomington: University of Indiana Press, 1995.

Bevins, Vincent. *The Jakarta Method: Washington's Anticommunist Crusade and the Mass Murder Program That Shaped Our World*. New York: Public Affairs, 2020.

Bitar, Sergio. *El Gobierno de Allende: Chile, 1970–1973*. Santiago: Pehuén, 2013.

Black, Jan Knippers. *United States Penetration of Brazil*. Philadelphia: University of Pennsylvania Press, 1977.

Blanc, Jacob. *Searching for Memory: Aluízio Palmar and the Shadow of Dictatorship in Brazil*. Chapel Hill: University of North Carolina Press, 2025.

Blume, Norman. "Pressure Groups and Decision-Making in Brazil." *Studies in Comparative International Development* 3, no. 11 (1967): 2025–223.

Bohoslavsky, Ernesto. "Contra el hombre de la calle: Ideas y proyectos del corporativismo católico chileno (1932–1954)." *Revista de Estudios Transfronterizos* 8, no. 1 (2006): 105–25.

———. "Los mitos conspirativos y la Patagonia en Argentina y Chile durante la primera mitad del siglo XX: Orígenes, difusión y supervivencias." PhD diss., Universidad Complutense de Madrid, 2006.

Boisard, Stéphane. "La matriz antiliberal en las derechas radicales: El caso del Frente Nacional Patria y Libertad en Chile (1971–1973)." *Nuevo Mundo, Mundos Nuevos*, 2017, https://journals.openedition.org/nuevomundo/69124.

Boizard, Ricardo. *El último día de Allende*. Santiago: Del Pacífico, 1973.

Bonnefoy Miralles, Pascale. *Terrorismo de estadio: Prisioneros de guerra en un campo de deportes*. Santiago: ChileAmérica, CESOC, 2005.

Boorstein, Edward. *Allende's Chile: An Inside View*. New York: International, 1977.

Borba, Marco Aurélio. *Cabo Anselmo: A luta armada ferida por dentro*. São Paulo: Global, 1981.

Bortone, Elaine de Almeida. "O Instituto de Pesquisas e Estudos Sociais (IPES) na construção da reforma do estado autoritário (1964–1968)." *Tempos Históricos* 18 (2012): 44–72.

Braga, Políbio. *Ahú: Diário de uma prisão política*. Porto Alegre, Brazil: Movimento XXI, 2004.

Brands, Hal. *Latin America's Cold War*. Cambridge, MA: Harvard University Press, 2010.

Brito, Angela Neves-Xavier de. "Brazilian Women in Exile: The Quest for an Identity." *Latin American Perspectives* 13, no. 2 (1986): 58–80.

Brito, Maria do Carmo. "Embaixada do Panamá." In *68, a geração que queria mudar o mundo: Relatos*, edited by Eliete Ferrer, 592–97. Brasília: Ministério da Justiça / Comissão da Anistia / Projeto Marcas da Memória, 2011.

Brown, Jonathan C. *Cuba's Revolutionary World*. Cambridge, MA: Harvard University Press, 2017.

Brum, Maurício Marques. "Um jacarandá em Santiago: O radicalismo político no Chile pela trajetória militante de Nilton Rosa da Silva (1971–1973)." PhD diss., Universidade Federal do Rio Grande do Sul, 2016.

Buitrago, Francisco Leal. "La doctrina de seguridad nacional: Materialización de la Guerra Fría en América del Sur." *Revista de Estudios Sociales* 15 (June 2003): 74–87.

Burns, E. Bradford. *A History of Brazil*. New York: Columbia University Press, 1993.

———. "Tradition and Variation in Brazilian Foreign Policy." *Journal of Inter-American Studies* 9 (April 1967): 185–208.

Burns, Mila. "Dictatorship across Borders: The Brazilian Influence on the Overthrow of Salvador Allende." *Revista Estudios de Seguridad y Defensa* (Departamento de Investigación de la Academia Nacional de Estudios Políticos y Estratégicos de Chile), no. 3 (July 2014): 165–87.

———. "Ditadura tipo exportação: A diplomacia brasileira e a queda de Salvador Allende." In "Dossiê Autoritarismos e conservadorismos políticos," special issue of *Revista História e Cultura* (Universidade Estadual Paulista) 5, no. 3 (December 2016): 175–98.

———. *Dona Ivone Lara's "Sorriso Negro."* New York: Bloomsbury Academic, 2019.

———. "El modelo brasileño: La influencia de Roberto Campos y Câmara Canto en la dictadura chilena." *Nuevo Mundo, Mundos Nuevos* [Online], Debates, October 10, 2016, http://nuevomundo.revues.org/69707.

Bustos Díaz, Carlos Ignacio. *Diplomacia chilena: Una perspectiva histórica*. Santiago: RIL, 2018.

Caldas, Álvaro. *Tirando o capuz*. Rio de Janeiro: Garamond, 2006.

Calirman, Claudia. *Brazilian Art under Dictatorship: Antonio Manuel, Artur Barrio, and Cildo Meireles*. Durham, NC: Duke University Press, 2012.

Campero, Guillermo. "Los empresários chilenos en el militar y el post-plebiscito." In *El difícil camino a la democracia en Chile, 1982–1990*, edited by Paul Drake and Iván Jaksic, 243–306. Santiago: Flacso, 1993.

————. *Los gremios empresariales en el período 1970–1983: Comportamiento sociopolítico y orientaciones ideológicas*. Santiago: Instituto Latinoamericano de Estudios Transnacionales, 1984.

Campos, Luiz Felipe. *O massacre da Granja São Bento*. Recife: Cepe, 2017.

Campos, Roberto. *A lanterna na popa*. Rio de Janeiro: Topbooks, 1994.

————. *A moeda, o governo e o tempo*. Rio de Janeiro: APEC, 1964.

————. *Política econômica e mitos políticos*. Rio de Janeiro: APEC, 1965.

————. *O século esquisito*. Rio de Janeiro: Topbooks, 1990.

Cardoso, Fernando Henrique, and Enzo Faletto. *Dependência e desenvolvimento na América Latina*. Rio de Janeiro: Zahar, 1970.

Carvalho, Apolônio de. *Vale a pena sonhar*. Rio de Janeiro: Rocco, 1997.

Carvalho, José Murilo de. *Cidadania no Brasil: O longo caminho*. Rio de Janeiro: Civilização Brasileira, 2001.

Carvalho, Luiz Maklouf. *Mulheres que foram à luta armada*. São Paulo: Globo, 1998.

Carvalho, Marco Antonio Batista. "Paulo Freire e o exílio no Chile: Uma contribuição recíproca para uma visão de mundo." *Educere et Educare* 4, no. 7 (2000): 191–201.

Carvalho, Renée France de. *Renée France de Carvalho: Uma vida de lutas*. São Paulo: Editora da Fundação Perseu Abramo, 2012.

Castañeda, Jorge G. "Latin America's Left Turn." *Foreign Affairs* 85, no. 3 (2006): 28–43.

Castello Branco, Carlos. *A renúncia de Jânio: Um depoimento*. Rio de Janeiro: Revan, 2008.

Castilho, Alessandra Beber. "Diplomacia e repressão política: A atuação do Centro de Informações do Exterior e da Divisão de Segurança e Informações do Ministério das Relações Exteriores no Chile (1968–1973)." Master's thesis, Universidade do Estado do Rio de Janeiro, 2015.

Castro, Celso. *O espírito militar: Um antropólogo na caserna*. Rio de Janeiro: Zahar, 1990.

————. *Os militares e a República: Um estudo sobre cultura e ação política*. Rio de Janeiro: Jorge Zahar, 1995.

Castro, Celso, and Maria Celina d'Araújo. *Ernesto Geisel*. Rio de Janeiro: Editora da Fundação Getúlio Vargas, 1997.

Castro, Fidel. "Castro Announces the Revolution." In *The Cuba Reader*, edited by Aviva Chomsky, Barry Carr, and Pamela Maria Smorkaloff, 367–72. Durham, NC: Duke University Press, 2003.

Cavalcanti, Pedro Uchôa, Pedro Celso, and Jovelino Ramos, eds. *Memórias do exílio, 1964/19??: De muitos caminhos*, vol. 1. São Paulo: Livramento, 1978.

Cavallo, Ascanio, Manuel Salazar, and Oscar Sepúlveda. *La historia oculta del régimen militar: Chile, 1973–1988*. Barcelona: Debolsillo, 2004.

Cepik, Marco. "Sistemas nacionais de inteligência: Origens, lógica de expansão e configuração atual." *Dados* 46, no. 1 (2003): 7–40.

Cerda, Luis. "Aspectos internacionales de la revolución latinoamericana." *Correo de la Resistencia*, no. 9 (July–August 1975): 60–61.

Chagas, Carlos. *A ditadura militar e os golpes dentro do golpe, 1964–1969*. Rio de Janeiro: Record, 2015.

Chase, Michelle. *Revolution within the Revolution: Women and Gender Politics in Cuba, 1952–1962*. Chapel Hill: University of North Carolina Press, 2015.

Chavkin, Samuel. *The Murder of Chile: Eyewitness Accounts of the Coup, the Terror, and the Resistance Today*. New York: Everest House, 1982.

Chirio, Maud. *A política dos quartéis*. Rio de Janeiro: Zahar, 2012.

Chomsky, Aviva, Barry Carr, and Pamela Maria Smorkaloff, eds. *The Cuba Reader*. Durham, NC: Duke University Press, 2003.

Clifford, James. *Routes: Travel and Translation in the Late Twentieth Century*. Cambridge, MA: Harvard University Press, 1997.

Cockcroft, James. *Neighbors in Turmoil: Latin America*. New York: Harper & Row, 1989.

Codarin, Higor. *O MR-8 na luta armada: As armas da crítica e a crítica das armas*. São Paulo: Alameda, 2019.

Castro, Fidel. *Cuba-Chile, Encuentro simbólico entre dos procesos históricos*. Havana: Comisión de Orientación Revolucionaria del Comité Central del Partido Comunista de Cuba, 1972.

Comisión Nacional de Verdad y Reconciliación. *Informe de la Comisión Nacional de Verdad y Reconciliación*. Vol. 1. Santiago de Chile: Andros/Corporación Nacional de Reparación y Reconciliación, 1996. www.derechoshumanos.net/lesahumanidad/informes/Informe-Rettig-tomo1.pdf.

Comisión Nacional sobre Prisión Política y Tortura. *Informe de la Comisión Nacional sobre Prisión Política y Tortura (Informe Valech)*. Santiago, Chile: Ministerio del Interior, 2005.

Comissão Especial sobre Mortos e Desaparecidos Políticos. *Direito à memória e à verdade*. Brasília: Secretaria Especial dos Direitos Humanos, 2007. www.dhnet.org.br/dados /livros/a_pdf/livro_memoria1_direito_verdade.pdf.

Comissão Nacional da Verdade. *Relatório*. Vol. 3, *Mortos e desaparecidos políticos*. Brasília: Comissão Nacional da Verdade, December 2014. https://apublica.org/wp-content /uploads/2020/01/relatorio-final-comissao-nacional-da-verdade.pdf.

Compagnon, Olivier, and Caroline Moine. "Introduction: Pour une histoire globale du 11 septembre 1973." *Monde(s)*, no. 8: 9–26.

Cordeiro, Janaina Martins. *Direitas em movimento: A Campanha da Mulher pela Democracia e a ditadura no Brasil*. Rio de Janeiro: Editora da Fundação Getúlio Vargas, 2009.

———. "Direitas e organização do consenso sob a ditadura no Brasil: O caso da Campanha da Mulher pela Democracia (Camde)." *Nuevo Mundo, Mundos Nuevos* (2017). https://journals .openedition.org/nuevomundo/71513.

Correa, Gonzalo Vial. *Libro blanco del cambio de gobierno en Chile*. Santiago: Lord Cochrane, 1973.

Costa, Albertina de Oliveira, Maria Teresa Porciúncula de Moraes, Norma Marzola, and Valentina da Rocha Lima, eds. *Memórias das mulheres do exílio*, vol. 2. Rio de Janeiro: Paz e Terra, 1980.

Cowan, Benjamin A. *Securing Sex: Morality and Repression in the Making of Cold War Brazil*. Chapel Hill: University of North Carolina Press, 2016.

Crandall, Russell. *The United States and Latin America after the Cold War*. Cambridge, MA: Cambridge University Press, 2008.

Crenzel, Emílio Ariel. *Memory of Argentina Disappearances: The Political History of Nunca Más*. New York: Routledge, 2011.

Crummett, María de los Ángeles. "El Poder Feminino: The Mobilization of Women against Socialism in Chile." *Latin American Perspectives* 4, no. 4 (1977): 103–13.

Cruz, Fábio Lucas da. "Frente Brasileño de Informaciones e Campanha: Os jornais de brasileiros exilados no Chile e na França (1968–1979)." Master's thesis, Universidade de São Paulo, 2010.

Cuya, Esteban. "Las comisiones de la verdad en América Latina." *KO'AGA ROÑE'ETA*, ser. 3 (1996), www.derechos.org/koaga/iii/1/cuya.html.

Cysne, Rubens Penha. "A economia brasileira no período militar." *Estudos Econômicos* 23, no. 2 (May–August 1993): 185–226.

Dantas, San Tiago. *Política externa independente*. Brasília: Fundação Alexandre de Gusmão, 2011.

Dattwyler, Rodrigo Hidalgo. "La vivienda social en Santiago de Chile en la segunda mitad del siglo XX: Actores relevantes y tendências espaciais." In *Santiago en la Globalización: ¿Una nueva ciudad?*, edited by Carlos A. de Mattos, 219–42. Santiago: SUR Corporación de Estudios Sociales y Educación, 2004.

d'Avila, Ney Eduardo Possapp. *Um olhar sobre a legalidade, 1961*. Porto Alegre, Brazil: Rígel, 2011.

Davis, Nathaniel. *The Last Two Years of Salvador Allende*. Ithaca, NY: Cornell University Press, 1985.

Debray, Régis. *Conversación con Allende*. Mexico City: Siglo XXI, 1971.

della Vechia, Renato da Silva. "Origem e evolução do Partido Comunista Brasileiro Revolucionário (1967–1973)." PhD diss., Universidade Federal do Rio Grande do Sul, 2005.

Deutsch, Sandra McGee. *Las Derechas: The Extreme Right in Argentina, Brazil, and Chile, 1890–1939*. Stanford, CA: Stanford University Press, 1999.

DeWitt, John. "The Alliance for Progress: Economic Warfare in Brazil (1962–1964)." *Journal of Third World Studies* 26, no. 1 (2009): 57–76.

Díaz Nieva, José. "'Patria y Libertad' y el nacionalismo chileno durante la Unidad Popular, 1970–1973." *Bicentenario* 2, no. 2 (2003): 155–83.

Dinges, John. *The Condor Years: How Pinochet and His Allies Brought Terrorism to Three Continents*. New York: New Press, 2004.

Domingos, Charles Sidarta Machado. "A política externa independente do governo João Goulart (1961–1964): Movimentos 'quentes' de uma guerra fria." *MÉTIS: História & Cultura* 7, no. 13 (January–June 2008): 257–76.

Drake, Paul, and Iván Jaksic, eds. *El difícil camino hacia la democracia en Chile, 1982–1990*. Santiago: Editora FLACSO, 1993.

Dreifuss, René Armand. *A Internacional Capitalista: Estratégias e táticas do empresariado transnacional, 1918–1986*. Rio de Janeiro: Espaço e Tempo, 1987.

———. *1964: Conquista do estado: Ação política, poder e golpe de classe*. Petrópolis, Brazil: Vozes, 1981.

———. *O jogo da direita*. Petrópolis, Brazil: Vozes, 1989.

Drummond, Aristóteles. *Memórias: Fatos e fotos de uma vida*. São Paulo: PoloBooks, 2021.

Duarte-Plon, Leneide, and Clarisse Meireles. *Um homem torturado: Nos passos de Frei Tito de Alencar*. Rio de Janeiro: Civilização Brasileira, 2014.

Eidelman, Ariel Esteban. "El desarrollo de los aparatos represivos del estado argentino durante la 'Revolución argentina,' 1966–1973." PhD diss., Universidad de Buenos Aires, 2010.

Eisenber A., Raul Husid, and Juan E. Luco. "A Preliminary Report: The July 8, 1971, Chilean Earthquake." *Bulletin of the Seismological Society of America* 62, no. 1 (1972): 423–30.

Elizondo, José Rodríguez. "El invierno del Mesías." *Caretas*, no. 1695 (November 8, 2001).

Evans, Leslie, ed. *Disaster in Chile: Allende's Strategy and Why It Failed*. New York: Pathfinder, 1974.

Fajardo, Margarita. *The World That Latin America Created: The United Nations Economic Commission for Latin America in the Development Era.* Cambridge, MA: Harvard University Press, 2022.

Farias, Rogério de Souza. "Industriais, economistas e diplomatas: O Brasil e as negociações comerciais multilaterais, 1946–1967." PhD diss., Institute of International Relations, University of Brasília, 2012.

Fermandois, Joaquín. *Chile y el mundo, 1970–1973: La política exterior del gobierno de la Unidad Popular y el sistema internacional.* Santiago: Ediciones Universidad Católica de Chile, 1985.

———. "Chile y la 'Cuestión Cubana,' 1959–1964." *Historia* 17 (1982): 143–44.

———. *La revolución inconclusa: La izquierda chilena y el gobierno de la Unidad Popular.* Santiago: Centro de Estudios Públicos, 2013.

Fernandes, Ananda Simões. "A reformulação da doutrina de segurança nacional pela Escola Superior de Guerra no Brasil: A Geopolítica de Golbery do Couto e Silva." *Antíteses* 2, no. 4 (July–December 2009): 831–56.

Ferraz, Lucas. *Injustiçados: Execuções de militantes nos tribunais revolucionários durante a ditadura.* São Paulo: Companhia das Letras, 2021.

Ferreira, Jorge. *João Goulart: Uma biografia.* Rio de Janeiro: Civilização Brasileira, 2011.

Ferreira, Jorge, and Ângela de Castro Gomes. *Jango: As múltiplas faces.* Rio de Janeiro: Editora da Fundação Getúlio Vargas, 2007.

———. *1964: O golpe que derrubou um presidente, pôs fim ao regime democrático e instituiu a ditadura no Brasil.* Rio de Janeiro: Civilização Brasileira, 2014.

Ferreira, Sónia. "Anthropology of Exile: Mapping Territories of Experience." *Anthropology Today* 36, no. 5 (October 2020): 22–23.

Fico, Carlos. *Como eles agiam: Os subterrâneos da ditadura militar—Espionagem e polícia política.* Rio de Janeiro: Record, 2001.

———. *O grande irmão: Da Operação Brother Sam aos Anos de Chumbo.* Rio de Janeiro: Civilização Brasileira, 2008.

Fico, Carlos, Maria Paula Araújo, and Monica Grin, eds. *Violência na história: Memória, trauma e reparação.* Rio de Janeiro: Ponteio, 2013.

Field, Thomas C., Jr. *From Development to Dictatorship: Bolivia and the Alliance for Progress in the Kennedy Era.* Ithaca, NY: Cornell University Press, 2014.

Field, Thomas C., Jr., Stella Krepp, and Vanni Pettinà. *Latin America and the Global Cold War.* Chapel Hill: University of North Carolina Press, 2020.

Figueiredo, Lucas. *Lugar nenhum: Militares e civis na ocultação dos documentos da ditadura.* São Paulo: Companhia das Letras, 2015.

Foxley, Alejandro. *Latin American Experiments in Neoconservative Economics.* Berkeley: University of California Press, 1983.

Frank, André Gunder. *Autobiographical Essays (1991–1995).* Róbinson Rojas Archive. http://rrojasdatabank.info/agfrank/online.html#auto (accessed September 9, 2024).

Frazier, Lessie Jo. *Salt in the Sand: Memory, Violence, and the Nation-State in Chile, 1890 to the Present.* Durham, NC: Duke University Press, 2007.

Freire, Paulo. *Pedagogy of the Oppressed.* New York: Penguin, 1968.

Friedman, Milton, and Rose D. Friedman. *Two Lucky People: Memoirs.* Chicago: University of Chicago Press, 1998.

Furtado, Alencar. *Salgando a terra.* Rio de Janeiro: Paz e Terra, 1977.

Furtado, Celso. *Teoria e política do desenvolvimento econômico*. São Paulo: Nacional, 1967.

Gabeira, Fernando. *O que é isso, Companheiro?* São Paulo: Companhia das Letras, 1979.

Galeano, Eduardo. *As veias abertas da América Latina*. São Paulo: Paz e Terra, 1976.

Gárate Chateau, Manuel. *La revolución capitalista de Chile (1973–2003)*. Santiago: Ediciones Universidad Alberto Hurtado, 2012.

García, Patricio. *El Caso Schneider*. Santiago: Nacional Quimantú, 1972.

García, Pío, ed. *Las fuerzas armadas y el golpe de estado en Chile*. Mexico City: Siglo XXI, 1974.

Garrido Soto, Luis. *La "vía chilena" al socialismo (1970–1973): Un itinerario geohistórico de la Unidad Popular en el sistema-mundo*. Santiago: Ediciones Universidad Alberto Hurtado, 2015.

Gaspari, Elio. *A ditadura encurralada*. São Paulo: Companhia das Letras, 2003.

———. *A ditadura envergonhada*. São Paulo: Companhia das Letras, 2003.

———. *A ditadura escancarada*. São Paulo: Companhia das Letras, 2003.

———. *O sacerdote e o feiticeiro: A ditadura derrotada*. São Paulo: Companhia das Letras, 2003.

Gaudichaud, Franck. *Chile, 1970–1973, mil días que estremecieron al mundo: Poder popular, cordones industriales y socialismo durante el gobierno de Salvador Allende*. Barcelona: Sylone, 2017.

Gerrett-Schesch, Pat. "The Mobilization of Women during the Popular Unity Government." *Latin American Perspectives* 2, no. 1 (Spring 1975): 101–3.

Giambiagi, Fabio, Jennifer Hermann, Lavínia Barros de Castro, and André Villela, eds. *Economia brasileira contemporânea, 1945–2004*. Rio de Janeiro: Campus, 2004.

Gillmore, Juan. "Bolivia y la solución brasileña." *Mensaje* 21, no. 210 (July 1972): 406–9.

Gilroy, Paul. *The Black Atlantic: Modernity and Double Consciousness*. Cambridge, MA: Harvard University Press, 1993.

Glennon, John P., ed. *Foreign Relations of the United States, 1958–1960*. Vol. 5, *American Republics*, edited by N. Stephen Kane and Paul Claussen. Washington, DC: Government Printing Office, 1991.

Godoy, Marcelo. *A Casa da Vovó*. São Paulo: Alameda, 2014.

Gomés, Gabriela. "Héroes y demonios: Los jóvenes del Frente Nacionalista Patria y Libertad en el Chile de la Unidad Popular (1970–1973)." *Revista de la Red Intercátedras de Historia de América Latina Contemporánea: Segunda Época* 4 (2016): 57–73.

Gomes, Paulo César. *Os bispos católicos e a ditadura militar brasileira: A visão da espionagem*. Rio de Janeiro: Record, 2014.

Gómez, Sergio. *Organizaciones empresariales rurales: Los casos de Brasil y de Chile*. Santiago: FLACSO, 1987.

Gonçalves, Leandro Pereira, and Odilon Caldeira Neto. *O fascismo em camisas verdes: Do integralismo ao neointegralismo*. Rio de Janeiro: Editora da Fundação Getúlio Vargas, 2020.

González, Mónica. *Chile: La conjura—Los mil y un días del golpe*. Santiago: Ediciones B, 2000.

González Errázuriz, Francisco Javier. *Partido Demócrata Cristiano: La lucha por definirse*. Valparaíso, Chile: Instituto de Estudios Generales, 1989.

Gonzalo Monsálvez Araneda, Danny. "Discurso y legitimidad: La doctrina de seguridad nacional como argumento legitimatorio del golpe de estado de 1973 en Chile." *Revista Derecho y Ciencias Sociales*, October 2012, 111–29.

Gorender, Jacob. *Combate nas trevas*. São Paulo: Ática, 1987.

Grael, Dickson M. *Aventura, corrupção e terrorismo: À sombra da impunidade*. Petrópolis, Brazil: Vozes, 1985.

Graham, Jessica Lynn. *Shifting the Meaning of Democracy: Race, Politics, and Culture in the United States and Brazil*. Oakland: University of California Press, 2019.

Gramsci, Antonio. *Prison Notebooks*, vols. 1, 2, and 3. New York: Columbia University Press, 2011.

Grandin, Greg. *Empire's Workshop: Latin America, the United States and the Rise of the New Imperialism*. New York: Owl, 2006.

———. *The Last Colonial Massacre: Latin America in the Cold War*. Chicago: University of Chicago Press, 2011.

Green, James N. "Clérigos, exilados e acadêmicos: Oposição à ditadura militar brasileira nos Estados Unidos, 1969, 1974." *Projeto História—Cultura e Poder: O Golpe de 1964, 40 Anos Depois*, no. 19 (July/December 2004): 13–34.

———. *We Cannot Remain Silent: Opposition to the Brazilian Military Dictatorship in the United States*. Durham, NC: Duke University Press, 2010.

Green, James N., and Abigail Jones. "Reinventing History: Lincoln Gordon and His Multiple Versions of 1964." *Revista Brasileira de História* 29, no. 57 (2009): 67–89.

Green, James N., Luis Roniger, and Pablo Yankelevich. *Exile and the Politics of Exclusion in the Americas*. Sussex, UK: Sussex Academic, 2012.

Gualazzi, Eduardo Lobo Botelho, and Jânio Quadros Neto. *Jânio Quadros: Memorial à história do Brasil*. São Paulo: Rideel, 1996.

Guarany, Reinaldo. *Os fornos quentes*. São Paulo: Alfa-Omega, 1980.

———. *A fuga*. São Paulo: Brasiliense, 1984.

Guardiola-Rivera, Oscar. *Story of a Death Foretold: The Coup against Salvador Allende, 11 September 1973*. New York: Bloomsbury, 2013.

Güell, Pedro. "El Estallido Social de Chile: Piezas para un rompecabezas." *Mensaje* 68, no. 685 (2019): 8–14.

Guena, Márcia. *Arquivo do horror—Documentos secretos da ditadura do Paraguai (1960–1980)*. São Paulo: Memorial da América Latina, 1996.

Guerra, Lillian. *Visions of Power in Cuba: Revolution, Redemption, and Resistance, 1959–1971*. Chapel Hill, NC: University of North Carolina Press, 2012.

Guimarães, Luiz Carlos. "45 dias prisioneiro da junta militar no Chile." In Eliete Ferrer, ed., *68, a geração que queria mudar o mundo: Relatos*, 565–72. Brasília: Ministério da Justiça / Comissão da Anistia / Projeto Marcas da Memória, 2011.

Gustafson, Kristian. "CIA Machinations in Chile in 1970." *Studies in Intelligence* 47, no. 3 (2003).

———. *Hostile Intent: U.S. Covert Operations in Chile, 1964–1974*. Lincoln, NE: Potomac, 2007.

Guttmann, Aviva. *The Origins of International Counterterrorism: Switzerland at the Forefront of Crisis Negotiations, Multilateral Diplomacy, and Intelligence Cooperation (1969–1977)*. Leiden, the Netherlands: Brill, 2017.

Guzmán, Patrício, dir. *The Battle of Chile*. DVD. New York: Icarus Films, 2009.

Habermas, Jürgen. "Kant's Idea of Perpetual Peace: At Two Hundred Years' Historical Remove." In *The Inclusion of the Other: Studies in Political Theory*, edited by C. Cronin and P. DeGreiff, 165–202. Cambridge, MA: MIT Press, 1998.

Bibliography

Harmer, Tanya. *Allende's Chile and the Inter-American Cold War.* Chapel Hill: University of North Carolina Press, 2011.

Haslam, Jonathan. *The Nixon Administration and the Death of Allende's Chile: A Case of Assisted Suicide.* New York: Verso, 2005.

Heller, Milton Ivan. *Resistência democrática: A repressão no Paraná.* Rio de Janeiro: Paz e Terra, 1988.

Herler, Thomaz Joezer. "Formação e trajetória do primeiro MR-8: Possibilidades e limites de construção de uma vanguarda revolucionária político-militar (1964–1969)." Master's thesis, Universidade Estadual do Oeste do Paraná, Marechal Cândido Rondon, 2015.

Herman, Edward S. *The Real Terror Network: Terrorism in Fact and Propaganda.* Washington, DC: South End, 1982.

Hermann, Jennifer. "Reformas, endividamento externo e o 'milagre econômico' (1964–1973)." In *Economia brasileira contemporânea, 1945–2004,* edited by Fabio Giambiagi, Jennifer Hermann, Lavínia Barros de Castro, and André Villela, 69–92. Rio de Janeiro: Campus, 2004.

Herrera, Eva, and Katherine Reyes. "El rol de las radios opositoras frente a la censura instaurada durante la dictadura cívico-militar en Chile." Museo de la Memoria y los Derechos Humanos, November 2018. http://www.cedocmuseodelamemoria.cl/wp -content/uploads/2018/11/Informe-Projeto-Radios.pdf.

Hershberg, James G. "Soviet-Brazilian Relations and the Cuban Missile Crisis." *Journal of Cold War Studies* 22, no. 1 (2020): 175–209.

———. "The United States, Brazil, and the Cuban Missile Crisis, 1962 (Part 1)." *Journal of Cold War Studies* 6, no. 2 (2004): 3–20.

Hoeveler, Rejane Carolina. "(Neo)liberalismo, democracia e 'diplomacia empresarial': A história do Council of the Americas (1965–2019)." PhD diss., Universidade Federal Fluminense, 2020.

———. "René Dreifuss e o golpe de 1964: Sobre teorias e 'conspiracionismos.'" *Anais do XVI Encontro Regional de História da Anpuh-Rio: Saberes e práticas científicas.* Rio de Janeiro: Anpuh-Rio, 2014.

Hopenhayn, Daniel, ed. *Así se torturó en Chile (1973–1990).* Santiago: Copa Rota, 2019.

Howard, Adam, ed. *Foreign Relations of the United States, 1969–1976.* Vol. 21, *Chile, 1969–1973,* edited by James McElveen and James Siekmeier. Washington, DC: Government Printing Office, 2014.

———. ed. *Foreign Relations of the United States, 1969–1976.* Vol. E-11, part 2, *Documents on South America, 1973–1976,* edited by Sara Berndt, Halbert Jones, and James Siekmeir. Washington, DC: Government Printing Office, 2015.

Hurtado-Torres, Sebastián. *The Gathering Storm: Eduardo Frei's Revolution in Liberty and Chile's Cold War.* Ithaca, NY: Cornell University Press, 2020.

Hurtado-Torres, Sebastián, and Joaquín Fermandois. *An International History of South America during the Era of Military Rule.* New York: Routledge, 2023.

Iber, Patrick. *Neither Peace nor Freedom: The Cultural Cold War in Latin America.* Cambridge, MA: Harvard University Press, 2015.

Jaquette, Jane, ed. *The Women's Movement in Latin America: Feminism and the Transition to Democracy.* New York: Routledge, 1994.

Jiménez-Yañez, César. "#Chiledespertó: Causas del estallido social en Chile." *Revista Mexicana de Sociología* 82, no. 4 (2020): 949–57.

Joffily, Mariana. "A política externa dos EUA, os golpes no Brasil, no Chile e na Argentina e os direitos humanos." *Topoi* 19, no. 38 (May/August 2018): 58–80.

Johnson, Carlos. "Dependency Theory and the Processes of Capitalism and Socialism." *Latin American Perspectives* 8, no. 3/4 (1981): 55–81.

Jones, Peter. *Track Two Diplomacy in Theory and Practice.* Stanford, CA: Stanford University Press, 2015.

Keefer, Edward C., ed. *Foreign Relations of the United States, 1964–1968.* Vol. 31, *South and Central America; Mexico,* edited by David C. Geyer and David H. Herschler. Washington, DC: Government Printing Office, 2004.

Keller, Renata. "The Latin American Missile Crisis." *Diplomatic History* 39, no. 2 (2015): 195–222.

———. *Mexico's Cold War: Cuba, the United States, and the Legacy of the Mexican Revolution.* Cambridge: Cambridge University Press, 2015.

Kissinger, Henry. *Years of Upheaval.* Boston: Little, Brown, 1982.

Klein, Naomi. *The Shock Doctrine: The Rise of Disaster Capitalism.* New York: Metropolitan, 2007.

Kornbluh, Peter. "Declassifying U.S. Intervention in Chile." *NACLA Report on the Americas* 32, no. 6 (1999): 36–42.

———. *The Pinochet File: A Declassified Dossier on Atrocity and Accountability.* New York: New Press, 2004.

Kurlansky, Mark. *1968: The Year That Rocked the World.* New York: Random House, 2005.

Kushnir, Beatriz. *Cães de guarda: Jornalistas e censores, do AI-5 à Constituição de 1988.* São Paulo: Boitempo, 2015.

Labarca Goddard, Eduardo. *Corvalán, 27 horas: El P.C. chileno por fora e por dentro.* Santiago: Quimantú, 1972.

Laguerre, Michel S. "Homeland Political Crisis, the Virtual Diasporic Public Sphere, and Diasporic Politics." *Journal of Latin American Anthropology* 10, no. 1 (April 2005): 206–25.

Langland, Victoria. *Speaking of Flowers: Student Movements and the Making and Remembering of 1968 in Military Brazil.* Durham, NC: Duke University Press, 2013.

Latham, Michael E. "Ideology, Social Science, and Destiny: Modernization and the Kennedy-Era Alliance for Progress." *Diplomatic History* 22, no. 2 (1998): 199–229.

Leacock, Ruth. *Requiem for Revolution: The United States and Brazil, 1961–1969.* Kent, OH: Kent State University Press, 1990.

Leonelli, Domingos, and Dante de Oliveira. *Diretas Já: 15 meses que abalaram a ditadura.* Rio de Janeiro: Record, 2004.

Loureiro, Felipe Pereira. *A Aliança para o Progresso e o governo João Goulart (1961–1964): Ajuda econômica norte-americana a estados brasileiros e a desestabilização da democracia no Brasil pós-guerra.* São Paulo: Unesp, 2021.

———. "O empresariado paulista e a política econômica do governo Castelo Branco (1964–1967)." In *Dimensões do empresariado brasileiro: História, organizações e ação política,* 207–28. Rio de Janeiro: Consequência, 2019.

Lumsden, David P. "Broken Lives? Reflections on the Anthropology of Exile and Repair." *Refuge* 18, no. 4 (November 1999): 30–39.

MacEoin, Gary. *No Peaceful Road: The Chilean Struggle for Dignity.* New York: Sheed and Ward, 1974.

Magalhães, Mário. *Marighella: O guerrilheiro que incendiou o mundo.* São Paulo: Companhia das Letras, 2012.

Magalhães, Marionilde Dias Brepohl de. "A lógica da suspeição: Sobre os aparelhos repressivos à época da ditadura militar no Brasil." *Revista Brasileira de História* 17, no. 34 (1997): 203–20.

Mahler, Anne Garland. *From the Tricontinental to the Global South: Race, Radicalism, and Transnational Solidarity.* Durham, NC: Duke University Press, 2018.

Malkki, Liisa H. "Refugees and Exile: From 'Refugee Studies' to the National Order of Things." *Annual Review of Anthropology* 24 (1995): 495–523.

Mallon, Florencia. *Courage Tastes of Blood: The Mapuche Community of Nicolás Ailío and the Chilean State, 1906–2001.* Durham, NC: Duke University Press, 2005.

Malloy, James, ed. *Authoritarianism and Corporatism in Latin America.* Pittsburgh: University of Pittsburgh Press, 1976.

Marchesi, Aldo. *Latin America's Radical Left: Rebellion and Cold War in the Global 1960s.* Cambridge: Cambridge University Press, 2017.

———. "Revolution beyond the Sierra Maestra: The Tupamaros and the Development of a Repertoire of Dissent in the Southern Cone." *Americas* 70, no. 3 (January 2014): 523–53.

Marini, Ruy Mauro. *Dialéctica de la dependencia.* Mexico City: Serie Popular ERA, 1973.

———. *Subdesarrollo y revolución.* Mexico City: Siglo XXI, 1969.

Markun, Paulo, and Duda Hamilton. *1961: O Brasil entre a ditadura e a guerra civil.* São Paulo: Benvirá, 2011.

Marques, Teresa Cristina Schneider. "O exílio e as transformações de repertórios de ação coletiva: A esquerda brasileira no Chile e na França (1968–1978)." *DADOS: Revista de Ciências Sociais* 60, no. 1 (2017): 239–79.

———. "Lembranças do exílio: As produções memorialísticas dos exilados pela ditadura militar brasileira." In *A construção da memória política,* edited by Elias Medeiros Vieira and Naiara Molin, 119–37. Pelotas, Brazil: UFPEL, 2011.

———. "Militância política e solidariedades transnacionais: A trajetória política dos exilados brasileiros no Chile e na França (1968–1979)." PhD diss., Universidade Federal do Rio Grande do Sul, 2009.

Martins Filho, João Roberto. *O golpe de 1964 e o regime militar.* São Carlos: Editora EdUFSCar, 2014.

McPherson, Alan. *Ghosts of Sheridan Circle: How a Washington Assassination Brought Pinochet's Terror State to Justice.* Chapel Hill: University of North Carolina Press, 2019.

McSherry, J. Patrice. *Predatory States: Operation Condor and Covert War in Latin America.* Lanham, MD: Rowman and Littlefield, 2005.

Medina, Eden. *Cybernetic Revolutionaries: Technology and Politics in Allende's Chile.* Cambridge, MA: MIT Press, 2011.

Meirelles, Domingos. *As noites das grandes fogueiras.* Rio de Janeiro: Record, 1995.

Melo, Demian Bezerra de. "Ditadura 'civil-militar'? Controvérsias historiográficas sobre o processo político brasileiro no pós-1964 e os desafios do tempo presente." *Espaço Plural* 13, no. 27 (2012): 39–53.

Mendes, Ricardo Antonio Souza. "As direitas e o anticomunismo no Brasil: 1961–1965." *Locus: Revista de História* 10, no. 1 (2005): 79–97.

Merlino, Tatiana, and Igor Ojeda, eds. *Direito à memória e à verdade: Luta, substantivo feminino.* São Paulo: Caros Amigos, 2010.

Michaels, Albert L. "The Alliance for Progress and Chile's 'Revolution in Liberty,' 1964–1970." *Journal of Interamerican Studies and World Affairs* 18, no. 1 (February 1976): 74–99.

Miranda, Nilmário, and Carlos Tiburcio. *Dos filhos deste solo.* São Paulo: Boitempo, 1999.

Mistral, Carlos. *Chile: Del triunfo popular al golpe fascista.* Mexico City: Era, 1974.

Moreira, Cássio Silva. "O projeto de nação do governo João Goulart: O Plano Trienal e as reformas de base (1961–1964)." PhD diss., Universidade Federal do Rio Grande do Sul, 2011.

Moreira, Cristiano da Silva. "Em defesa da Igreja: Religião e política na construção da propaganda da Campanha da Mulher pela Democracia (1962–1964)." *Revista de Trabalhos Acadêmicos: Campus Niterói* 3 (2018). http://revista.universo.edu.br/index.php.

Moreira, Fernanda Teixeira. "O partido do empresariado: O IPÊS-SP, os empresários paulistas e a construção de consenso na década de 1960." PhD diss., Fundação Getúlio Vargas CPDOC, History, Politics, and Cultural Heritage, 2023.

Mota, Urariano. *Soledad no Recife.* São Paulo: Boitempo, 2009.

Motta, Rodrigo Patto Sá. "O anticomunismo nas pesquisas de opinião: Brasil, 1955–1964." *Nuevo Mundo, Mundos Nuevos: Colloques*, January 14, 2014. http://journals.openedition .org/nuevomundo/68817.

———. *As universidades e o regime militar.* Rio de Janeiro: Zahar, 2014.

Moulian, Tomás. *Conversación interrumpida con Allende.* Santiago: LOM Ediciones, 1998.

Moura, Gerson. *O alinhamento sem recompensa: A política externa do governo Dutra.* São Paulo: Edusp, 2021.

———. *Sucessos e ilusões: Relações internacionais do Brasil durante e após a Segunda Guerra Mundial.* Rio de Janeiro: Editora da Fundação Getúlio Vargas, 1991.

Muñoz, Betilde V. "Where Are the Women? The Case of Chilean Women, 1973–1989." *International Social Science Review* 74, no. 1/2 (1999): 3–19.

Muñoz, Heraldo, Joseph S. Tulchin, and David G. Becker. *Latin American Nations in World Politics.* Boulder, CO: Westview, 1984.

Napolitano, Marcos. *1964: História do regime militar brasileiro.* São Paulo: Contexto, 2014.

Nashashibi, Rami. "Ghetto Cosmopolitanism: Making Theory at the Margins." In *Deciphering the Global: Its Spaces, Scalings and Subjects*, edited by Saskia Sassen, 241–62. New York: Routledge, 2007.

Navarro, Luis Eduardo González. "*Fiducia* y su cruzada en contra de la democracia cristiana: Chile, 1962–1967." *Revista Divergencia*, no. 1 (January–June 2012): 24–25.

Necochea, Hernán Ramírez. "El fascismo en la evolución política de Chile hasta 1970." In *Seis artículos de prensa*, edited by Manuel Loyola T., 9–34. Santiago: Ariadna, 2005.

Nery, Vanderlei Elias. *Diretas Já: A luta pela redemocratização.* Curitiba, Brazil: Prismas, 2015.

Neto, Lira. *Castello: A marcha para a ditadura.* São Paulo: Contexto, 2004.

———. *Getúlio 3 (1945–1954): Da volta pela consagração popular ao suicídio.* São Paulo: Companhia das Letras, 2014.

Nunes, Edson. *A Revolta das Barcas.* Rio de Janeiro: Garamond, 2000.

Nuñez M., Ricardo. *El gran desencuentro: Una mirada al socialismo chileno—La Unidad Popular y Salvador Allende.* Santiago: FCE, 2017.

Oliveira, Nilo Dias de. "Os primórdios da doutrina de segurança nacional: A Escola Superior de Guerra." *História* 29, no. 2 (2010): 135–57.

Padilla, Fernando Camacho. "Los asilados de las embajadas de Europa Occidental en Chile tras el golpe militar y sus consecuencias diplomáticas: El caso de Suecia." *European Review of Latin American and Caribbean Studies*, no. 81 (2006): 21–41.

Padrós, Enrique Serra, and Sílvia Simões. "A ditadura brasileira e o golpe de estado chileno." *Outros Tempos* 10, no. 16 (2013): 229–55.

Paiva, Márcia de. *BNDES: A Bank with a History and a Future*. São Paulo: Museu da Pessoa, 2012.

Pagliarini, Andre. "'De Onde? Para Onde?' The Continuity Question and the Debate over Brazil's 'Civil'-Military Dictatorship." *Latin American Research Review* 52, no. 5 (2017): 760–74.

Palmar, Aluízio. *Onde foi que vocês enterraram nossos mortos?* Curitiba, Brazil: Travessa dos Editores, 2006.

Parker, Phyllis R. *1964: O papel dos Estados Unidos no golpe de estado de 31 de março*. Rio de Janeiro: Civilização Brasileira, 1977.

Pedemonte, Rafael. "Castro's Position on the 'Chilean Path to Socialism' and Cuban-Soviet Relations." *Monde(s)* 8, no. 2 (2015): 27–44.

Penna Filho, Pio. "O Itamaraty e a repressão além-fronteiras: O Centro de Informações do Exterior—CIEX (1966–1986)." In *1964–2004—40 anos do golpe—Ditadura militar e resistência no Brasil*, edited by Carlos Fico, Maria Paula Araújo, Celso Castro, Ismênia de Lima Martins, Jessie Jane Vieira de Sousa, and Samantha Viz Quadrat, 163–69. Rio de Janeiro: Viveiros de Castro—7 Letras, 2004.

———. "O Itamaraty nos anos de chumbo: O Centro de Informações do Exterior (CIEX) e a repressão no Cone Sul (1966–1979)." *Revista Brasileira de Política Internacional* 52, no. 2 (July–December 2009): 43–62.

Pereira, Anthony W. *Political (In)justice: Authoritarianism and the Rule of Law in Brazil, Chile, and Argentina*. Pittsburgh: University of Pittsburgh Press, 2005.

Pereira, Marco Antônio Machado Lima. "Apolônio de Carvalho: Trajetória, memórias e militância política na era do antifascismo (1937–1947)." *Antíteses* 13, no. 25 (2020): 181–206.

Pericás, Luiz Bernardo. *Caio Prado Júnior: Uma biografia política*. São Paulo: Boitempo, 2016.

Perotti, Germán. *Harald Edelstam, héroe del humanismo, defensor de la vida*. Santiago: LOM Ediciones, 2013.

Petras, James, and Morris Morley. *The United States and Chile: Imperialism and the Overthrow of the Allende Government*. New York: Monthly Review Press, 1975.

Piñera, José. *Camino nuevo: Porque me confieso culpable de creer en Chile*. Santiago: Economia y Sociedad, 1993. www.josepinera.org/zrespaldo/camino_nuevo.pdf.

Pinheiro, Milton, ed. *Ditadura: O que resta da transição*. São Paulo: Boitempo, 2014.

Pinto, António Costa, and Francisco Carlos Palomanes Martinho, eds. *O passado que não passa: As sombras das ditaduras na Europa do Sul e na América Latina*. Rio de Janeiro: Civilização Brasileira, 2013.

Pio Corrêa, Manoel. *O mundo em que vivi*. Rio de Janeiro: Expressão e Cultura, 1996.

Poggi, Tatiana. "A política é a arma do negócio: O papel dos EUA e das corporations na construção da ditadura chilena." *Estudos Ibero-Americanos* 42, no. 2 (2016): 633–60.

Pollanah, Stella M. Senra. "D. Amélia Molina Bastos ou como e onde marcha a CAMDE." livro de cabeceira da mulher 1, no. 5 (1967): 157–74.

Pontes, José Alfredo Vidigal. *Julio de Mesquita Filho*. Recife: Fundação Joaquim Nabuco, Editora Massangana, 2010.

Power, Margaret. "The Engendering of Anticommunism and Fear in Chile's 1964 Presidential Election." *Diplomatic History* 32, no. 5 (November 2008): 931–53.

———. *Right-Wing Women in Chile: Feminine Power and the Struggle against Allende, 1964–1973*. University Park: Pennsylvania State University Press, 2002.

———. "Who but a Woman? The Transnational Diffusion of Anti-Communism among Conservative Women in Brazil, Chile and the United States during the Cold War." *Journal of Latin American Studies* 47, no. 1 (February 2015): 93–119.

Qureshi, Lubna Z. *Nixon, Kissinger, and Allende: U.S. Involvement in the 1973 Coup in Chile*. New York: Lexington, 2009.

Rabe, Stephen G. *Eisenhower and Latin America: The Foreign Policy of Anticommunism*. Chapel Hill: University of North Carolina Press, 1988.

———. *Kissinger and Latin America: Intervention, Human Rights, and Diplomacy*. Ithaca, NY: Cornell University Press, 2020.

———. *The Most Dangerous Area in the World: John F. Kennedy Confronts Communist Revolution in Latin America*. Chapel Hill: University of North Carolina Press, 1999.

Rabêlo, José Maria, and Tereza Rabêlo. *Diáspora: Os longos caminhos do exílio*. São Paulo: Geração, 2001.

Ramírez, Hernán. "Trayectoria intelectual y política de Roberto Campos desde su narrativa del yo." *Revista Esboços* 24, no. 38 (2017): 488–510.

Recondo, Felipe. *Tanques e togas: O STF e a ditadura militar*. São Paulo: Companhia das Letras, 2018.

Reed, John. *Ten Days That Shook the World*. Rev. ed. New York: Penguin Classics, 2007.

Reis, Daniel Aarão. "Ditadura, anistia e reconciliação." *Estudos Históricos* 23, no. 45 (January–June 2010): 171–86.

———. *Ditadura e democracia no Brasil: Do golpe de 1964 à constituição de 1988*. Rio de Janeiro: Zahar, 2014.

Reis, Daniel Aarão, and Jair Pereira de Sá, eds. *Imagens da revolução: Documentos políticos das organizações clandestinas de esquerda dos anos 1961–1971*. São Paulo: Expressão Popular, 2006.

Reis, Daniel Aarão, Marcelo Ridenti, and Rodrigo Patto Sá Motta, eds. *A ditadura que mudou o Brasil: 50 anos do golpe de 64*. Rio de Janeiro: Zahar, 2014.

Resende, André Lara. "A política brasileira de estabilização: 1963/68." *Pesquisa e Planejamento Econômico* 12, no. 3 (December 1982): 757–806.

Ribeiro, Maria Cláudia Badan. *Mulheres na luta armada: Protagonismo feminino na ALN (Ação Libertadora Nacional)*. São Paulo: Alameda, 2018.

Rocha, Zildo. *Helder, O Dom: Uma vida que marcou os rumos da Igreja no Brasil*. Curitiba, Brazil: Vozes, 2000.

Rodrigues, Flávio Luís. *Vozes do mar: O movimento dos marinheiros e o golpe de 64*. São Paulo: Cortez, 2004.

Rodrigues, José Honório. *Aspirações nacionais: Interpretação histórico-política*. Rio de Janeiro: Civilização Brasileira, 1970.

Rojas, Alejandra. *Salvador Allende: Una época en blanco y negro*. Buenos Aires: El País/Aguilar, 1998.

Rojas Aravena, Francisco. "Chile: Mudança política e inserção internacional, 1964–1997." *Revista Brasileira de Política Internacional* 40, no. 2 (1997): 49–75.

Rollemberg, Denise. "The Brazilian Exile Experience: Remaking Identities." *Latin American Perspectives* 34, no. 7 (2007): 81–105.

———. "Cultura política brasileira: Redefinição no exílio (1964–1979)." *Hispanic Research Journal* 7, no. 2 (2006): 163–72.

———. *Exílio: Entre raízes e radares*. Rio de Janeiro: Record, 1999.

———. "As trincheiras da memória: A Associação Brasileira de Imprensa e a ditadura (1964–1974)." In *A Construção social dos regimes autoritários: Legitimidade, consenso e consentimento no século XX*, edited by Denise Rollemberg and Samantha Viz Quadrat, 97–144. Rio de Janeiro: Civilização Brasileira, 2011.

———. "Uma vida, duas autobiografias." *Estudos Históricos* 37 (2006): 190–200.

Roniger, Luis. "Reflexões sobre o exílio como tema de investigação: Avanços teóricos e desafios." In *Caminhos cruzados: História e memória dos exílios latino-americanos no século XX*, edited by Samantha Viz Quadrat, 31–61. Rio de Janeiro: Editora da Fundação Getúlio Vargas, 2011.

Sá, Karolina Kneip de. "Ação Popular do Brasil: Da JUC ao racha de 1986." Master's thesis, Universidade Federal de Pernambuco, 2015.

Sáenz Rojas, Orlando. *Testigo privilegiado: Anécdotas, curiosidades, revelaciones, indiscreciones y peripecias de un espectador afortunado del pasado reciente*. Santiago: Erasmo, 2017.

Sales, Camila Maria Risso, and João Roberto Martins Filho. "*The Economist* and Human Rights Violations in Brazil during the Military Dictatorship." *Contexto Internacional* 40, no. 2 (May/August 2018): 203–27.

Sales, Jean Rodrigues. "A Ação Libertadora Nacional, a Revolução Cubana e a luta armada no Brasil." *Tempo* 14, no. 27 (2009): 199–217.

———. *Entre a revolução e a institucionalização: Uma história do Partido Comunista do Brasil (PCdoB)*. São Paulo: Edusp, 2020.

San Francisco, Alejandro, René Millar Carvacho, and Ángel Soto. *Camino a La Moneda: Las elecciones presidenciales en la historia de Chile, 1920–2000*. Santiago: Ediciones Instituto de Historia, Pontificia Universidade Católica de Chile—Centro de Estudios Bicentenario, 2005.

Sander, Roberto. *O verão do golpe*. São Paulo: Maquinária, 2013.

Santos, C. MacDowell, Edson Teles, and Janaína de Almeida Teles, eds. *Desarquivando a ditadura: Memória e justiça no Brasil*. Vols. 1–2. São Paulo: Hucitec, 2009.

Santos, Deijenane, and Jean de Mulder Fuentes. "Celso Furtado, da materialização do pensamento ao exílio." *Procondel Sudene*, February 2015. http://procondel.sudene.gov.br/ArtigosDetalhes.aspx?Id=1006.

Santos, Everton Rodrigo. *Poder e dominação no Brasil: A Escola Superior de Guerra (1974–1989)*. Porto Alegre, Brazil: Sulina, 2010.

Santos, José Anselmo dos. *Cabo Anselmo: Minha verdade*. São Paulo: Matrix, 2015.

Santos, Ralph G. "Brazilian Foreign Policy and the Dominican Crisis: The Impact of History and Events." *Americas* 29, no. 1 (July 1972): 39–55.

Santos, Theotônio dos. *Dependencia y cambio social*. Santiago: Centro de Estudios Socio-económicos, 1970.

Sattamini, Lina Penna. *A Mother's Cry*. Durham, NC: Duke University Press, 2010.

Scelza, Maria Fernanda Magalhães. "Entre o controle e a resistência: O presídio da Ilha das Flores como espaço de luta e afirmação de identidade de ex-prisioneiros políticos." Conference presentation at Associação Nacional de História—ANPUH XXIV Simpósio Nacional de História, 2007. https://anpuh.org.br/uploads/anais-simposios/pdf/2019 -01/1548210412_d123e786e8ab5b356729258754e283be.pdf.

Schlotterbeck, Marian E. *Beyond the Vanguard: Everyday Revolutionaries in Allende's Chile.* Berkeley: University of California Press, 2018.

Schoultz, Lars. *National Security and United States Policy toward Latin America.* Princeton, NJ: Princeton University Press, 1987.

Schwarcz, Lilia M. *Brazil: A Biography.* New York: Farrar, Straus and Giroux, 2018.

Semán, Ernesto. *Ambassadors of the Working Class: Argentina's International Labor Activists and Cold War Democracy in the Americas.* Durham, NC: Duke University Press, 2017.

Serbin, Kenneth P. *Diálogos na sombra.* São Paulo: Companhia das Letras, 2002.

———. *From Revolution to Power in Brazil: How Radical Leftists Embraced Capitalism and Struggled with Leadership.* Notre Dame, IN: University of Notre Dame Press, 2019.

Serra, José. *Cinquenta anos esta noite: O golpe, a ditadura e o exílio.* Rio de Janeiro: Record, 2014.

Sigmund, Paul E. "The CIA in Chile." *Worldview* 19, no. 4 (1976): 11–17.

———. "The 'Invisible Blockade' and the Overthrow of Allende." *Foreign Affairs* 52, no. 2 (January 1974): 322–40.

———. *The Overthrow of Allende and the Politics of Chile, 1964–1976.* Pittsburgh: University of Pittsburgh Press, 1977.

Sikkink, Kathryn. *Mixed Signals: U.S. Human Rights Policy and Latin America.* Ithaca, NY: Cornell University Press, 2004.

Silva, Alexandra de Mello e. *A política externa de JK: Operação Pan-Americana.* Rio de Janeiro: CPDOC, 1992.

Silva, Carla Luciana. "Vanguarda Popular Revolucionária: Massas, foquismo e repressão." *Revista História: Debates e Tendências* 19, no. 3 (2019): 494–512.

Silva, Cátia Cristina de Almeida. "Resistência no exterior: Os exilados brasileiros no Chile (1969–1973)." Conference paper, XII Encontro Regional de História, ANPUH-RJ, 2006.

Silva, Eduardo. "La política económica del régimen chileno durante la transición: Del neo-liberalismo radical al neoliberalismo pragmático." In *El difícil camino hacia la democracia en Chile, 1982–1990,* edited by Paul Drake and Iván Jaksic, 193–242. Santiago: FLACSO, 1993.

Silva, Hélio. *1964: Golpe ou contragolpe?* Porto Alegre, Brazil: L&PM, 2014.

Silva, Lautaro. *Allende: El fin de una aventura.* Santiago: Patria Nueva, 1974.

Silva, Ricardo Santos da. "Os não-anistiados: Os militares da Associação dos Marinheiros e Fuzileiros Navais do Brasil." Master's thesis, Universidade Estadual Paulista, 2011.

Silveira, Éder da S. "Dissidência comunista: Da cisão do PCB à formação do PCBR na década de 1960." *Anos 90* 20, no. 37 (2012): 291–322.

Silveira, Emilia, dir. *Setenta.* DVD. Rio de Janeiro: Globo Filmes, 2014.

Silveira, Fabio Vidigal Xavier da. *Frei, el Kerensky chileno.* Buenos Aires: Cruzada, 1968.

Simili, Ivana Guilherme. "Tecidos, linhas e agulhas: Uma narrativa para Zuzu Angel." *Revista Tempo e Argumento* 7, no. 15 (2015): 177–201.

Simon, Roberto. *O Brasil contra a democracia: A ditadura, o golpe no Chile e a Guerra Fria na América do Sul.* São Paulo: Companhia das Letras, 2021.

Sirkis, Alfredo. *Roleta chilena*. Rio de Janeiro: Record, 1981.

Skidmore, Thomas E. *Politics in Brazil, 1930–64: An Experiment in Democracy*. New York: Oxford University Press, 2007.

———. *The Politics of Military Rule in Brazil, 1964–85*. New York: Oxford University Press, 1988.

Slack, Keith M. "Operation Condor and Human Rights: A Report from Paraguay's Archive of Terror." *Human Rights Quarterly* 18 (1996): 492–506.

Soares, Fabiana de Menezes, Tarciso dal Maso Jardim, and Thiago Brazileiro Vilar Hermont. "Lei de Acesso à Informação no Brasil." Universidade Federal de Minas Gerais, Senado Federal. https://www12.senado.leg.br/transparencia/arquivos/sobre/cartilha-lai/ (accessed September 16, 2024).

Solari Orellana, Francisco Salvador. "Una voz que vino de lejos: Memorias de la comunicación de los programas radiales *Escucha Chile* y *Radio Magallanes*, durante la dictadura de Augusto Pinochet (1973–1990)." Bachelor's thesis, Facultad de Periodismo y Comunicación Social, Universidad Nacional de La Plata, September 15, 2015.

Soto Ángel, Rogelio Núñez, and Cristián Garay. *Las relaciones chileno-brasileñas: De la amistad sin límites al pragmatismo del gigante (1945–1964)*. Santiago: RiL Editores, 2012.

Souza, Percival de. *Autópsia do medo*. São Paulo: Globo, 2000.

———. *Eu, Cabo Anselmo*. Rio de Janeiro: Globo, 1999.

Spektor, Matias. *Kissinger e o Brasil*. Rio de Janeiro: Zahar, 2009.

———. "Origens e direção do pragmatismo ecumênico e responsável (1974–1979)." *Revista Brasileira de Política Internacional* 47 (2004): 191–222.

Spooner, Mary Helen. *The General's Slow Retreat: Chile after Pinochet*. Berkeley: University of California Press, 2011.

Stallings, Barbara. *Class Conflict and Economic Development in Chile, 1958–1973*. Stanford, CA: Stanford University Press, 1979.

Starling, Heloisa. "Golpe militar de 1964." Brasil Doc, Universidade Federal de Minas Gerais. https://www.ufmg.br/brasildoc/temas/1-golpe-militar-de-1964/ (accessed September 17, 2024).

Stepan, Alfred C. *The Military in Politics: Changing Patterns in Brazil*. Princeton, NJ: Princeton University Press, 1971.

Stern, Steve J. *Remembering Pinochet's Chile: On the Eve of London 1998*. Durham, NC: Duke University Press, 2006.

Swyngedouw, Erik. "Globalisation or Glocalisation? Networks, Territories and Rescaling." *Cambridge Review of International Affairs* 17, no. 1 (2004): 25–48.

Taffet, Jeffrey. *Against Aid: A History of Opposition to U.S. Foreign Aid Spending*. New York: Routledge, 2021.

———. *Foreign Aid as Foreign Policy: The Alliance for Progress in Latin America*. New York: Routledge, 2007.

Taffet, Jeffrey, and Dustin Walcher. *The United States and Latin America: A History with Documents*. New York: Routledge, 2017.

Tavares, Flávio. *1964: O golpe*. Porto Alegre, Brazil: L&PM, 2014.

Tinsman, Heidi. *Buying into the Regime: Grapes and Consumption in Cold War Chile and the United States*. Durham, NC: Duke University Press, 2014.

———. *Partners in Conflict: The Politics of Gender, Sexuality, and Labor in the Chilean Agrarian Reform, 1950–1973*. Durham, NC: Duke University Press, 2002.

Toledo, Caio Navarro de. "1964: O golpe contra as reformas e a democracia." *Revista Brasileira de História* 24, no. 47 (2004): 13–28.

Tollerson, Cos. "Developing Democracy through Dictatorship: Race-Thinking, Modernization, and Authoritarianism in Cold War Brazil." PhD diss., New York University, 2020.

Townsend, Camilla. "Refusing to Travel La Via Chilena: Working-Class Women in Allende's Chile." *Journal of Women's History* 4, no. 3 (Winter 1993): 43–63.

Trumper, Camilo D. *Ephemeral Histories: Public Art, and the Struggle for the Streets of Chile.* Berkeley: University of California Press, 2016.

Tulchin, Joseph S., and Augusto Varas. *From Dictatorship to Democracy: Rebuilding Political Consensus in Chile.* Boulder, CO: Lynne Rienner, 1991.

Ulianova, Olga, Manuel Loyola, and Rolando Álvarez, eds. *1912–2012: El siglo de los comunistas chilenos.* Santiago: LOM Ediciones, 2012.

United Nations. *Proceedings of the United Nations Conference on Trade and Development: Geneva, 23 March–16 June 1964.* Vol. 2, *Policy Statements.* New York: United Nations, 1964. https://unctad.org/en/Docs/econf46d141vol2_en.pdf.

United Nations Department of Economic and Social Affairs. *International Merchandise Trade Statistics: Compilers Manual.* IMTS 2010-CM. New York: United Nations, 2017.

Uribe, Armando. *The Black Book of American Intervention in Chile.* Boston: Beacon, 1975.

US Senate. *Covert Action in Chile: 1963–1973.* Staff report of the Senate Select Committee on Intelligence Activities. Washington, DC: US Government Printing Office, 1975. https://www.intelligence.senate.gov/sites/default/files/94chile.pdf.

Valdés, Jorge Tapia. *El terrorismo de estado: La doctrina de la seguridad nacional en el Cono Sur.* Mexico City: Nueva Imágen, 1980.

Valdés, Juan Gabriel. *Pinochet's Economists: The Chicago School in Chile.* New York: Cambridge University Press, 1995.

Valente, Nelson. *Jânio Quadros: Face a face com a renúncia.* Rio de Janeiro: Panorama do Saber, 1997.

Valente, Rubens. *Os fuzis e as flechas: A história de sangue e resistência indígenas na ditadura.* São Paulo: Companhia das Letras, 2017.

Valenzuela, Arturo. *Political Brokers in Chile: Local Government in a Centralized Polity.* Durham, NC: Duke University Press, 1977.

———. "Six Years of Military Rule in Chile: A Rapporteur's Report." Latin American Program, Wilson Center. www.wilsoncenter.org/sites/default/files/media/documents/publication/wp109_six_years_of_military_rule_in_chile.pdf (accessed September 16, 2024).

Valenzuela, Arturo, and J. Samuel Valenzuela. "Visions of Chile." *Latin American Research Review* 10, no. 3 (1975): 155–75.

Valle, Maria Ribeiro do. *1968: O diálogo é a violência—Movimento estudantil e ditadura militar no Brasil.* Campinas, Brazil: Editora Unicamp, 2008.

Varas, Florencia. *Conversaciones con Viaux.* Santiago: Impresiones EIRE, 1972.

Vazquez, Ana. "Des troubles d'identité chez les exilés." *Amérique Latine* 12 (1982): 76–87.

Velasco, Alejandro. *Barrio Rising: Urban Popular Politics and the Making of Modern Venezuela.* Oakland: University of California Press, 2015.

Veloso, Fernando A., André Villela, and Fabio Giambiagi. "Determinantes do 'milagre' econômico brasileiro (1968–1973): Uma análise empírica." *Revista Brasileira de Economia* 62, no. 2 (April/June 2008): 221–46.

Ventura, Zuenir. *1968: O ano que não terminou*. Rio de Janeiro: Nova Fronteira, 2006.

Vera, Cristián Garay, and José Díaz Nieva. "Frente Nacionalista Patria y Libertad (1970–1973). Caracterización de una identidad política." In "Partis, mouvements et organisations patronales: Les droites dans le Cône Sud latino-américain (1950–2016)," special issue of *Cahiers ALHIM* 32 (2016). https://journals.openedition.org/alhim/5589.

Verdugo, Patricia. *Interferencia secreta: 11 de septiembre de 1973*. Buenos Aires: Sudamericana, 1998.

Vianna, Martha. *Uma tempestade como a sua memória: A história de Lia, Maria do Carmo Brito*. Rio de Janeiro: Record, 2003.

Vidal, Virginia. *La emancipación de la mujer chilena*. Santiago: Quimantú, 1972.

Vieira, Rosa Maria. "Celso Furtado e o Nordeste no pré-64: Reforma e ideologia." *Projeto História—Cultura e Poder: O Golpe de 1964, 40 Anos Depois* 19 (July/December 2004): 53–86.

Villa, Marco Antônio. *Ditadura à brasileira*. Alfragide, Portugal: LeYa, 2014.

Villegas, Sergio. *Chile—El Estadio: Los crímenes de la junta militar*. Buenos Aires: Cartago, 1974.

Vizentini, Paulo Fagundes. "Da barganha nacionalista à política externa independente: Uma política exterior para o desenvolvimento, 1951–64." PhD diss., University of São Paulo, 1993.

———. *A política externa do regime militar brasileiro: Multilateralização, desenvolvimento e a construção de uma potência média (1964–1985)*. Porto Alegre, Brazil: Editora UFRGS, 1998.

———. *Relações internacionais do Brasil: De Vargas a Lula*. São Paulo: Editora Fundação Perseu Abramo, 2003.

von der Weid, Carolina, and Eduardo Uziel. "Odette de Carvalho e Souza (1904–1970)." In *Diplomatas: Sete trajetórias inspiradoras de mulheres diplomatas*, edited by Thais Mesquita and Guilherme José Roeder Friaça, 89–124. Brasília: FUNAG, 2023.

Waissbluth, Mario. "Orígenes y evolución del estallido social en Chile." Santiago: Centro de Estudios Públicos, Universidad de Chile, 2020.

Wasserman, Claudia. "Transição ao socialismo e transição democrática: Exilados brasileiros no Chile." *História Unisinos* 16, no. 1 (January/April 2012): 82–92.

Weis, W. Michael. *Cold Warriors and Coups d'État: Brazilian-American Relations, 1945–1964*. Albuquerque: University of New Mexico Press, 1993.

Wexler, Haskell. *Brazil: A Report on Torture*. Directed by Hannah Eaves, Haskell Wexler, and Saul Landau. YouTube, 1971.

White, Judy, ed. *Chile's Days of Terror: Eyewitness Accounts of the Military Coup*. New York: Pathfinder, 1974.

William, Wagner. *Uma mulher vestida de silêncio: A biografia de Maria Thereza Goulart*. Rio de Janeiro: Record, 2019.

Wolpin, Miles D. *Cuban Foreign Policy and Chilean Politics*. New York: Heath Lexington, 1972.

Yoma, Marisi Pérez Zujovic. *La gran testigo: El asesinato de mi padre durante la Unidad Popular*. Santiago: Catalonia, 2013.

Young, Robert J. C. "Disseminating the Tricontinental." In *The Routledge Handbook of the Global Sixties: Between Protest and Nation-Building*, edited by Naomi Haynes and Piya Chatterjee, 517–47. New York: Routledge, 2018.

Zolov, Eric. *The Last Good Neighbor: Mexico in the Global Sixties.* Durham, NC: Duke University Press, 2020.

———. *Refried Elvis: The Rise of the Mexican Counterculture.* Berkeley: University of California Press, 1999.

Zolov, Eric, and Terri Gordon-Zolov, eds. *The Walls of Santiago: Social Revolution and Political Aesthetics in Contemporary Chile.* New York: Berghahn Books, 2022.

INDEX

Page numbers in italics refer to illustrations.

Angel Jones, Stuart, 46, 176nn64–65
Anselmo dos Santos, José (Cabo
    Anselmo), 59, 63–68, 64, 180n24,
    181nn38–39
anticommunism: Anticommunist
    Movement, 84; and authoritarian
    nationalism, 72; Bolsonaro's elec-
    tion, 148; as Brazilian state policy,
    1–2, 16; Commission of Summary
    Investigation (Brazil), 75; guerrilla
    groups, 84, 102; opinions on, 167n22;
    Patria y Libertad, 6, 33, 78, 87, 90,
    124, 132; shifting opinions regarding,
    167n22; US support for, 19–20. See also
    Campaign of Women for Democracy
    (CAMDE); CIEX (Brazilian Foreign
    Office Intelligence Center); Institute
    for Social Studies and Research
    (IPES)
Aragão, Cândido da Costa, 62–63, 123
archival sources. See documentation
Archives of Terror, 62. See also torture
Argentina: as axis of power, 94; and Chile,
    support for, 5; and Chilean border, 102;
    CIEX participation of, 61; and Cuba,
    approach to, 22, 23; dictatorship in,
    6, 10, 29, 49, 149; exiles from, 49;
    OLAS, 27; Operation Condor, 6; PCB
    outreach in, 36; SOFOFA, 82; and US
    interventionism, 105
Arraes, Miguel, 63
Arriagada, Genaro, 69
Arruda, Marcos, 109
asilados, 40. See also exile; exiles
Assis Riberito, Paulo, 96
Association of Industrialists of Valparaíso,
    90
Association of Metallurgical Industries
    (Chile), 90
Association of Sailors and Marines, 63
asylum status. See exile
Atlantic Community Development Group
    for Latin America (ADELA), 78, 82–83,
    88, 98
authoritarianism, 99–100; and economic
    policy, 97–98; exile from, 49; legacy

of, 13–14; and nationalism, 72; socialist,
    94; and violence, 176n78
author's methodology: chapter outlines,
    11–14; terminology used, 8. See also doc-
    umentation; primary sources
Azevedo, Ricardo de, 144

Balestiero, Leovigildo, 86
Bambirra, Vânia, 3, 42, 156
Bandeira, Luiz Alberto Moniz, 72
Bangu neighborhood (Rio de Janeiro), 60
Banzer Suárez, Hugo, 90, 153, 191n11
Barbosa, Mário Gibson, 101–2, 110, 112, 151
Barbosa, Wilson, 44, 45, 47, 52–53, 62,
    128–29, 146, 155
Barcelos, Maria Auxiliadora Lara "Dora,"
    54, 130, 139, 155
Barrett, Jorge, 67–68
Barrett, Rafael, 67
Barros, Ademar de, 112
Bastos, Paulo de Mello, 41
Bastos, Solange, 41, 140, 144–45, 152
Bay of Pigs, 21
Bazán Dávila, Raúl, 23, 25
Beaulac, Willard L., 172n110
Belaunde, Fernando, 94
Benedetti, Mario, 59
Beraldo Laune, Elaine Maria, 138–39
Berle, Adolf A., 19
The Black Pimpernel (film), 198n25
Bogotá Conference, 15–16, 165n5
Bolívar, Simón, 21
Bolivia, 104; and CIEX participation, 61;
    coup (1971), 72; and Cuba, approach to,
    23; dictatorship in, 10; exiles from, 49;
    Operation Condor, 6
Bolsonaro, Jair, 14, 148
Bonnefoy Miralles, Pascale, 145
Bordaberry, Juan María, 148, 153
Boric, Gabriel, 147–48
Braden Copper (mining company), 21
Brady, Herman, 76
Brazil: Amnesty Law (1979), 154; Army,
    103; Army Intelligence Service, 9;
    Aviation Information Service, 163n51;
    business sector involvement in

Câmara, Dom Hélder, 50, 177n84

Câmara Canto, Antônio Cândido da: on Allende, opposition to, 6, 31–33; and Allende and Popular Unity, surveillance of, 30; as ambassador, 7, 27, 70, 96; analysis of Frei Montalva's leadership, 27; on Castro's visit, 115–16; and Chilean coup, role in, 5, 73–76, 75, 126–27, 128; and Chilean dictatorship, role in, 149–50, 151–52, 155; on Frei Montalva's leadership, 27

Camargo, Edmur Péricles, 69, 70

Campaign of Women for Democracy (CAMDE), 13, 78, 80, 86–87

Campos, Roberto, 12, 15, 77, 79, 92–96, 93, 166n14, 189n107; Chilean contacts, 96; influence, loss of, 97–98; on nationalism, opposition to, 99

Canales, Alfredo, 125

capitalism: and democratic society, 42–43; and efficiency, 99–100; integrated, 82

Capozzi, Sérgio, 136

carabineros (military police), 31

"Caravan of Death," 75–76

Cardoso, Fernando Henrique, 3, 42, 157

Cardoso, Jaime, 46, 130, 140

Carnation Revolution, 154

Carrasco, Pepe, 136

Carvalgo e Souza, Odette de, 61

Carvalho, Apolônio de, 40, 46, 154, 173n16, 174n32, 176n62

Carvalho, José Murillo de, 57

Carvalho, Renée de, 46

Carvalho, René-Louis de, 40, 44–46, 67, 129–30, 131–32, 154

Carvalho Pinto, Carlos Alberto de, 26

Casa da Moeda (Brazilian Mint), 98

Castelo Branco, Humberto de Alencar, 61, 93, 95, 111, 112; economic policy of, 97–98; and IPES policies, 96; National Security Council (CSN), 15

Castro, Fidel, 21, 111; visit to Chile (1971), 114–20, 115, 117

Castro, João Augusto de Araújo, 71

Catholic Church: and anticommunism, 86; and Brazilian conservatives,

inspiration for, 78; clergy, 103; and leftist militant groups, 43; and social justice and left-wing leadership, 50

Cavalcanti, Pedro Celso Uchôa, 55

CENIMAR (Navy Intelligence Center) (Brazil), 9, 38, 62, 145, 173n19, 191n4

censorship, 4, 28, 55–57, 108

Center for the Economic and Social Development of Latin America, 52

Central Intelligence Agency (CIA) (United States.), 61; and anticommunist election interference in, Brazil, 19–20; and assassination of General René Schneider, 113–14; role of, 2; spoiling operations of, 13, 20–21, 81, 113

Cerda, Aguirre, 63

Chadwick, Andrés, 14

Chateaubriand, Assis, 84

Chicago Boys, 79, 96–98, 149

Chile: before Allende's election, 15–18, 21; and Brazilian guerrillas, 43; Central Bank, 127; constitution, rejection of (2022), 148; copper industry, 21; as "democratic axis," 94; economic models, 74, 85, 92–93; election (2021), 147–48; Estallido Social, 13–14; and financial aid from international agencies (early 1960s), 25; Health Program for Schools, 37; housing policies in, 112–13; internal migration in, 113; Left, cooperation with Brazilian guerrillas, 43; Ministry of Housing and Urbanism, 112–13; preceding Allende's election, 15–18, 21; presidential terms in, 170n70; and trade with Brazil, 186–87n55; transnational efforts to isolate, 114; and United States, diplomacy pre-Allende, 23–24. *See also* Chilean coup (September 11)

Chilean Chamber of Construction (Chile), 90

Chilean Communist Party (PCCh), 68–69, 103

Chilean coup (September 11): "Brazil Connection," 73; Brazilian casualties, 132–39; Brazilian involvement in,

102–6, 126–28; and business class, role of, 88–89; day of coup, 128–32; days preceding, 126–28; military junta, leaders after, 127; military plotting, 123–26; political prisoners taken during, 121–23; and torture in National Stadium, 1, 3, 5, 133–35, 139–46; and US cooperation, 110–11; xenophobic attitudes after, 129–32

Chilean National Commission for Truth and Reconciliation, 9, 136, 137

Chilean National Commission on Political Prison and Torture, 140

Chilean Society for the Defense of Tradition, Family, and Property, 103

Christian Democratic Party (Partido Demócrata Cristiano), 28, 31, 43, 69, 87, 91, 103, 113–14

Christian Left, 50

Church Committee (1975), 2, 105, 159–60n2, 162n30

CIA (Central Intelligence Agency) (United States), 61; and anticommunist election interference in Brazil, 19–20; and assassination of General René Schneider, 113–14; role of, 2; spoiling operations of, 13, 20–21, 81, 113

CIEX (Brazilian Foreign Office Intelligence Center), 123; on Castro's visit to Chile, 115–16; creation and early history of, 60–62; employees of, 68; focus on Chile, 8; infiltration of, 5, 38; operations, 70; reports from Chile, 69, 103–4

citizenship: principles and definitions, 40, 47, 57, 174n26

Clifford, James, 176n75

Coimbra, Jaques de Souza, 52

Cold War in Latin America: Brazil's role in, 24–25, 105, 112; multidimensional aspect of, 119; and National Security Doctrine, 29; overview of, 6–11, 99, 162n31; polarizing aspect of, 112

Colombia, 94, 148, 165n5

Commission of Summary Investigation (Brazil), 75

Committee Carlos de Ré for Truth and Justice of Rio Grande do Sul, 3, 133

Companhia Rio-Grandense de Telephones, 94

"concentric circles," theory of, 71

Concepción University, 118

Confederation of Industry (CNI) (Brazil), 88–89

Confederation of Truck Owners (SIDUCAM), 87, 90

Conference of the Latin American Solidarity Organization, 65

Connally, John, 106

Contreras, Manuel, 11, 133

copper industry, 21, 32, 91

Correio Braziliense (newspaper), 68

Cortes, Marcos, 151

Costa e Silva, Artur da, 4, 36, 97–98

Council of the Americas (COA), 78, 91

Cowan, Benjamin A., 172n111

Cuba, 21–22; and anti-Castro asylum seekers in Chile, 25; boycott of, 18; and Castro's visit to Chile (1971), 114–20, 115, 117; rejection of from OAS, 22

Cuban Missile Crisis, 21

Cuban Revolution, 19

Dantas, Francisco San Tiago, 23, 86

Dauster, Bruno, 45

Davis, Nathaniel, 6, 73

Debray, Régis, 36, 65

Deferre, Gaston, 116

Delfim Netto, Antonio, 89, 98

Democratic Military Liberation Crusade, 84

Department of Internal Operations (DOI) (Brazil), 141

Department of Political and Social Order (DOPS) (Brazil), 11, 46, 66

Dependência e desenvolvimento na América Latina (Cardoso & Faletto), 3

dependency theory, 3, 22

Diários Associados (media group), 84

Dias Costa, Luiz Loureiro, 145

Díaz, Gustavo, 63

dictatorships. See authoritarianism

Dino, Flávio, 149
Dirección de Inteligencia Nacional
  (Chile), 11
Diretas Já, 57, 157
divorce, 86, 187b59
documentation: eyewitness accounts, 2–3;
  lack of, 8–9, 105; recent availability of,
  2. *See also* primary sources
Dominican Republic, 112
Dourado, Rui, 60
Doutrina de Segurança Nacional (DSN), 7
Dreifuss, René, 12, 88, 100
Drummond, Aristóteles, 84, 85
Dutra, Eurico Gaspar, 18

Echeverría, Luis, 155
Economic Commission for Latin America
  and the Caribbean (ECLAC), 22, 42, 51,
  92–94, 150, 169n57
Ecuador, 15, 22, 23, 30, 84, 155
Edelstam, Harald, 152, 157, 198n25
Eisenhower administration, 18–19, 167n23
Elbrick, Charles Burke, 28, 48, 108
Eletrobras (Brazilian energy company), 25
El Mercurio (Chilean newspaper), 24, 90,
  199n39
El Poder Feminino (Female Power)
  organization, 13, 78, 86, 87
El Siglo (Chilean newspaper), 24
EMFA (General Staff of the Armed
  Forces) (Brazil), 30, 62, 73
Enríquez, Miguel, 43
Estadio de Chile, 141
Estadio Nacional, 138, 195n39
Estado Novo, 154
Estallido Social (Chile), 13–14
exile: of academics, 175n36; asylum status,
  39–40, 155–56; citizenship and rights,
  47; historiography of, 55–57, 174n23;
  myth of intellectual exchange, 41–42;
  outlines and definitions, 39–40,
  174n26; women in, 178n121
exiles: *asilados*, 40; Brazilian in Chile,
  3, 35–39; avoidance of engagement,
  44; *caixinha* (financial support fund
  for), 51–54; Chilean in Brazil, 78–79;

citizenship and rights of, 47; definitions of, 39–40; difficulty of return of,
  41; estimated numbers of, 132–33; exile,
  state of, definitions, 39–40; identity
  formation of, 47–49; major waves of,
  3–4; nationalism of, 49; Quarento,
  44–45; return of to Brazil, 57; second
  wave (post AI-5), 50–51; Setenta (political prisoners), 39, 43, 45, 45–47,
  102; surveillance of Brazilian, 4–5, 7;
  targeting of by Brazilian intelligence
  services, 38; torture of during Chilean
  coup, 121–23; in Uruguay, 60; written
  accounts by, 55–57
exiles, Brazilian: difficulty of return of,
  41; surveillance of, 7; as target of
  Brazilian intelligence services, 38; in
  Uruguay, 60
exiles, Chilean in Brazil, 78–79

Fajardo, Margarita, 169n57
Faletto, Enzo, 3
Fauné, Angélica, 66
Fazio, Hugo, 127
Federation of Chilean Industry
  (SOFOFA), 5, 78, 82, 88–90, 150
Federation of Industries of the State of
  São Paulo (FIESP), 20
Ferraz, Antônio Paulo, 144
Ferreira de Araújo, José María, 67
Ferreira de Souza, Evaldo Luiz, 67
Ferrer, Eliete, 130, 140–41, 157
Fiducia (Chilean periodical), 103
Figueiredo, João, 80
Fischer, Carmen, 138
Fleury, Sérgio, 11, 66, 68, 69
Folha de. S. Paulo (newspaper), 33
Fonseca, Edmur, 52, 177n99
Fontaine, Jorge, 150
foquismo, 36–37, 43, 65
Ford, Gerald R., 105
Fort Leavenworth, KS, 80
France: and Allende, support for, 32; exile
  in, 39, 154, 157, 160n6
Frei Montalva, Eduardo, 4, 7, 16, 26–27,
  30, 32, 69, 87, 91, 94, 103–4, 112–13

Valenzuela, Arturo, 98–99
Valés Subercaseaux, Gabriel, 166n13
Valle Silva, Murillo Vasco do, 114
Vandré, Geraldo, 62
Vanini, Jane, 135–37, 196n53
Vargas, Alfredo, 139
Vargas, Getúlio, 18, 70, 167n17
VAR-Palmares (Palmares Armed
    Revolutionary Vanguard), 14, 41, 139,
    181–82n41
Vasconcelos, Amarílio, 62–63, 69
Vazquez, Ana, 178–79n125
Veja (magazine), 150
Velasco Alvarado, Juan, 94, 126
Veloso, Caetano, 157
Vendas Promotion SA (advertising
    agency), 84
Venezuela, 15, 18, 28, 94, 155,
    165n5
Vial Correa, Gonzalo, 199n39
Vidal, Gustavo, 68
Viedna, Soledad Barrett, 67–68
Vieira, Luiz Carlos, 138
Vilarín, León, 87, 188n76

violence: against Brazilians in Chile,
    132–39; Brazil's use of, 106. *See also*
    human rights violations; torture
Vital Brasil, Vera, 51, 157
Vizentini, Paulo Fagundes, 70, 166n7
Von Appen, Ernesto Huber, 125
Von der Weid, Jean Marc, 40–41, 43, 45,
    46, 124
von Holleben, Ehrenfried, 30, 45, 66, 108
VPR (Popular Revolutionary Vanguard),
    37, 65, 66, 108, 133

Washington Post (newspaper), 28, 83, 109
Women's Civic Union, (São Paulo), 80
women's roles, 86, 87; women in exile,
    178–79nn124–25, 178n121. *See also*
    Campaign of Women for Democracy
    (CAMDE)
Working Circles, 80
World Bank, 106
World Council of Churches, 52

Young Catholic Students, 50
Youth Student Front (Asunción), 67